Understanding and Using Financial Data: An Ernst & Young Guide for Attorneys

Also from Ernst & Young

The Ernst & Young Guide to Total Cost Management
The Complete Guide to Special Event Management
The Ernst & Young Guide to Raising Capital
The Ernst & Young Guide to Expanding in the Global Market

Forthcoming from Ernst & Young

The Ernst & Young Guide to Mergers & Acquisitions, Second Edition
The Ernst & Young Business Plan Guide, Second Edition
The Ernst & Young World Markets Resource Guide 1993–1994
The Ernst & Young Guide to Managing Information Strategically

Understanding and Using Financial Data: An Ernst & Young Guide for Attorneys

VINCENT J. LOVE

JOHN WILEY & SONS
New York * Chichester * Brisbane * Toronto * Singapore

This text is printed on acid-free paper.

Copyright © 1992 by Ernst & Young
Published by John Wiley & Sons, Inc.

All rights reserved. Published simultaneously in Canada.

Reproduction or translation of any part of this work beyond
that permitted by Section 107 or 108 of the 1976 United
States Copyright Act without the permission of the copyright
owner is unlawful. Requests for permission or further
information should be addressed to the Permissions Department,
John Wiley & Sons, Inc., 605 Third Avenue, New York, NY
10158-0012.

This publication is designed to provide accurate and
authoritative information in regard to the subject
matter covered. It is sold with the understanding that
the publisher is not engaged in rendering legal, accounting,
or other professional services. If legal advice or other
expert assistance is required, the services of a competent
professional person should be sought. *From a Declaration
of Principles jointly adopted by a committee of the
American Bar Association and a Committee of Publishers.*

Library of Congress Cataloging in Publication Data:
Understanding and using financial data: an Ernst & Young guide for attorneys / Ernst & Young.
    p.   cm.
  Includes bibliographical references (p.) and index.
  ISBN 0-471-55878-8 (cloth)
    1. Lawyers--Accounting. 2. Financial statements. I. Ernst &
Young.
  HF5686.L35F56   1992
  657' .834--dc20   92-14888
                                                          CIP

Printed in United States of America

10 9 8 7 6 5 4 3 2 1

SUBSCRIPTION NOTICE

This Wiley product is updated on a periodic basis with supplements to reflect important changes in the subject matter. If you purchased this product directly from John Wiley & Sons, we have already recorded your subscription for this update service.

If, however, you purchased this product from a bookstore and wish to receive (1) the current update at no additional charge, and (2) future updates and revised or related volumes billed separately with a 30-day examination review, please send your name, company name (if applicable), address and the title of the product to:

Supplement Department
John Wiley & Sons, Inc.
One Wiley Drive
Somerset, NJ 08875
1-800-225-5945

Acknowledgments

This book had its genesis in the work performed over the years by Ernst & Young professionals who serve the legal profession. These outstanding men and women developed and taught courses on financial accounting for law firms and legal professional organizations. In their wake, they left materials and a spirit of enthusiasm that have culminated in the writing of this book. To this legion of professionals, in particular David A. Wilson and Terry M. Lloyd, I owe an immeasureable debt of gratitude.

The technical accuracy of the financial accounting information was assured by the able and extraordinarily helpful support of Judith A. Kudla from the Ernst & Young National Accounting Services Department. I would also like to acknowledge Mort Meyerson, National Director of Public Communications, for his support and encouragement and Richard Sasanow, Assistant Director, for nurturing the project along to completion.

Whatever grace of language and style I have achieved is the direct result of many long hours of editorial assistance from Tammy Mitchell. A special thanks goes to Dan Goldwasser of Vedder, Price, Kaufman, Kammholz & Day for his advice on accounting language in legal documents.

Last, but not least, I want to acknowledge my wife, Lorraine, who showed the patience of a saint in dealing with the long and difficult hours I devoted to this book.

This book is dedicated to all the Ernst & Young professionals who provide expert, audit, tax, consulting, and education services to the legal profession.

Vincent J. Love

March 27, 1992

About Ernst & Young

With more than 65,000 people worldwide, including 20,000 people in over 100 U.S. cities, Ernst & Young is the leading international professional services firm. It serves the legal profession through a vast range of accounting, tax, and management consulting services to individuals, law firms, corporate legal departments, and public sector law offices of all sizes. Its Litigation Services professionals have served as expert witnesses and consultants for virtually every major law firm on matters ranging from damages in contract disputes to liability issues in intellectual property cases, and its Legal Consulting Group is a national leader in providing office systems, information systems, and management consulting to law departments and firms. The Corporate Finance Group works with attorneys on a broad range of merger, acquisition and divestiture transactions (including due diligence), while the Restructuring and Reorganization Group has provided assistance to bank lenders, public debt holders, troubled companies and other parties—and their attorneys—in virtually every major troubled company situation. Full-time Valuation professionals provide diversified services to help businesses and investors—and their legal advisors—with a broad spectrum of valuation and appraisal services.

About the Author

Vincent J. Love is national director of litigation services for Ernst & Young. Mr. Love is a certified public accountant, as well as a certified fraud examiner and chartered bank auditor. He is a frequent speaker, lecturer, panelist, and writer on accounting, reporting, and auditing issues. He has also written and lectured on damage strategies, expert preparation, accountants' liability, understanding financial statements, and other legal-accounting subjects for various legal organizations. Mr. Love is active in a number of professional organizations and currently serves on the professional ethics committee of the New York State Society of CPAs and is a member of the board of directors and executive committee of the American Arbitration Association.

Introduction: How to Use This Book

Financial documents can appear to be written in a code known only to accountants and other specialists. The truth is, however, that with a bit of guidance, anyone can master the conventions that govern the presentation of financial information.

The purpose of this book is to help attorneys understand, analyze, and use financial statements and other financial data. You will be able to make the numbers come to life and perform the basic analytic computations that create a detailed, multifaceted picture of a company's financial situation. Is it viable? Is it profitable? Can the company meet its current payments, make capital improvements, and stay in business?

For attorneys, whether in-house or in private practice, understanding financial statements has become as essential as knowledge of the law. A better grasp of financial relationships will improve the quality of the business advice you can offer to clients. It will help answer questions you may have about the management and fiscal health of any company. It will clarify the merits of various proposed transactions and aid you in offering viable structural alternatives that offer a more favorable financial statement presentation.

A wealth of information is available on the financial operations of an entity. This book will tell you where to find the information you need, how to compare it to the information provided by other companies in the same industry or geographic location, and how to corroborate the information in the basic statements. Litigation attorneys will find guidance here in locating the primary internal documents upon which financial statements are based. In proving liability and damages, these documents are frequently more important than the financial statements themselves.

The book is divided into three parts. Part I addresses the raw financial data that is cited in financial statements and other public disclosures. It guides the reader though a wealth of information, which, when pieced together, creates a picture of the entity's financial situation. Chapters 1 through 5 contain the basic principles of financial reporting, an item-by-item analysis of basic financial statements, an explanation of the notes to financial statements and Management's Discussion and Analysis (MD&A), and a description of the work of the outside auditor.

Part II begins with Chapter 6 "Putting the Pieces Together." This is a walk through a set of financial statements, which points out ways to begin piecing together the mosaic of an entity's financial history and prospects. This chapter will help you understand the interrelationships among the various disclosures in the financial statements. Once you understand these relationships, you will have important clues to the company's underlying policies, goals, and corporate culture.

Chapter 7 expands the analysis of financial statements to include, in simple terms, the ratios and other analytical tools that accountants use to evaluate an entity's liquidity, leverage, operations, and management. Chapter 8 explains the theories and mechanics of determining the present and future value of money, a critical concept for lawyers in negotiating deals or settlements for their clients.

Part III deals with how lawyers can apply financial analysis and data in their everyday dealings with clients or in court. Chapters 9 and 10 discuss the use of financial language in legal documents, the financial basis of damage strategies, the financial aspects of discovery, how to select an expert, and how to present financial data to judges and juries.

In the Appendices, I have provided reference material which the reader will find helpful in making sense of financial information. This includes a glossary of accounting and financial terminology and jargon, sample financial statements, a sample Form 10-K, a listing of authoritative accounting literature, and a bibliography.

The book is best read in order of the chapters. Readers with a strong knowledge of accounting might want to start with Chapter 6, which is a guided tour through a set of financial statements. Part III can be used as a source for attorneys who need to apply financial knowledge to various legal situations. You may want to read the chapter on financial language in legal documents when you are drafting covenants or warranties for inclusion in clients' (or your own) agreements. Chapter 10 on discovery of financial data will prove valuable when you are drafting requests for documents or interrogatories.

Every effort has been made to write this book in a style and vocabulary that will be clear to a nonfinancial professional. At the same time, I have been scrupulous in maintaining the technical precision required to make the book a reliable reference tool.

Of course, no book can transform an attorney into an accountant—any more than reading a legal text can qualify a lay reader as an attorney. For legal situations that involve complex financial information, I advise attorneys to hire an accounting expert.

CONTENTS

APPENDICES

PART I

Reading and Understanding Financial Statements and Other Disclosures

CHAPTER ONE

The Basics: Financial Reporting Fundamentals

§1.1 GAAP

Financial statements summarize an entity's transactions on a given date and for a stated period of time. For public companies, the Securities and Exchange Commission (SEC) is concerned that statements "fairly represent" the financial condition of the company to the users of the statements, which include stockholders, bankers, suppliers, and others.

The rules companies must follow in preparing their financial statements are set by a body called the Financial Accounting Standards Board (or FASB, which is often pronounced "fazbee"). The FASB's rules, which fill many volumes with technical details, are known as Generally Accepted Accounting Principles, or GAAP. GAAP encompasses various conventions, rules, and procedures that accountants follow in recording the financial effect of various business transactions. The first official body that issued accounting pronouncements was the Committee on Accounting Procedure, which dates back to 1938. This committee of the American Institute of Certified Public Accountants (AICPA) issued Accounting Research Bulletins (ARBs).

In 1959, the committee was reorganized as the Accounting Principles Board, and the opinions expressed by this body are called APB opinions. As pressure mounted from government and business for more timely and independent standard setting, the FASB was established in 1973 as the authoritative organization responsible for producing GAAP.

The FASB is an independent organization whose members serve five-year terms and are fully compensated for their work. They are supported by a staff of researchers and other assistants. The FASB issues Statements of Financial Accounting Standards (SFAS), which are often referred to as FASB statements, or as SFAS #1, SFAS #2, etc.

The accounting profession recognizes a hierarchy among GAAP's principles, rules, and pronouncements. Certain concepts of financial accounting and reporting serve as the underlying basis for all GAAP. The basic concepts address such issues as the qualitative characteristics of accounting, the objectives of financial reporting, the elements of financial statements, when economic events should be recorded, and how to financially measure an event. Included among these basics are the concepts of cost and accrual accounting, materiality, conservatism, the "going concern" concept, substance over form, and others that will be addressed in this and later chapters.

Exhibit 1-1

Level	Literature[1]	Authority
5	Accounting textbooks, articles, all other publications of U.S. standard setting groups, and pronouncements of the IASC.	Lowest
4	AICPA accounting interpretations, Q&As issued by the FASB staff, and prevalent industry practices.	
3	EITF Consensus Positions and AICPA Practice Bulletins	
2	AICPA industry audit and accounting guides, AICPA statements of position, and FASB technical bulletins.	
1	FASB statements and interpretations, APB opinions, and AICPA accounting research bulletins.	Highest
Foundation	Basic concepts and conventions, including qualitative characteristics of financial statements, recognition and measurement of economic transactions, objectives of financial reporting, and elements of financial statements.	Bases for all GAAP

The first level above the foundation consists of the pronouncements of the FASB, APB, and ARB, which are set forth in FASB Statements and Interpretations, APB Opinions, and Accounting Research Bulletins. These documents include the interpretations issued by these three bodies, which remain valid until the pronouncement or the interpretation is amended or superseded.

The next level has less authority but is applicable if the first level does not address a particular issue. This level includes AICPA statements of position, AICPA industry audit and accounting guides, and FASB technical bulletins. If a question is not addressed at this level, the next places to look for an answer are the FASB's Emerging Issues Task Force (EITF) Consensus, AICPA accounting interpretations, FASB staff ques-

---

[1] SAS #69, issued in January 1992, "The Meaning of Present Fairly in Conformity With Generally Accepted Accounting Principles," AICPA, 1992.

tions and answers (Q & As), and practices that are prevalent in the applicable industry.

The least authoritative places to look for an answer are accounting texts and articles, APB statements (as distinguished from APB opinions), the AICPA's issues papers and Accounting Standards Executive Committee (AcSEC) practice bulletins, FASB concept statements, and International Accounting Standards Committee (IASC) statements.

The principles articulated in all of these levels are based on underlying foundational concepts and conventions. Understanding these concepts and conventions is necessary to understanding recent FASB statements about such issues as pensions, other postretirement benefits, and taxes. The FASB tries to align its pronouncements with the classical concepts and conventions. (In Exhibit 1-1, the authority of the literature goes down as the level goes up.)

For the most part, we will focus on public disclosures of financial data. But it is important for attorneys to recognize that this is only a small part of the financial and operating data that an entity generates and uses in its operations. In litigation, other valuable financial data may be available to attorneys upon request or through the discovery process. See Chapter 9.

The following basic GAAP concepts form the foundation and framework for all financial statements.

§1.2   Reporting Entity

The first step in understanding financial statements is to determine the nature and composition of the reporting entity. Statements can be prepared for an individual, sole proprietorship, partnership, corporation, trust, or other legal entity. Some statements, called "consolidated," consist of specific combinations of related entities. Though these may appear simple and straightforward, they often are not. In the case of a major international organization, the nature of the entity may be quite complex and difficult to determine from the face of the financial statements.

The name of the entity being reported on can, of course, be found at the top of the financial statements. Additional information about the composition, legal status, and type of business is generally found in the notes to the statements.

§1.3 Reporting Period

The basic financial statements are usually prepared for each operating cycle of an entity, and this is usually one year. For internal operating purposes, most commercial enterprises prepare monthly statements. Companies that report to the Securities and Exchange Commission (SEC) are required to report quarterly financial information to the public. Quarterly reporting is also a common practice for many other large enterprises. In addition to the SEC, banks and other lending institutions normally require quarterly reports from commercial borrowers as a condition in their lending agreements.

Because of the many judgments and estimates that are used in preparing financial statements, some precision is sacrificed in order to produce financial information on a timely basis. A common example of an estimate is the amount of receivables that, for various reasons, will not be collected. If the preparer of the financial statements waited until the disposition of the receivable balance was known, the reserve for uncollectible receivables would be accurate, but, in all likelihood, the statements would be useless. They would have been issued so far after the reporting date that the data would be too stale to make reasonable judgments on the current business operations and condition of the entity. Too many changes would have occurred in the interim.

§1.4 "Going Concern"

A basic assumption underlying financial statements is that the entity is a "going concern" and will continue normal operations into the future. When evaluating an entity's ability to continue normal operations, an auditor usually looks at a period of one year from the date of the financial statement. This exemplifies one of the many judgments an auditor has to make. If it looks as if the entity will survive, the values placed on the assets apparently will be "realized," i.e., used up in operations or converted into cash.

This is a key assumption, since the value assigned to the assets under GAAP would probably be overstated if the entity were forced to liquidate them. The asset value of items like equipment depends upon their use in producing goods or services. If the company is forced to sell the equipment, the entity may receive only a fraction of the book value.

If an entity's outside auditor doubts the entity's ability to continue as a going concern, the auditor's opinion on the financial statements must be qualified. If there is substantial doubt that the company is a going concern, the auditor's report will be expanded to explain that concern. If a company adopts a plan of liquidation, it must value the entity on a liquidation basis and must prepare different types of financial statements.

The "going" concern concept is also important because it serves as a foundation for deferring costs and recording intangible assets such as goodwill. As with fixed assets like machinery, it is assumed that the entity will survive and recover the value of the deferred costs and intangibles in the process of its operations.

§1.5   Historical Cost vs. Current Value

Recording of business transactions in an entity's accounting records is customarily done at the cost at the date of the transaction. With limited exceptions, the recorded amount is not changed to recognize changes in value, unless there has been a permanent impairment in the value of the assets and the value will not be recovered through operations. This "historical cost" principle has its roots in the need for objectivity in financial accounting.

Generally, a change in value is recorded without a transaction only to lower the value of an asset, never to value the asset above its historical cost. For example, marketable equity securities change value every day. At the valuation date, if the total current value of the portfolio is less than its cost, the portfolio is written down in value. If the portfolio has increased in value, however, the value is currently not increased above cost. This is called the "lower of cost or market" method of valuing assets. Although entities in the securities industry, and a few others, are permitted to keep their portfolios at market regardless of cost, that is the exception and not the rule.

The lower of cost or market (LCM) rule has been called a one-way street by some and "hysterical cost" by others, since it requires companies to value assets at what might be decades-old amounts. For example, a film or music library (like Disney's) or real estate (like Santa Fe Southern Pacific's) may be carried on the books at only a fraction of its fair market value.

On the other hand, the value of some long-term investments, such as bonds, may be overstated by some companies, using the argument that these investments will be held to term, when their full value will be realized. The actual market value of some assets will be disclosed on the face of the statements or in the accompanying notes. However, to properly understand an entity's financial position, you have to look at all the data in the financial statements, notes, and other disclosures. Do not limit yourself to only part of the picture.

The use of historical cost is a U.S. accounting principle. In some other countries, particularly those with hyper-inflationary economies, the accounting conventions allow companies, with the help of independent appraisers, to write up the value of assets as their value increases. When these companies are consolidated subsidiaries of U.S. companies, they typically value those assets in their U.S. statements at their historical dollar-value cost.

§1.6 Consistency

Consistency in the way transactions are recorded and summarized in financial statements is essential to comparability. Comparability between companies is one of the objectives of GAAP and one of the reasons why GAAP limits the way transactions can be recorded. When GAAP allows flexibility (as in the choice of methods for depreciating long-lived assets), it requires disclosure of the method that the preparer of the statements used in recording the transaction.

Another aspect of consistency, the application of the same GAAP for all similar transactions in different financial reporting periods, is essential for the purpose of comparing an entity's financial data from period to period. Deviations from the consistent application of GAAP by an entity must be disclosed in the notes and in the independent auditors' opinion.

GAAP can change when the FASB issues new pronouncements, or when the entity changes its selection of alternative GAAP and discloses the change properly. Thus, when drafting legal documents that contain clauses about financial information, attorneys may want to specify that GAAP *at the date of the agreement* must be applied to a particular contract.

§1.7   Substance over Form

A transaction must be accounted for based on its substance, regardless of its form. For example, in the past, a company could acquire assets by using leases that gave the company the right to those assets for their economic life, or the right to buy the assets at the end of the lease at a bargain price. At that time, this allowed the company to keep the asset—and the debt—off its balance sheets because the transaction was not a purchase *in form*.

The Financial Accounting Standards Board dealt with this issue early in its history by requiring that the economic substance of the transaction dictates how it is treated in the company's financial records. The leases, in substance, were acquisitions of an asset which involved the incurring of debt. The company would have the use of the asset for its economic life (or, because of a bargain purchase price provision, would acquire the asset at the end of the lease), and the payments on the lease would, in substance, be payments on the financing.

Todays sophisticated and extremely complex transactions and financial instruments make the application of substance over form more challenging than ever before. Personal computers, which are more powerful than the massive mainframes of two decades ago, enable business and financial professionals to design and monitor these complex transactions. Often, for example, it is difficult to distinguish between equity and debt, and between an asset or obligation and a contingent asset or obligation. Attorneys are sure to face this issue more and more when advising clients on the legal form of transactions and the need for disclosure.

It is especially important to remember that while the legal form may suffice for legal issues, that is not necessarily so for accounting issues. If the substance of the transaction is at odds with its legal form, the accounting will follow the substance. A client may be disappointed to find that a transaction did not accomplish what was intended. For example, in the lease situation described above, the intent may have been to keep the debt off the financial statements because of other pre-existing debt covenants. This will not work, and it may cause problems in complying with the debt covenants.

Increasing pressures on independent auditors have placed additional emphasis on this principle of substance over form. Court decisions have forced auditors to consider more than "the rule" of GAAP in applying accounting standards to questionable transactions and situations. The

Court of Appeals for the Second Circuit ruled that an accountant could be held liable for false financial statements notwithstanding compliance with GAAP.[2] In a subsequent decision, the same court held that to the extent form over substance is allowed, it is a misapplication of GAAP.[3]

§1.8   Conservatism

Frequently, assets and liabilities are measured in the presence of business conditions that are quite uncertain. Accountants make every effort to avoid overly optimistic presentations of financial data. They do this by anticipating and recording losses, even though they may be somewhat less than certain; at the same time, they do not record gains until they are certain of their realization.

This guiding principle has become known as conservatism in the preparation of financial statements, and it sometimes leads accountants to understate income, assets, and equity. For example, even though Texaco recorded an expense when it lost its appeal in the *Pennzoil v. Texaco* litigation, Pennzoil did not record the income until a settlement was reached and approved by the court in the following year.

§1.9   Accrual vs. Cash Basis

Virtually all financial statements use the accrual and not the cash basis of accounting. In accounting on an accrual basis, income and expense are recognized when they are incurred, not necessarily when the actual payment or receipt of cash occurs. Receivables and payables are established to record the amounts owed by and to an enterprise.

With the accrual method, even if payment is made in advance of receiving the goods or services in question, the amount is not included as an expense. Instead, a prepayment account is established. Although it may appear contrary to intuition, the party making the payment carries this prepayment as an asset, while the party receiving the payment carries it as a liability for services or goods owed. For instance, if a party has prepaid its insurance, this is an asset to the payor, which is owed

---

[2] *U.S. v. Simon*, 425 F.2d 796 (2d Cir. 1969).

[3] *Herzfeld v. Laventhol Krekstein, Horwath & Horwath*, 540 F.2d 27 (2d Cir. 1976).

insurance protection, and a liability for the payee, since it represents an obligation to provide insurance. If, in this example, the insurance policy is cancelled early, the insurer owes the insured a refund.

The accrual concept gives rise to a number of other "book" entries to make financial statements more representative of the actual financial condition of an enterprise. When a company acquires equipment, buildings, and other long-lived assets, the accrual concept requires capitalization of the asset and its subsequent depreciation (reduction in the carrying value of the asset as it is used in the business).

The advantage of the accrual basis is that it more closely reflects the true condition and activities of the entity. However, the accrual basis requires accountants to make a number of reasoned judgments: for instance, estimating income and expense for transactions that have not settled, and estimating costs that have been incurred but not consumed in operations and contingencies. Examples of transactions that have not settled are those related to long-term construction contracts and to potential bad debts and receivables. Costs that have been incurred but not consumed in operations are exemplified by supplies that have not been used. Since these estimates are not "fact" but rather depend upon judgment, they are subject to mistakes and manipulation.

A financial statement preparer can make statements look stronger by minimizing accrued expenses and maximizing accrued income. There are many examples of companies aggressively attempting to accrue income, then going out of business because the income accrued earlier failed to materialize or did not produce enough cash to keep the company solvent. However, a reader of financial statements can often find disclosures of income and expense policies in the notes to the financial statements or other published financial data. Such disclosures can assist the reader in determining whether any aggressive practices were used in recording accruals.

§1.10   Recognition of Income and Revenue

Some company managers prefer to accrue, or "recognize," income on their financial statements as soon as possible and to defer recording expenses as long as possible. (Reporting on income tax returns is about the only activity in which this preference is not followed.) Often, this means recognizing or recording the income before the payment is actually received. According to GAAP, however, to recognize income, the earnings process must be substantially complete. If there are significant contingencies, warranties, or other services to be performed before, or after, a product is sold or a service is complete, GAAP requires that all (or, in the case of long-term contracts, some) of the income cannot be recognized.

Even when the transaction is virtually complete, certain contingencies or warranties may exist, and their costs have to be estimated. The anticipated cost should be "reserved," which means that the anticipated cost is charged to earnings and a liability or contra-account is set up when the transaction is recorded. Two common examples are reserves for uncollectible receivables and product repair warranties. The situation becomes more complex if the transaction in question involves long-term contracts that span several years, or if there is no reasonable basis for estimating sales returns, allowances, or other subsequent expenses.

§ 1.11 Matching

The principle of matching requires the recording ("recognizing") of revenue and all related costs in the same time period. This concept gives rise to the deferral of costs that will generate future revenue. For instance, if a company acquires a machine to produce revenue-generating products or services in future periods, the machine is booked as an asset and depreciated (expensed) over the productive life of the machine.

By accelerating the reporting of its income or by deferring the reporting of payment of its expenses, a company could misstate the results of its operations. For this reason, the principle of matching, which uses accruals and deferrals, requires entities to reflect all expenses in their proper accounting period.

The matching principle requires that, in a multi-year construction or other long-term contract, income and expense must be allocated to each year of the contract. On the other hand, because of the principle of conservatism, companies must immediately recognize (i.e., record) any estimated loss on a contract.

As with all matters that require judgment, the process of properly matching income and expenses is subject to mistakes and intentional distortions.

§1.12   Current and Long-Term Assets and Liabilities

On a balance sheet (also called a statement of financial position), assets and liabilities are generally divided into current and long-term. Current assets are those that are expected to be used or converted into something else within one year. Most (if not all) receivables, for example, should be converted into cash within one year of the balance sheet date. Prepaid insurance will be used over time and the asset will no longer exist. Current assets are listed in order of their declining liquidity (cash first, followed by investments maturing within one year, listed securities held for trading purposes, receivables, etc.).

Long-term assets are those that will not be converted within one year. These include income-producing assets such as property, plant, and equipment. It should be noted that the ensuing year's depreciation (cost of the property, plant, and equipment charged to income) is not included in current assets, even though these assets will be used in production within the next year.

Like current assets, current liabilities are those that are expected to be honored or converted within one year. Some examples are short-term debt, trade accounts payable, and currently payable income taxes. Also included in this category is any portion of long-term debt that will come due within one year.

Any asset or liability that is not classified as current is long-term. Typical long-term liabilities include noncurrent portions of debt (mortgages, bonds, etc.) and deferred taxes.

The classification of assets and liabilities as current or long-term is important for attorneys who draft agreements and who develop covenants or warranties related to balance sheet ratios such as working capital. To be sure that the debtor will properly classify assets and liabilities, and to avoid later disagreements, such attorneys may want to specify unusual classifications. It is important to note that the movement of assets or liabilities between categories will affect ratios and relationships. See Chapter 7.

§1.13   Capitalized Costs

Many assets are capitalized costs. They are the result of expenditures that are considered to carry value into the future. This is in contrast with expenditures that are consumed during the current operating cycle. Common examples of capitalized costs are real estate, equipment, inventory, and intangibles like copyrights and patents.

In a commercial enterprise, all disbursements are related to the cost of doing business. Since accounting is by nature conservative, GAAP requires that balance sheets carry only those costs or assets that have continuing value. All other costs are used to reduce income ("charged" or "expensed") on the income statement during the period that ends at the balance sheet date. Assets that have no continuing value (referred to in accounting as "permanently impaired") must be reduced in value to the amount that is expected to be received when they are sold or disposed of.

§1.14   Recognition of Liabilities

The accounting principle of conservatism dictates that liabilities be recognized, when it is probable that a company has an obligation to perform or pay, and the amount is reasonably determinable.

Some liabilities—such as those relating to pensions, other postretirement benefits, and taxes not currently due—are subject to special treatment. The rules for when to record pension and postretirement benefit obligations allow companies to defer recording the estimated costs that were incurred before the effective dates of the FASB pronouncements, or before the effective date of companies' amendments to their plans ("prior service costs"). These prior service costs are an expense that will reduce the companys' revenue on future financial statements. See Sections 3.10 and 3.11.

Another major liability is taxes that a business must pay. Income for tax purposes frequently differs from income for financial reporting purposes. This is because companies take advantage of provisions of the Internal Revenue Code and claim expenses sooner, or less frequently, delay reporting of certain revenues. A common example of acceleration of expenses is the use for tax purposes of an asset depreciation method that differs from the book method. This tax asset depreciation method allocates a larger portion of the depreciation expense to the earlier years of an assets economic life. As tax laws grow more complex and as they are used to forge social and economic policy, it is often difficult to determine what the real tax expense will be—especially if it is paid in the future based on the current *book* income before taxes. The problem of how to account for taxes payable in future years has been analyzed extensively by the accounting profession for more than fifty years, and will probably be an issue for the next fifty years as well.

Liability issues can be very complex, and it takes time to investigate obligations that are not evident on the face of financial statements. Also, lawyers need to be sensitive to problems that arise when the FASB sets new accounting standards, which can have a significant effect on the financial statements. For instance, to comply with FASB statements on pension and postretirement benefits, companies face the prospect of booking very significant liabilities. In many cases, these liabilities have caused companies to be in violation of their loan covenants because of ratios in those covenants that involved computing liabilities.

From the standpoint of an attorney drafting such a covenant, a good way to protect the client against future changes in the rules is to add a clause stating that the GAAP used to compute any ratio will be that which was in effect at the date of the agreement.

§1.15 Contingent Liabilities

Not all uncertainties are contingencies. Financial statements are replete with uncertainties, since much of the information they contain is based on a variety of estimates. A contingency, however, is defined as uncertainty about possible gain or loss to an enterprise as a result of one or more future events. Significant differences can result from the tremendous uncertainty and the range of judgment involved in deciding whether or not to record contingent liabilities.

Contingent gains usually are not recorded as income before they occur; however, they should be disclosed in notes to the financial statements, and the disclosure should avoid misleading implications about the likelihood of the event actually occurring. On the other hand, a charge against earnings for an estimated loss arising from contingency is required if both of the following conditions exist:

- It is *probable* that an asset has been impaired or a liability has been incurred as of the date of the financial statements, and

- The amount of the loss can be *reasonably estimated*.

"Reasonably estimated" does not mean that it will be possible to determine a single amount. Typically, an estimate consists of a range of amounts. The amount that appears in the financial statements should be either the one within the range that seems to be the best estimate at the time, or, if no amount within the range seems better than another, the lowest amount within the range.

Pending and threatened litigation are examples of contingencies that are highly relevant to attorneys. It is important to note that just because a lawsuit has been filed does not mean that a loss has to be recognized in the defendant's financial statements. Recognition of a loss is required only if an unfavorable outcome is probable and the amount of the loss can be reasonably estimated.

Contingencies must be disclosed in notes to the financial statements if the amount in question is material. If the loss is not recognized in the financial statements and the amount is material, the auditors are required to express an adverse opinion, stating that the financial statements are not in conformity with generally accepted accounting principles and the reason why.

If a loss is only reasonably possible or if a reasonable estimate of the loss cannot be made, the auditors may have to expand their opinion to include an explanatory paragraph. For example:

> "As discussed in Note _____ to the financial statements, the Company is a defendant in a legal action alleging that it failed to deliver under a purchase agreement and claiming general and punitive damages. The Company has filed a counterclaim, and discovery proceedings are in progress. Since the ultimate outcome of this litigation cannot be determined at this time, no provision for any liability that may result therefrom has been made in the accompanying financial statements."

§1.16   Accrued Income and Expenses

For financial statements to be meaningful, they should be published within a reasonable time after the balance sheet date. Statements that are a year old are of little value. Since most entities have transactions that are incomplete at any one date, some adjustments, including estimates based on judgments, must be made at the balance sheet date so that all transactions are taken into account.

Many of these adjustments are for items that can be easily calculated, such as interest to date on debt. A company may have debt that calls for interest and principal payments on July 1 of each year. On December 31, interest on the outstanding principal will be recorded as a liability for accrued interest payable. The amount of the interest is easily determined in this example by multiplying the principal by the interest rate and dividing by 2.

Other adjustments are more difficult to determine, because there is no set formula. An example is uncollectible receivables. Prior experience is one indicator of the factors that go into evaluating a receivable balance, but the process is often complicated and requires a significant amount of judgment. Even the best attempt could be far off the mark if an unexpected event occurs that affects the ability of a customer to pay. This type of "soft" reserve should be given special consideration when analyzing a financial statement.

§1.17   Deferred Income and Expenses

Deferred income is a claim against the company by the prepayer. Thus, if an attorney receives a retainer and has not yet performed services, the income is deferred until the service is performed or the money is returned. Deferred expenses are also called "prepaid expenses."

GAAP does not allow losses to be deferred except in very limited cases. For example, oil and gas companies can capitalize "dry holes" under a comprehensive program of income recognition. Under certain circumstances, GAAP may allow the deferral of the loss recognition of long-term investments, but only when the decline in value (loss) is only temporary and the asset is being held as an investment. The entity must demonstrate its ability to hold the investment to maturity.

§1.18   Full Disclosure

The principle of full disclosure requires financial statements to clearly report all material relevant information about the economic affairs of the entity. The information must be understandable and comprehensive, but not so detailed that it masks the truly relevant data.

Once again, the preparer has to exercise a significant amount of judgment in deciding what to include and what to leave out. Hindsight assures accuracy, but waiting for the completion of transactions and events assures "stale" and meaningless information.

Users of financial statements should be aware that a "complete package" for financial reporting purposes may include more than the basic financial statements and the notes. For public companies, important information is also contained in management's discussion and analysis (MD&A), and in sections of the company's Form 10-K filing with the SEC. Form 10-K contains some additional information that an annual report will not, including schedules of changes in certain asset accounts, a discussion of the entity's business, and a listing of properties it owns.

§1.19 Materiality

Materiality is defined in terms of a reasonable user of financial statements. A material item is one that would cause a reasonable person to change his or her judgment. Materiality is both qualitative and quantitative, and it is relative. For example, if there was a $500,000 misstatement of cost of goods sold for IBM, it would not influence the judgment of a user of its financials. That same amount would be material, however, to a small business with revenues of only $2 million.

To some degree, materiality is a judgment call. If a junior officer was involved in a fraud and the amount was not significant, the fraud probably would not be material. But if the chairman of the board was involved, even when the amount is not significant, the fraud may be material, as the mental attitude of the chairman may affect other decisions or dealings with shareholders or the public.

Materiality in financial statements must be distinguished from materiality in an audit. In an audit, the auditor sets a dollar estimate of the size of an error the auditor is willing to tolerate at a level below what it would be on a financial statement. Materiality dictates the dollar value of the transactions the auditor selects for testing. It takes into consideration not only qualitative and quantitative measures, but also the risk that an error or irregularity will occur. These judgments are based on the inherent nature of the transaction and on the entity's system of internal accounting controls.

In this chapter, we have outlined the basic principles that underlie financial statements. These basic accounting principles prepare the reader to read financial statements in their proper context. The next chapter will lead you, step by step, through a typical set of financial statements.

CHAPTER TWO

Introduction to Financial Statements

§2.1 Purposes and Limitations of Financial Statements

The purpose of financial statements is to organize, summarize, and present to the public the financial performance and condition of a business. They are directed toward the common interest of a broad spectrum of users, ranging from shareholders to creditors and bankers, with the intent of providing information that will help them make business decisions. Financial statements are designed to be understandable to readers who have a reasonable grasp of business and economics, and who examine the statements with care.

As noted in Chapter 1, the conventions for financial statement preparation are set forth and modified as necessary by the FASB, an independent body that is privately funded by accounting firms and corporations. The financial reporting rules of the FASB are targeted to the needs of users. The FASB has formulated three basic criteria for financial statements: They must be relevant, reliable, and comparable. To be relevant, the information must be timely and capable of making a difference in the decision-making process. To be reliable, it must be based on a faithful representation of the economic impact of events on the entity. When exact amounts are not available, the information must be based on reasonable estimates. The FASB also requires that statements be presented in a way that is internally consistent, as well as comparable to information in the statements of other companies.[1]

Since financial statements are a summary, they have definite limitations. They report on the activities of a business, without reference to the larger context of the industry or the economy. Readers should evaluate a company's financial statements in light of industry and economic trends. Information on industries can be obtained from industry and trade associations, the U.S. government, and certain universities. The information is based on approximations, and these, in turn, stem from judgments made by management. It is important to remember that financial statements are only one source of information for making decisions about a business enterprise. Besides the information published by the company in annual reports and other publications, interested parties may consult other sources. The SEC and other regulatory agencies require filings for

---

[1] See FASB Statements of Financial Accounting Concepts Nos. 1 through 6:

No.   Title
1   Objectives of Financial Reporting by Business Enterprise
2   Qualitative Characteristics of Accounting Information
3   Elements of Financial Statements of Business Enterprises
4   Objectives of Financial Reporting by Nonbusiness Organizations
5   Recognition and Measurement in Financial Statements of Business Enterprises
6   Elements of Financial Statements (replaces FASB Concepts Statement No. 3 and incorporates an amendment of FASB Concepts Statement No. 2).

publicly held companies. Analysts with securities and investment firms produce research information and reports on specific companies and industries. Rating agencies, such as Moody's and Standard & Poor's, also evaluate the financial strength of individual companies. Finally, in some cases, the company's management may respond to individual requests for information.

The following financial statements are required under GAAP as a basic minimum for any entity. The basic information is standard and is prescribed by GAAP, but the names of the statements and the way the information is depicted may vary. The basic statements include:

- Balance sheet (or statement of financial position),

- Statement of operations (or income statement),

- Statement of cash flows,

- Statement of changes in retained earnings,

- Disclosure of any other changes in stockholders' equity,

- Other disclosure needed to provide the reasonable user with all material financial information necessary to understand the basic financial statements.

§2.2   The Balance Sheet

A balance sheet, often referred to as a statement of financial position, is a "snapshot" of an entity at a specific point in time. The balance sheet summarizes the entity's financial position—assets, liabilities, and owners' equity—*as of one date:* the date when the balance sheet was prepared. It takes between one and three months to prepare, examine, and distribute annual audited statements. Inevitably, therefore, by the time a company issues its balance sheet, its situation and its account balances will have changed.

The balance sheet represents the end result of all of an entity's financial decisions—how it obtained its money, how it spent its money, and the cumulative effect of those decisions. That information includes:

- What the business owns (assets),

- What the business owes (liabilities), and

- What residual interest the owners have in the business (owners' equity).

The basis of the balance sheet is the classic accounting equation, Assets = Liabilities + Capital (A = L + C). Capital is sometimes called "equity" or "owners' equity," and it represents the excess (or deficit) of assets over liabilities. This equation holds true for any entity's financial statements, since, by definition, the assets of any business equal its liabilities plus its owners' equity. The formula applies also to personal financial statements and to ownership of any asset, such as a car, a home, or a business.

Assets are generally valued and shown on the balance sheet at historical cost, i.e., the price in dollars at the date acquired. In some instances and in certain industries, the assets may be valued either at the lower of cost or market, or at market. When these less conventional valuations occur, the financial statement will say so.

A balance sheet breaks down the major classifications, especially the assets and liabilities, into separate categories. All balance sheets will not look exactly alike, since they contain a variety of different accounts. The factors that influence the accounts shown on a balance sheet include the nature of the business, industry practice, relative size of the various categories of accounts, and GAAP specifications.

To illustrate the basic types of accounts and classifications you can expect to see, Exhibit 2-1 shows an example of a balance sheet for ABC, Inc.

The following is a brief description of the captions you will see on a typical balance sheet.

§2.3 Assets

Assets are resources the company owns or controls that will probably produce future economic benefits.[2] Assets are presented on the left

---

[2] For a technical definition, see Statement of Financial Accounting Concepts No.6, "Elements of Financial Statements," par. 25.

side of a balance sheet, or on top if the presentation is vertical. Within the general category of assets, there are two subcategories: current assets and long-term (noncurrent or fixed) assets. Current assets are generally listed in order of decreasing liquidity. (Liquidity is the relative ease and time it takes to convert an asset into cash). Here is a description of the typical accounts you will find in each asset category.

Exhibit 2-1

ABC, Inc.
Consolidated Balance Sheets

	December 31	
	19X5	19X4
	(In Thousands)	
Assets		
Current assets:		
Cash and cash equivalents *(Note 5)*	$ 7,500	$ 6,000
Accounts receivable, less allowances of		
$300,000 in 19X5 and $250,000 in 19X4	29,000	28,000
Inventories *(Note 3):*		
Finished products	17,000	16,000
Products in process	35,000	29,000
Raw materials and supplies	7,000	6,000
	59,000	51,000
Prepaid expenses	500	500
Total current assets	96,000	85,500
Investment in affiliated company	4,200	4,100
Property, plant, and equipment *(Note 10):*		
Land	6,000	5,000
Buildings	38,350	30,850
Machinery and equipment	59,700	47,200
	104,050	83,050
Accumulated depreciation and amortization	35,550	30,550
	68,500	52,500
Other assets	800	1,400
Total assets	$169,500	$143,500

Exhibit 2-1 *(continued)*

ABC, Inc.
Consolidated Balance Sheets

	December 31	
	19X5	*19X4*
	(In Thousands)	
Liabilities and shareholders equity		
Current liabilities:		
Notes payable to banks *(Note 5)*	$ **3,000**	$ 7,000
Commercial paper *(Note 5)*	**3,000**	2,000
Accounts payable and accrued expenses	**23,600**	20,200
Income taxes	**5,000**	2,000
Deferred income taxes	**700**	—
Current portion of long-term debt and capital lease obligations	**1,400**	1,350
Total current liabilities	**36,700**	32,550
Long-term debt, less current portion *(Note 6)*	**35,000**	21,000
Capital lease obligations, less current portion *(Note 10)*	**14,500**	14,900
Accrued pension cost *(Note 9)*	**2,000**	2,100
Deferred income taxes *(Note 8)*	**3,000**	2,000
Lease commitments *(Note 10)*		
Shareholders' equity *(Notes 6 and 7)*:		
Common stock, $1 par value:		
Authorized shares − 5,000,000		
Issued and outstanding shares − 3,000,000 in 19X5 and 2,900,000 in 19X4	**3,000**	2,900
Additional paid-in capital	**15,000**	14,100
Retained earnings	**59,300**	54,950
Currency translation adjustments	**1,000**	(1,000)
Total shareholders' equity	**78,300**	70,950
Total liabilities and shareholders' equity	**$169,500**	$143,500

See accompanying notes.

(This exhibit with accompanying notes also appears in Appendix B)

(a)   Current Assets

Cash includes coin, currency, and money in the bank. Most entities also define as cash or "cash equivalents" any time deposits that convert into cash within 90 days.

Marketable securities are short-term investments that can be converted into cash within a few days. Rather than maintaining cash in excess of operating needs, most companies invest a portion of their cash in securities that give a better yield. Some companies may also seek a gain in market value. "Marketable securities" can include U.S. government and corporate securities, and are shown at the lower of cost or market in most companies' statements.

Accounts receivable represent the uncollected amounts due from sales or services rendered to customers. Since some customers may be poor credit risks, a company probably will not collect all of its receivables. The standard balance sheet recognizes this by providing an allowance for "doubtful accounts."

While the amount of a receivable is readily determinable from the accounting records, the calculation of the allowance (reserve) for doubtful accounts is based on an estimate. An attorney who is representing a client acquiring a company would do well to find out what method the seller used to determine the allowance for doubtful accounts. From the buyers point of view, the method used should be made part of any warranty concerning the value of the company's assets.

The adequacy of this allowance is almost always in contention after a deal is consummated. Time spent addressing this issue properly before the closing date will be more than compensated for by the time saved in arguing over who owes whom how much as a result of an allegedly inadequate reserve.

Inventories generally consist of the goods the company has manufactured for sale and the raw materials the company uses in the manufacturing process. Inventory can lose value rather abruptly, and most companies have some obsolete inventory. Obsolete inventory is potentially a major issue with high technology companies because of the rapid rate of technological change.

Under GAAP, inventory is to be valued at the lower of cost or market. This means that when the market value of a product drops below its cost, the inventory value must be reduced to the lower amount.

As with allowances for doubtful accounts receivable, inventory reserves are estimates. In an acquisition, the same precautions that apply to bad debt or accounts receivable reserves are also appropriate here.

(b)   Investments

In contrast with marketable securities, the primary purpose for acquiring investments is to hold them for long-term business purposes, rather than for current income. However, they affect current income because they produce interest, dividends and, under certain circumstances discussed below, equity in earnings of investees.

Investments are often made to exercise voting control over other businesses or to provide resources for paying long-term obligations. On the balance sheet, investments are recorded at cost, unless there has been a permanent impairment in their value, or unless a company owns 20 percent or more of another company that is not consolidated. (A consolidated company's statements are combined with those of another reporting entity for financial reporting purposes.) Permanent impairment is a decline in value that is not expected to reverse itself during the life of the investment. GAAP requires that a permanent impairment be recognized by writing down the value of the investment. When a company owns over 20 percent of an investee, that investment is accounted for using the equity method, i.e., the original cost of the investment is adjusted for the investor's proportionate share of the investee's income, loss, or capital activities (stock sales, dividends, etc.).

(c)   Property, Plant, and Equipment

Property, plant, and equipment (PP&E) includes land, buildings, machinery, equipment, tools, trucks, computers, furniture, etc. These assets are expected to be used in the business for more than one year after the date they were purchased. They lose their usefulness as time passes. "Depreciation" is an attempt to account for this loss in relation to the asset's cost.

Depreciation applies to all property, plant, and equipment, except land. Land is generally not considered to decline in usefulness over time and therefore is not depreciated. The exception is land that is used for such resources as oil, timber, iron, etc. Such land does decline in usefulness, so its value is reduced as its resources are depleted.

Depreciation can be calculated in one of several alternative ways, and this calculation can change the company's operating results in a given reporting period. To avoid drawing erroneous conclusions, especially when comparing companies, a reader of financial statements should be aware of which depreciation method is used. The notes to the statements will disclose the method or methods, if they are not shown on the face of the statement.

In acquisitions, an attorney should be sure to include warranties protecting the buyer against environmentally contaminated land, and against PP&E that is no longer used in production and that has a value below its depreciated cost.

(d) Other Assets

"Other assets" on a balance sheet might include such items as patents, copyrights, or other intangible (nonphysical) assets that are generally being "amortized" over a period of years. Amortization is the equivalent of depreciation for these assets. It is based on the assumption that the economic usefulness of both tangible and intangible assets declines over a period of time.

The precautions for intangible assets are similar to those for depreciation. Especially when making comparisons with other companies, a reader should understand the amortization method that was used in evaluating intangible assets. However, unlike tangible assets, some intangible assets may not lose their value, even though they may be amortized for accounting purposes.

This description of asset categories and accounts is for illustrative purposes only. Depending on their significance to the business, numerous other asset accounts and categories may appear on a balance sheet. Financial institutions, service-oriented firms like law firms, and other types of businesses have accounts that reflect their unique activities. For example, a law firm would not have inventory, but would have an account for unbilled time that was incurred in its engagements.

§2.4 Liabilities

Liabilities are claims against an entity that must be satisfied with cash, other assets, new obligations, or services.[3] The components of *current* liabilities are usually loans, accounts and notes payable, accrued expenses, currently maturing portions of long-term debt, and dividends and taxes payable. *Long-term* liabilities include long-term debt (notes, bonds, and mortgages), leases with more than one year to run, pension obligations, deferred taxes, and redeemable stock (usually preferred). Several accounts require special accounting consideration, including deferred taxes, redeemable stock, pension liabilities, minority interests, and contingencies.

Here is a brief explanation of the typical accounts in each liability category.

(a) Current Liabilities

Current liabilities usually include:

Loans payable. These are short-term borrowings, usually from banks, such as revolving lines of credit and loans that the company expects to pay within one year.

Short-term notes payable. Such notes arise from commercial transactions and are due within one year from the date of the balance sheet.

Current portions of long-term debt and capital leases. These obligations are also called "funded debt." Amounts included in the "current liabilities" section represent the principal payments that must be made within one year.

Trade accounts payable. This type of obligation is incurred for goods or services that are purchased in the normal course of business. Such goods and services might include raw material, inventory, utilities, and professional fees.

Accrued expenses. These are costs incurred for which bills have not been received. In accounting, the concept of accrual requires obligations that have been incurred to be recognized on the balance sheet when the entity becomes liable for them. Accrued expenses typically include wages, commissions, interest, and taxes.

---

[3] Ibid., par. 35, contains the technical definition.

Cash dividends payable. Once declared, dividends become a binding obligation to the company and are recorded as payable until they are actually paid. Cash dividends payable are amounts payable to shareholders for dividends that have been declared before the balance sheet date and have not been paid.

Unearned revenues. Defined as payments received before the end of the year for goods or services that have not yet been provided, unearned revenues include subscriptions, insurance premiums, and similar payments received. As the amount is earned, it becomes part of income. At the time of the balance sheet, however, it represents an obligation to refund the money or to provide some type of service. On law firms' balance sheets, unused retainers against fees are an example of this type of liability.

Income taxes payable. These are taxes on earnings that must be paid within one year of the balance sheet date. Most companies record income taxes and other taxes separately.

(b) Long-Term Liabilities

Any obligations that cannot be classified as short term are classified as long-term liabilities. These are liabilities that are not expected to be liquidated within the ensuing year. The following is a brief explanation of items that typically appear under this heading.

Notes payable are note obligations with more than a year to go before the principal must be repaid.

Bonds payable are comparable to notes, but are sold through the financial markets. They represent borrowing, not from one institution or individual, but from hundreds or thousands of investors.

Mortgages are collateralized borrowings that are due more than a year from the balance sheet date. They are secured by physical assets such as real property and equipment.

Obligations under capital leases are much like mortgages, and the amounts represent the principal portions of debt that has been incurred to acquire specific assets (rights). Leasehold rights from capitalizeable leases are obtained by secured financings (i.e., lease payments are secured by the leasehold), and consequently they operate much the same way as purchases of assets financed with debt.

Deferred taxes. When classified as long-term liabilities, deferred taxes are income taxes payable to any taxing authority at a future date, which is usually more than one year from the balance sheet date. The delay in paying the tax is caused by the difference in accounting under GAAP and under tax laws. For example, some depreciation methods for tax purposes are much more liberal than those typically used for GAAP. This discrepancy results in greater expenses—and currently lower taxes—in the early years of the assets' lives. In theory, this difference "turns around" at a later date, eliminating the deferral.

Some financial professionals argue that at least *some* of the amounts shown on balance sheets for deferred tax obligations are not really liabilities, but are *permanent* deferrals of obligations. Consider, for example, a company that is replacing assets and adding assets as it grows. Assume that the assets are depreciated under allowable tax methods at rates that are in excess of rates appropriate under GAAP. If the company continues to grow and replace assets, it may always have tax depreciation expense in excess of financial statement depreciation. However, if the company's growth levels off or declines, it will find itself paying taxes that it previously deferred, since tax depreciation will be lower than GAAP depreciation.

To the extent that a liability is not being paid, it is beneficial to the company. In fact, some financial statement users view deferred taxes as an interest-free loan from the government. They contend that the actual liability is less than the face value of the deferment, due to the time value of money.

Equity with debt characteristics presents a challenge for accountants. Some "hybrid" financial instruments are closer to debt than to equity.

For purposes of reporting to the SEC, any equity instrument issued with redemption provisions outside the control of the issuer is to be shown on the balance sheet between debt and equity in a separate, or "plateau," account.

Other characteristics of equity shares that *could* cause them to be treated as debt for purposes of analysis include a high, fixed yield, a superior treatment in liquidation or in payment of dividends, and no conversion-to-common provision.[4]

Pension plan and retirement benefit deficiencies have received significant press coverage in recent years. Under existing accounting standards, companies must report on their balance sheets any unfunded obligations they have to a pension plans they sponsor. To help companies make the

---

[4] See SEC Accounting Series Release (ASR) 268.

transition from earlier years, when GAAP did not require them to record this obligation, GAAP allows plan sponsors to amortize the full amount of the obligation onto the balance sheet over a minimum of a 15-year period.

Contingent liabilities are obligations that may or may not exist. Lawsuits are perhaps the best example of contingent liabilities. According to accounting standards, a loss must be charged to income if two conditions exist:

- It is *probable* that an asset had been impaired or a liability had been incurred at the date of the financial statements, and

- The amount of loss can be *reasonably estimated.*

Whether or not the amount can be estimated, a contingent liability whose occurrence is "reasonably possible" must be disclosed in a footnote. Two examples of typical contingent liabilities that appear on balance sheets are accruals for warranty costs on products and some costs of self insurance.

Minority interest appears on the face of the balance sheet when a company does not own 100 percent of all its consolidated subsidiaries. When a company owns more than 50 percent of another entity, it consolidates that entity's balance sheet with its own. Since it does not own all of the other entity, however, the parent company shows a separate minority claim against the consolidated assets. That claim represents the equity interest in the subsidiary held by the minority shareholders. This is neither debt nor the equity of the parent.

§2.5 Shareholders' Equity

Arithmetically, equity is the difference between what is owned (the assets) and what is owed (the liabilities). The items in the equity section of the balance sheet represent what the owners would receive if the entity were liquidated. This theoretical liquidation assumes that the assets can be sold and the liabilities can be satisfied for the amounts shown on the balance sheet.

The typical components of the equity section of a corporate balance sheet are:

- Capital stock

- Additional amounts paid for capital stock

- Retained (undistributed) earnings of the entity

- Treasury stock

- Cumulative foreign currency translation adjustment for companies with foreign operations

- Net unrealized losses on long-term investments in equity securities. (The loss in value does not pass through the income statement until the investment is sold or is permanently impaired.)

It is highly unusual for assets to be worth precisely the values shown. Accounting convention requires that those values be set at cost on the day they were acquired, and that they continue to be recorded on a cost basis.[5] Thus, at any given time, some assets may be worth more than their book value and others less. Forced liquidations usually result in significant losses from book values.

The balance sheet of ABC, Inc. (**Exhibit 2**) contains a category of shareholders' equity called "additional paid in capital." This means that the shareholders of ABC, Inc. paid more than the stated face value (par value) of the common stock when they bought their shares. Sometimes "additional paid in capital" is called capital in excess of par value.

The balance sheet of ABC, Inc. shows three million issued shares (i.e., 3 million shares have been sold to the shareholders at December 31, l9x5). These shares have a par value of $1, and three million shares at $1 par value equals $3 million of issued common stock. The ABC, Inc. balance sheet also shows $15 million of paid-in capital. Consequently, the shareholders of ABC, Inc. actually paid an average of $6 ($18 million divided by $3 million) for each share they purchased.

§2.6   The Income Statement

The income statement, which is also called the "statement of operations" or "operating statement," presents a far different view of the

---

[5] See **Chapter 1**, especially § 1.5 on the cost basis of accounting and § 1.4 on the concept of the going concern.

business from that of a balance sheet. The balance sheet is a status report at one point in time, like a snapshot. The income statement presents the results of operations over a period of time, usually one year. In addition to annual statements, most companies produce monthly and quarterly statements known as interim statements.

A balance sheet cannot tell a reader very much about a company's ability to make a profit. An income statement, however, by summarizing how much income a business earned and by what means, becomes a first step in assessing profitability. How a business makes a profit is of interest to an investor or to a creditor, since it provides a basis for further analysis of whether or not profits are likely to continue in the future.

Like the balance sheet, however, the income statement is limited because it shows only one year's operations. Thus, it is not a reliable predictor of what will occur in the future. To evaluate a company's management and determine its ability to continue earning profits, an investor must analyze trends and changes from year to year, as well as other data. This type of analysis of financial statements is discussed in Chapters 6 and 7.

Exhibit 2-2 is an example of an income statement for ABC Inc.

The income statement and notes offer varying amounts of detail about revenues and expenses. Additional information on public companies is available in the Form 10-K Annual Report filed with the SEC. The following is a brief description of each line item on many corporate income statements.

Net sales is the amount of gross income a company generates by selling goods or services. Service companies may identify their revenues as "fees" or as "income." Assuming that costs remain relatively constant, increasing or decreasing sales is a major indicator of the vitality of the business in the competitive marketplace. Unless sales are rising at a rate higher than inflation, the company is probably stagnating or declining.

An interesting measure of a company's growth is not found in public financial statements. Units sold, or hours sold for some service companies, is a better indicator of growth, but often this information is difficult to obtain.

Cost of goods sold is used in traditional manufacturing and retailing operations, and is simply what it states. Since service firms do not sell specific products, this item will not appear on their income statements.

Exhibit 2-2

ABC, Inc.
Consolidated Statements of Income

	Year ended December 31	
	19X5	*19X4*
	(In Thousands)	
Net sales	**$150,000**	$125,000
Cost of products sold	**111,500**	90,300
Selling and administrative expenses	**19,950**	22,100
	18,550	12,600
Other income (expense):		
Interest expense	**(5,550)**	(4,400)
Other income	**1,000**	800
Income before income taxes	**14,000**	9,000
Income taxes *(Note 8)*	**6,700**	4,000
Net income	**$ 7,300**	$ 5,000
Earnings per share:[6]		
Primary	**$2.42**	$1.69
Fully diluted	**$2.32**	$1.67

See accompanying notes.

(This exhibit and accompanying notes also appears in Appendix B)

Gross profit, also known as gross margin, is the amount by which sales exceed the direct costs of the products or services sold. Direct costs are essentially the material, labor and overhead that is used to manufacture the product or deliver the service. The gross margin indicates how much the company marks up its products or services. Typically, companies dealing with unique products can maintain higher margins; conversely, as a product becomes more of a commodity (e.g., sugar or flour), the margin usually shrinks.

Selling, general, and administrative expenses are frequently referred to by the acronym SG&A. This line item contains all costs other than interest and cost of goods sold. It normally includes office and sales sala-

---

[6] Earnings per share is not required for nonpublic enterprises. FASB Statement No. 21.

ries, rent, depreciation, non-income-producing assets, and other non-manufacturing or service delivery costs. Because many companies do not provide more detail than this one line on the face of their income statements, it can be difficult to tell what expenses are contained in the amount without reading the notes and SEC filings.

Interest expense is the cost of borrowing. It may or may not represent the actual cash paid, since the financial statements are on an accrual basis.

Other income is revenue earned from activities other than the main business activity. It typically includes items such as interest income, rent, and profits on the sale of property, plant and equipment.

Federal and state income tax are based on the income before taxes that appears on the income statement, adjusted for "permanent differences." The amount on the income statement is usually not the amount that is payable to the tax authorities for that year. The income statement is a summary of all earnings transactions, recorded in accordance with GAAP. The income tax return is a summary of all earnings transactions recorded in accordance with the applicable tax regulations. There are three types of differences between GAAP and tax accounting: permanent, timing, and temporary differences.

- *Permanent differences* arise from tax law provisions that differ from GAAP and that will not be offset in the future. For example, interest on state or municipal bonds is included in GAAP income, but not in tax return income (except possibly in minimum tax computations).

- *Timing differences*, on the other hand, relate only to a difference between the time period in which the income or expense item is recognized for tax purposes and the time period in which it is recorded on the financial statements. For example, an addition to a reserve for uncollectible receivables is recorded as an expense for GAAP accounting, but not until the receivable is completely beyond collection and written off is the expense allowed for tax purposes. When the reporting period for the reserving of the uncollectible account differs from the time of the actual tax writeoff of the uncollectible account, a timing difference arises.

- *Temporary differences*, which are similar to timing differences, represent the difference between the tax basis of an asset or liability and its reported amount in the financial statements that will be taxable or tax deductible in future years. (This term is used in the latest FASB statements on taxes, SFAS #96 and #106.)

The financial statements or the notes will disclose both the currently payable and the deferred (payable at some time beyond one year from the date of the statement) portions of the income tax expense.

Extraordinary items are those economic events that are material, significantly different in nature from the typical or customary business activities, not expected to be repeated often, and not normally considered when evaluating the operations of a company. For example, if a foreign country nationalized the operations of a subsidiary of a U.S. company, it would be reported as extraordinary, if it was material. Extraordinary items are usually designated as such by informed professional judgment based on all the facts and circumstances of the event or events in question. Events that may be classified as extraordinary include gains on restructuring payables, gains or losses on the extinguishment of debt, and expropriations of property.

Earnings per share. This calculation shows how much of an entity's income or loss is attributable to an individual share of common stock. When a company has a simple capital structure, earnings per share (EPS) is computed by dividing net income by the average number of common shares outstanding during the period.

A company with a complex capital structure calculates two amounts for earnings per share. The first, called the "primary earnings per share," is income divided by the weighted average of all common stock and equivalents outstanding during the period. Common stock equivalents are those securities (such as convertible preferred stock, debt with conversion features, options, and warrants) that are considered common stock for purposes of this calculation. Whether a security is a common stock equivalent depends upon whether it is selling on the basis of its convertibility feature. Convertibility depends on the economics of the transaction at the time preferred stock or debt with conversion features is issued. The analyst looks at warrants and options at the balance sheet date and makes a judgment about whether they will be exercised, in light of market factors.

The second amount of EPS, "fully diluted earnings per share," considers all possible dilutions to earnings per share, such as conversions, exercises of options, and more. This is calculated even in a case where the economics of the conversion would not benefit the rights holder at that time. Dilution or decreased earnings per share occurs when net income (the numerator) stays the same or does not change significantly, while the number of shares (the denominator) increases. Only instruments that have a diluting effect on EPS are considered in calculating fully diluted EPS.

When dealing with common stock equivalents or making adjustments to average shares outstanding, one must also make an adjustment to compensate for any interest or dividends related to the shares. If, for example, you treat convertible debt as if it were common stock for purposes of determining EPS, you must add back to earnings the interest paid on that debt before you divide the earnings by the adjusted number of average shares outstanding.

§2.7   The Cash Flow Statement

Mandated since 1988, this statement is the FASB's most recent effort to help financial statement users understand the profitability and solvency of a business. If it is analyzed carefully, a cash flow statement can be one of the most helpful documents available to a reader of the financial statements. To an informed user, this statement is a summarized tour through the company's checkbook.

A cash flow statement reconciles the reported net income to the movement of cash into and out of the entity. It discloses the company's cash flow in three areas: operations, investing, and financing. Accrual basis financial statements have come a long way from cash basis statements, but now users can also see the movement of cash in an entity. Some call this a "where it came from and where it went statement." (See Exhibit 2-3 for an example of a cash flow statement.)

On statements of cash flow, activities are broken out into the following categories:

- *Investing activities* relate to making and collecting loans, as well as acquiring and disposing of debt, equity instruments, and assets that are used in the entity's production of goods or services.

Exhibit 2-3

___

ABC, Inc.
Consolidated Statements of Cash Flows
Year ended December 31

	19X5	19X4
	(In Thousands)	
Operating activities		
Net income	$ 7,300	$ 5,000
Adjustments to reconcile net income to net cash provided by operating activities:		
Depreciation and amortization	9,000	8,000
Deferred income taxes	1,700	850
Undistributed earnings of affiliates	(1,000)	(500)
Changes in operating assets and liabilities:		
Accounts receivable	(1,000)	(1,000)
Inventories	(8,000)	(5,000)
Accounts payable and accrued expenses	3,400	1,300
Income taxes payable	3,000	(350)
Net cash provided by operating activities	14,400	8,300
Investing activities		
Purchases of property, plant, and equipment	(13,800)	(5,900)
Acquisition of Future Corp.	(10,000)	—
Proceeds from disposal of property, plant, and equipment	1,000	200
Net cash used in investing activities	(22,800)	(5,700)
Financing activities		
Proceeds from issuance of 10% debentures	15,000	—
Proceeds from issuance of common stock	1,000	—
Payments of long-term debt	(1,200)	(860)
Payments of capital lease obligations	(350)	(300)
Net decrease in short-term borrowings	(3,000)	(1,000)
Dividends paid	(2,950)	(2,900)
Net cash provided (used) by financing activities	8,500	(5,060)

Exhibit 2-3 *(continued)*

ABC, Inc.
Consolidated Statements of Cash Flows
Year ended December 31

	19X5	19X4
	(In Thousands)	
Effect of exchange rate changes on cash	**1,400**	(840)
Net increase (decrease) in cash and cash equivalents	1,500	(3,300)
Cash and cash equivalents at beginning of year	6,000	9,300
Cash and cash equivalents at end of year	$ 7,500	$ 6,000

See accompanying notes.

(This exhibit and accompanying notes also appears in Appendix B)

- *Financing activities* include investing transactions by owners (sale of stock, payment of dividends, etc.), borrowing and repayment of money, and obtaining and paying for other resources on the basis of long-term credit.

- *Operating activities* are all transactions and other events that are not defined as investing or financing activities. These cash flows generally arise from an entity's income-producing activities, i.e., transactions and other events that become part of net income.

§2.8   The Statement of Shareholders' Equity

Statements of shareholders' equity summarize the various components of equity and how they have changed. They are usually omitted from the financial statements if the information is contained on the face of other statements or in the notes. Often, for example, if changes in equity all occurred as a result of earnings that are being retained in the business, the change in retained earnings may be shown at the bottom of the income statement. However, where there has been significant activity in stock, this statement can be quite extensive. Such statements usually show the opening balances, activity, and closing balances for the following categories of equity or special accounts:

Exhibit 2-4

ABC, Inc.
Consolidated Statements of Shareholders' Equity[7]

	Common Stock	Additional Paid-In Capital	Retained Earnings	Currency Translation Adjustments	Total
			(In Thousands)		
Balance at December 31, 19X3	$2,900	$14,100	$52,850	$ 500	$70,350
Net income for 19X4	—	—	5,000	—	5,000
Currency translation adjustments	—	—	—	(1,500)	(1,500)
Cash dividends ($1.00 per share)[8]	—	—	(2,900)	—	(2,900)
Balance at December 31, 19X4	2,900	14,100	54,950	(1,000)	70,950
Proceeds from issuance of 100,000 shares of common stock	100	900	—	—	1,000
Net income for 19X5	—	—	7,300	—	7,300
Currency translation adjustments	—	—	—	2,000	2,000
Cash dividends ($1.00 per share)[9]	—	—	(2,950)	—	(2,950)
Balance at December 31, 19X5	$3,000	$15,000	$59,300	$1,000	$78,300

See accompanying notes.

(This exhibit and accompanying notes also appears in Appendix B)

---

[7] It is also acceptable to present "Statements of Retained Earnings" or "Statements of Income and Retained Earnings," particularly when there are few transactions affecting shareholders' equity during the years presented.

[8] Disclosure of dividends per share is optional for nonpublic enterprises.

[9] See footnote 8.

- Common shares

- Preferred shares

- Capital in excess of par value

- Retained earnings

- Treasury shares

- Unrealized gain or loss on marketable equity securities

- Foreign currency translation adjustments

Exhibit 2-4 is an example of a statement of shareholders' equity.

This statement and its accompanying notes will disclose both the dollar value and the number of shares involved in any changes in all classes of stock—stock dividends, splits, reverse splits, new issues, acquisitions, and dispositions of the company's own stock (treasury stock activity), and exercises of rights, warrants and options.

CHAPTER THREE

Notes to the Financial Statements

§3.1   Introduction

The basic financial statements are actually very concise summaries of many underlying transactions. To understand the statements fully, however, a reader must be aware of certain significant details. Adding a lot of detail to the face of the statements would clutter them and confuse the reader, so these details, many of which are disclosures required by GAAP or the SEC, are contained in the notes.

Reading the notes is an important step in the process of understanding financial statements. It is a truism among accountants that the notes are a user's best friend. Indeed, no serious user of financial statements can claim to have read the financial statements without reading the notes. They help the reader understand the business, the accounting methods, and the financial statements themselves.

The notes must be consulted if a reader wishes to compare the financial statements of any two companies, since the two may use different accounting methods or may differ in other ways. Notes offer very important information about the financial position of the company, such as major events that occurred after the date of the statements, transactions with related parties, and methods of calculating inventory.

GAAP requires that the notes contain all material information that is necessary to understand the company's financial position and the results of its operations. Managers of companies differ greatly in the amount of detail they disclose in the notes, and the presence or lack of detail can be a clue to the management style of a company. This chapter explains some of the basic information that typically appears in the notes to the financial statements of manufacturing and retailing enterprises. This information does not have to follow any particular format, although certain conventions have evolved over the years.

The content of the notes will vary widely of course, depending on the line(s) of a company's business, the complexity of its finances, and other factors. When the information in any particular note is complicated, it may be split into two or more separate notes.

§3.2 Significant Accounting Policies

Normally the first note describes how the entity is structured, the basis on which the statements are presented (accrual, cash, or other) and how management has chosen to account for inventories, taxes, consolidation, and income recognition, among other elements. In a number of instances, different companies can treat a similar transaction, such as depreciation, differently by using disparate but equally acceptable accounting methods. Thus, this note can help you compare one company to another more accurately.

This note provides more than a laundry list of choices a company has made among various alternatives. It also gives a picture of management's "reporting personality." Perhaps all the expenses are being recognized as slowly as possible, and all of the income is being recognized as quickly as possible. This would suggest that management may not be conservative in selecting its accounting methods. An awareness of management's "personality" is helpful in comparing the company to others and to the industry standard.

Accounting should be consistent from year to year, but if it changes, the change must be disclosed in the footnotes. The note on "Significant Accounting Policies" can include information on changes in accounting principles, changes of estimates, and changes to correct errors in prior reports. If a change is extensive, it may be handled in a separate note.

Sometimes a company does not adopt a recently-issued accounting standard because of a delayed effective date. If the new standard is expected to have a material effect on future results of the company's operations or financial position, this note (or another note) should include a brief discussion of the new standard, indicating the date on which the company will adopt the standard and its impact on the financial statements or the financing and operations of the company.* Exhibit 3-1 shows a typical note on significant accounting policies.

§3.3 Inventory

Inventory is a significant part of the operations of many businesses. This note will disclose the components of the amount shown on the balance sheet, separating raw materials, work in process, and finished goods. This note, or sometimes the note on Significant Accounting Policies, also addresses any problems with obsolescence.

Users can find out here whether first-in first-out (FIFO) or last-in first-out (LIFO) is being used to calculate inventory. The numbers for the same physical amount of inventory in exactly the same condition can be very different, depending upon whether the company uses LIFO or

---

*Examples of notes shown in this Chapter are from the example for ABC, Inc. in Appendix B.

FIFO. This calculation can be important to a buyer of a business, and to anyone who is comparing two businesses. Exhibit 3-2 shows a typical note on inventory.

Exhibit 3-1

1. Accounting Policies

Description of Business

The Company manufactures and sells automotive parts primarily to original equipment manufacturers (OEMs) and automotive aftermarket customers. The Company performs periodic credit evaluations of its customers' financial condition and generally does not require collateral. At December 31, 19X5 and 19X4, accounts receivable from OEM customers were approximately $16 million and $12 million, respectively. Receivables generally are due within 60 days. Credit losses relating to OEM customers consistently have been within management's expectations and comparable to losses for the portfolio as a whole.

Principles of Consolidation

The consolidated financial statements include the accounts of the Company and its subsidiaries, all of which are wholly owned. Significant intercompany accounts and transactions have been eliminated in consolidation. The Company's 20%-owned affiliate is accounted for by the equity method.

Inventories

Inventories are carried at the lower of cost or market using the last-in, first-out (LIFO) method for domestic inventories and the first-in, first-out (FIFO) method for all other inventories.

Property, Plant, and Equipment

Property, plant, and equipment is stated at cost. Depreciation is computed principally by the straight-line method for financial reporting purposes.

Cash Equivalents

The Company considers all highly liquid investments with a maturity of three months or less when purchased to be cash equivalents.

Exhibit 3-1 *(continued)*

Income Taxes

All income tax amounts and balances have been computed in accordance with APB Opinion No. 11, "Accounting for Income Taxes." In December, 1987, the Financial Accounting Standards Board issued Statement of Financial Accounting Standards No. 96, "Accounting for Income Taxes." The Company will be required to comply with the new rules by 1992.

The Company has not completed all of the complex analyses required to estimate the impact of the new Statement, and it has not decided whether it will implement the Statement early or restate any periods. However, the adoption of Statement 96 is not expected to have an adverse impact on the Company's financial position.

Earnings Per Share*

Earnings per share is based on the average number of shares of common stock outstanding during each year. Fully diluted earnings per share assumes that the 7% convertible sinking fund debentures were converted into common stock as of the beginning of each year, and that the interest expense thereon, net of income taxes, was added to net income.

(This exhibit also appears in Appendix B.)

* *Earnings per share is not required for nonpublic enterprises (FASB Statement No. 21).*

---

§3.4   Debt

All outstanding debt and interest payments are shown in this note, including all debt payments for the next five years. Significant restrictive covenants are also described here. Since "capitalized leases" are essentially secured lending, this note may also cover lease provisions. If leases are material, however, they may be treated in a separate note.

The maturity of debt is important in determining cash flow, and restrictive covenants could affect the company's ability to pay dividends. This note is worth studying when analyzing financial data, since it will tell the reader how sensitive to interest rates the company is, and when

Exhibit 3-2

---

3. Inventories

Current cost exceeds the LIFO value of inventories by approximately $20.5 million and $14 million at December 31, 19X5 and 19X4, respectively. Year-end inventories valued under the LIFO method were $50 million in 19X5 and $43 million in 19X4.

(This exhibit also appears in Appendix B.)

---

debt matures and will need to be refinanced. Exhibit 3-3 is a representative note on debt.

§3.5 Capital Stock

Combined with the note on debt, the note on capital stock will give the reader a detailed picture of the company's capitalization. This note supplements the Statement of Changes in Owners' Equity and Retained Earnings, which can be part of the basic financial statements when the ownership of an entity is complicated. The note on capital stock describes issuances, repurchases, and changes of terms in the company's stock. It also contains a description of the company's stock option plan and a summary of the options issued under the plan. Exhibit 3-4 is a sample note on capital stock.

§3.6 Earnings per Share

Calculations of earnings per share of stock will be described in the notes if they are not evident on the face of the income statement. For a company with a complex capital structure (convertible securities, options, warrants, etc.), there will be two calculations: primary earnings per share and fully diluted earnings per share. Both calculations can be quite complicated, but this note will show how they were made. The ABC, Inc. example of financial statements in Appendix B does not include a separate earnings per share note, as the company does not have a very complicated capital structure. Instead, information on the process used to compute the amount is included in the Accounting Policies note.

Exhibit 3-3

6. Long-Term Debt

Long-term debt consisted of the following:

	19X5	19X4
	(In Thousands)	
10% notes due through 19Y6	**$15,000**	—
7% convertible sinking fund notes due through 19X8	**14,000**	$15,000
Other, principally at 12% due through 19X9	**7,000**	7,000
	36,000	22,000
Less current portion	**1,000**	1,000
	$35,000	$21,000

Maturities of long-term debt for the five years succeeding December 31, 19X5 are $1 million in 19X6, $1 million in 19X7, $15.5 million in 19X8, $5.5 million in 19X9, and $2 million in 19Y0. Through June 30, 19X8, the 7% debentures are convertible into shares of common stock at the rate of one share for each $40 face amount.

The loan agreements for both note issues include, among other things, provisions relative to additional borrowings, maintenance of working capital, and restrictions on the amount of retained earnings available for the payment of dividends. Under the most restrictive of these covenants, retained earnings in the amount of $32 million were free of such limitations at December 31, 19X5.

Interest payments were $6.175 million and $4.8 million in 19X5 and 19X4, respectively, of which $600,000 and $350,000, respectively, was capitalized as part of the cost of the Company's newly constructed manufacturing plant.

(This exhibit also appears in Appendix B.)

§3.7 Contingencies

Notes on contingencies discuss the expected results of litigation and environmental issues, along with other contingent assets or liabilities. The note should indicate the nature of the contingency and an estimate of the range of loss, or a statement that an estimate cannot be made. Whether or not the amount can be calculated or estimated, contingencies

Exhibit 3-4

7. Shareholder's Equity

At December 31, 19X5, 1 million shares of Series A Preferred Stock with a stated value of $10 per share were authorized, none of which have been issued.

At December 31, 19X5, the Company has reserved 350,000 shares for the conversion of the 7% convertible sinking fund notes.

A subsidiary of the Company is subject to debt agreements that limit cash dividends and loans to the Company. At December 31, 19X5, restricted net assets of the subsidiary were $20 million.

(This exhibit also appears in Appendix B.)

---

that are *reasonably possible* must be discussed in a note. Contingencies that can be *reasonably estimated* in amount and that are *probable*, must be both recorded on the books and included in the financial statements as a loss.

Reporting to the public about a probable loss arising from a lawsuit presents a dilemma for accountants and lawyers. On one hand, the law requires disclosure; on the other, the disclosure may weaken the company's position in court or in negotiation. Such situations require a tremendous amount of legal and managerial judgment. The following is an example of a contingencies note:

Exhibit 3-5

Contingencies

The company is involved in two environmental actions. The first at the Anytown site of its wholly owned subsidiary, Littleco, Inc., involved the contamination of groundwater at and near the plant. The Company denies responsibility, but provided $925,000 in fiscal year 19X4 which included the cost of bringing public water to the area and incurred $700,000 of expenses related to this matter in fiscal year 19X5. The Company has had continuing discussions with the State and the

Exhibit 3-5 *(continued)*

Environmental Protection Agency and has reached agreement on remediation steps required to alleviate the contamination.

Several residents near the plant have filed a complaint against Littleco, Inc. in the Circuit Court for Any County. The complaint alleges that the company is responsible for the above mentioned contamination. The plaintiffs seek $32,000,000 in compensatory damages and $64,000,000 in punitive damages. Management believes the case is without merit, and is vigorously contesting these claims.

In the second environmental action, the Company received notice by letter dated September 16, 19X5 from the Environmental Protection Agency that, together with over 66 other companies in the area, it may be a potentially responsible party for hazardous waste discovered at a landfill in Malborough. If found liable, the company would be required to perform or finance certain response activities. The Company denies responsibility, and is vigorously contesting all claims connected with the site.

During the fourth quarter of fiscal 19X5, the Company provided an additional $2,400,000 (net of anticipated insurance coverage) related to remediation expenses, legal, consulting and engineering fees, EPA response costs, and other expenses related to these environmental matters. As of December 31, 19X9 and December 31, 19X8, $2,320,000 and $900,000, respectively, is included in other accrued liabilities, relating to the above issues.

---

§3.8 Income Taxes

Accounting for tax purposes and for general reporting purposes almost always differ. Consequently, the amount shown on the income statement as income tax expense can vary significantly from the amount of taxes actually paid. This note describes the differences and gives more detail on how the taxes were calculated. The note also discusses other relevant tax information such as carryforwards, credits, and deferrals. Exhibit 3-6 shows a note on income taxes.

Exhibit 3-6

8. Income Taxes

Income before income taxes consisted of the following:

	19X5	19X4
	(In Thousands)	
Domestic	$10,000	$6,000
Foreign	4,000	3,000
	$14,000	$9,000

Federal, foreign, and state income taxes consisted of the following:

	19X5		19X4	
	Current	Deferred	Current	Deferred
	(In Thousands)			
Federal	$3,150	$1,400	$1,700	$550
Foreign	1,000	250	910	240
State	850	50	540	60
	$5,000	$1,700	$3,150	$850

The deferred tax provision relates to the following:

	19X5	19X4
	(In Thousands)	
Depreciation	$1,600	$800
Other	100	50
	$1,700	$850

Total income tax payments during 19X5 and 19X4 were $2 million and $3.5 million, respectively.

Provision has been made for U.S. federal income taxes to be paid on the portion of undistributed earnings of foreign subsidiaries expected to be remitted to the Company. Undistributed earnings intended to be invested indefinitely in foreign subsidiaries was $10 million and $8 million at the end of 19X5 and 19X4, respectively. Deferred income taxes have not been provided on such earnings; however, if such earnings were remitted, estimated withholding taxes would be $2 million and $1.6 million, respectively.

The effective income tax rate varied from the statutory federal income tax rate as follows:

Exhibit 3-6 *(continued)*

	19X5	19X4
Statutory federal income tax rate	34.0%	40.0%
Increases (decreases):		
State income taxes, net of federal tax benefit	5.5	3.6
Effect of foreign income tax rates	3.5	(1.6)
Alternative minimum tax	3.2	—
Research and experimentation credit	(1.1)	—
Other items	2.7	2.4
Effective income tax rate	47.8%	44.4%

(This exhibit also appears in Appendix B.)

§3.9 Segment Data

A note on segment data is required for certain companies that operate in more than one industry or type of business. It describes the various segments, or lines of business, and summarizes the revenues, earnings, and assets of each of the segments. Exhibit 3-7 is an example of this type of disclosure, which also appears in the sample Form 10-K in Appendix C. This note may also contain additional information on particular segments and international operations.

Exhibit 3-7

Industry Segment Data

The Company operates in three principal industries—construction materials, metal products, and paper products. The Company's construction materials division markets residential heating systems, electrical parts and motors, plumbing supplies and miscellaneous metal goods (including metal products division products) through a chain of wholesale supply warehouses. The Company's metal products, which are sold to its own and to independent wholesale supply warehouses, include vent systems, range hoods, flexible metal hose and light coverings. Paper product operations include the manufacture and distribution of boxes, cartons, and other packing materials for industrial uses. They are marketed directly to consumers.

Exhibit 3-7 *(continued)*

	Year Ended December 31		
	19X5	*19X4*	*19X3*
	(Thousands of dollars)		
Net Sales			
Construction materials	$110,000	$ 98,000	$ 90,000
Metal products			
Unaffliated customers	20,000	12,000	10,000
Intersegment	10,000	8,000	8,000
	30,000	20,000	18,000
Paper products	20,000	15,000	14,000
Other industries	10,000	8,000	8,000
Eliminations—intersegment sales	(10,000)	(8,000)	(8,000)
Total Revenue	$160,000	$133,000	$122,000
Operating Profit			
Construction materials	$ 9,000	$ 5,000	$ 9,100
Metal products	5,000	3,500	3,500
Paper products	4,000	3,000	2,000
Other industries	2,000	2,000	1,500
Total Operating Profit	20,000	13,500	16,100
Corporate expenses	(1,450)	(1,100)	(450)
Interest expense	(5,550)	(4,400)	(4,650)
Income Before Income Taxes	$ 13,000	$ 8,000	$ 11,000
Identifiable Assets			
Construction materials	$112,500	$ 90,000	$ 85,000
Metal products	20,000	20,000	18,000
Paper products	20,000	19,000	15,000
Other industries	10,000	8,000	6,000
	162,500	137,000	124,000
Corporate assets	7,000	6,500	6,000
Total Assets	$169,500	$143,500	$130,000

(This exhibit also appears in Appendix C.)

§3.10 Quarterly Results

Many large public companies are required to publish a summary of their quarterly results. This information, which is unaudited, will give the user a picture of the flow of revenue and expense over the year. The note provides insight into the seasonal fluctuations and other trends in the company's operations. Often these companies include the quarterly results of operations in the annual report to shareholders and incorporate it by reference in the SEC Form 10-K. Exhibit 3-8 is an example of this type of disclosure, and is also included in the sample Form 10-K in Appendix C.

§3.11 Pension Plans

This note describes the entity's pension plans and includes which employee groups are covered, the type of benefit formula, the funding policy, types of assets, and significant liabilities in the plan.

In this note you can find the total cost of pension plans included in the income statements, and a schedule that reconciles the funded status of the plan with the amounts reported on the balance sheet. This schedule shows the fair value of pension plan assets, benefit obligations, unrecognized prior service costs, and gain or loss on the plan's assets. This note also contains discount rates and estimated rates of compensation increase—two of the factors that are used to ascertain the current cost that is being charged against earnings and the funded (or unfunded) status of the plan. Exhibit 3-9 contains a note on pension plans.

§3.12 Postretirement Benefits Other Than Pensions

After December 15, 1992, for public and large privately held companies, and 1994 for all other companies, financial statements must recognize the costs and liabilities of postretirement benefits other than pensions. Among the more common types of these benefits for retired employees are health care, dental care, and life insurance benefits. Health care plans are by far the most expensive of the benefits given to retirees.

Exhibit 3-8

Quarterly Results of Operations

The following is a summary of the quarterly results of operations for the years ended December 31, 19X5 and 19X4.

	Three Months Ended			
	Mar. 31	Jun. 30	Sep. 30	Dec. 31
	(Thousands of dollars, except per-share data)			
19X5				
Net sales	$45,000	$30,000	$40,000	$35,000
Cost of products sold	36,000	24,500	32,000	28,000
Net income	2,400	1,600	2,150	1,850
Net income per common share:				
Primary	.80	.53	.71	.61
Fully diluted	.73	.49	.65	.59
19X4				
Net sales	$25,000	$37,500	$33,500	$29,000
Cost of products sold	19,500	29,500	26,000	22,500
Net income	1,000	1,500	1,300	1,200
Net income per common share:				
Primary	.34	.51	.46	.38
Fully diluted	.34	.49	.45	.37

The information in the note is similar in many respects to the extensive disclosures required for pension plans:

- Description of the plan, employee groups covered, and funding policies;

- The components of net postretirement benefit cost for each period;

- Key actuarial assumptions used in measuring the cost and the liability; and

- A reconciliation of the funded status of the plan to the amounts presented in the balance sheet.

Exhibit 3-9 is an example of a note on pension plans and other postretirement benefits (prior to the implementation of the new standard effective December 15, 1992).

Exhibit 3-9

9. Pension Plans and Postretirement Benefits

The Company and its subsidiaries have two defined benefit pension plans that cover substantially all nonunion employees, including certain employees in foreign countries. Benefits are based on years of service and each employee's compensation during the last five years of employment. The Company's funding policy is to make the minimum annual contributions required by applicable regulations.

The following table sets forth the funded status and amount recognized for the Company's defined benefit pension plans in the consolidated balance sheets at December 31:

	19X5	19X4
	(In Thousands)	
Actuarial present value of accumulated benefit obligation, including vested benefits of $24,800,000 in 19X5 and $23,700,000 in 19X4	**$(32,000)**	$(30,600)
Actuarial present value of projected benefit obligation for services rendered to date	**$(36,100)**	$(33,000)
Plan assets at fair value, primarily listed stocks and U.S. bonds	**29,100**	27,700
Projected benefit obligation in excess of plan assets	**(7,000)**	(5,300)
Unrecognized net loss from past experience different from that assumed and effects of changes in assumptions	**600**	200
Prior service cost not yet recognized in net periodic pension cost	**1,400**	1,000
Unrecognized net obligation at January 1, 19X5 and 19X4	**3,000**	2,000
Accrued pension cost	**$ (2,000)**	$ (2,100)

Net pension cost included the following components:

Exhibit 3-9 *(continued)*

	19X5	*19X4*
	(In Thousands)	
Service cost—benefits earned during the period	$ 800	$ 600
Interest cost on projected benefit obligation	3,300	3,000
Actual return on plan assets	(3,100)	(2,700)
Net amortization and deferral	500	700
Net pension cost	$1,500	$1,600

The Company also makes contributions to a union-sponsored multi-employer defined benefit pension plan. Such contributions were $1.2 million in 19X5 and $975,000 in 19X4.

Following is a summary of significant actuarial assumptions used:

	19X5	*19X4*
Discount rates	9%	10%
Rates of increase in compensation levels	6%	6%
Expected long-term rate of return on assets	10%	10%

The Company and its subsidiaries provide certain health care and life insurance benefits for retired employees. Substantially all of the Company's employees, including employees in foreign countries, may become eligible if they reach normal retirement age while still working for the Company. These benefits are provided through an insurance company whose premiums are based on the benefits paid during the year. The cost of retiree health care and life insurance benefits is recognized as expense as premiums are incurred. For 19X5 and 19X4, those costs approximated $225,000 and $200,000, respectively.

In December 1990, the Financial Accounting Standards Board issued new rules that require that the projected future cost of providing postretirement benefits, such as health care and life insurance, be recognized as an expense as employees render service instead of when paid. Companies can elect to record the cumulative effect of the accounting change as a charge against income in the year the rules are adopted, or alternatively, on a delayed basis as a part of the future annual benefit cost. The Company will be required to comply with the new rules by 1993. The Company has not yet completed the complex analysis required to estimate the financial statement impact of the new rules, nor has it decided how or when it will initially adopt them. In a related matter, the FASB is

Exhibit 3-9 *(continued)*

considering amending the accounting rules for income taxes, and the outcome of that consideration could have a significant impact on the financial statement effects of adopting the new rules on postretirement benefits.

(This exhibit also appears in Appendix B.)

§3.13 Related Party Transactions

Related party transactions include dealings between affiliated companies, and between the company and its employees, officers, and shareholders. If an entity is included in consolidated financial statements, its intercompany transactions will not appear on the statements because the sales and expenses cancel each other out.

This note therefore deals only with nonconsolidated affiliates. Since related party transactions often give rise to problems of substance over form, all related party transactions must be summarized in a footnote. Disclosure in the notes is not a substitute for accounting for the substance of the related party transactions. Related party transactions require greater scrutiny from auditors and readers of financial statements, because the parties' common control could enable them to artificially adjust the underlying economic event. Exhibit 3-10 is an example of a related party note.

§3.14 Subsequent Events

"Subsequent events" occur after the balance sheet date but before the financial statements and the auditors report are issued. To be reported, these events must be considered material to the user of the statements. The occurrence of an event dictates when and how it is accounted for. If an event occurs before the balance sheet date but is discovered afterward, the financial statements must be changed if the effect is material.

Examples of subsequent events include a fire in a plant, the death of a key employee, the sale of a capital stock issue, the loss of a contract, and losses on receivables due to conditions arising after the balance sheet date. Exhibit 3-11 is an example of a subsequent events note.

Exhibit 3-10

Related Party Transactions:

A director of the Company is associated with a law firm that rendered various legal services for the Company. The Company paid the firm, in the aggregate, approximately $352,000 and $297,000 during 19X5 and 19X4, respectively, for legal services.

The Company presently holds two notes receivable for a total of $672,500 from an officer of the Company. These notes arose from transactions in 19X2 and 19X3 whereby the Company loaned the officer money to purchase an aggregate of 350,000 shares of the Company's Class A common stock at the then fair market value. These notes, which bear interest ranging from 7% to 11%, are due in full on January 1, 19X5 and are collateralized by a second lien on real property. The amount of indebtedness shown on the balance sheets reflects the above amount discounted for the difference between the face value interest rate and the market rate at the transaction dates.

In December 19X4, the Company made a $920,000 interest free loan to the The Employee Stock Bonus Plan and Trust (the Plan) to fund benefit payments to Plan participants electing early distribution. Proceeds to the Plan from Company contributions and income from interest and dividends were used to repay the loan in 19X5.

Exhibit 3-11

Subsequent Events

On January 19, 19x5, the Company's Puerto Rican facilities suffered damage from Hurricane Bob. While the operations of those plants were interrupted, management feels that the damage caused by the storm was not material and will be substantially covered by insurance, and that, although there will be temporary production losses, there will be no significant loss of sales.

§3.15   Conclusion

This discussion does not address all possible notes. The content of the notes to the financial statements of any given company depends on the types of accounts and the transactions that are summarized in the financial statements. The general rule calls for disclosing information in the notes when disclosure would be necessary to avoid a misunderstanding of the statements. Materiality, too, is critical in deciding if a note is required.

Appendix C, "Sample Annual Report on Form 10-K," includes examples of additional notes not addressed in this chapter.

CHAPTER FOUR

Management's Discussion and Analysis

§4.1 Overview

After reading the financial statements and footnotes, people often ask what they mean. The SEC requires that public companies provide an explanation, which is known as Management's Discussion and Analysis or MD&A. Management's Discussion and Analysis of Financial Condition and Results of Operations is part of the annual 10-K filing of SEC registrants.[1] Though MD&A is separate from the financial statements,

---

[1] The regulations concerning the MD&A may be found in Item 303 of Regulation S-K. Though MD&A dates back to 1968, the current guidelines for MD&A were

many companies include it in the financial section of their annual reports. (For an example of a 10-K, see Appendix C.)

To a serious reader of financial statements, MD&A is a primary source of additional information about the companys financial condition.[2] The purpose of MD&A is not to repeat the numbers in the financial statements, but to add new information concerning, for example, operations, liquidity, and the effects of price changes. MD&A contains two basic types of information: management's analysis of the numbers in the financial statements, and managements commentary on the company's future prospects. The information covers the most recent three fiscal years.

MD&A is management's explanation of why things happened, what the trends are, and why changes occurred in the companys financial condition and results of operations. To give just one example, if sales rose in comparison with the previous year, MD&A should reveal whether more units were actually sold or whether the increase was due to an increase in price or to some other economic factor.

(a)   Emphasis on the Future

Perhaps the most unique aspect of MD&A is its emphasis on so-called "prospective information:" the impact in the future of what is happening at present. The SEC requires management to disclose in its MD&A any material "trends, events, and uncertainties" that would cause the financial statements not to be indicative of future operations. Nowhere else is this information publicly available, except perhaps in the press and in other outside reports by financial analysts.

Typically, MD&A will mention any factors that would cause the current financial information *not* to apply to future operations, as well as factors that will affect future operations, but did not affect past operations. Management is required to report its future projections, unless the trend or event is not "reasonably likely to occur" or unless its effect on the company will not be material. Because of the SEC's regulations, most analyses include all known events, transactions, and circumstances.

----

adopted in 1989. You will find the most recent interpretation in the codification of Financial Reporting Policies Section 501—FRR 36.

[2] It is a good idea to read the entire 10-K, which contains more information about the business, its operations, and the properties the company owns.

Thus, absence of certain information in the MD&A should give the reader some assurance that a particular scenario has not occurred.

The SEC monitors MD&A so carefully that it is not unusual for registrants to receive letters asking for changes in their MD&A, often on the basis of hindsight. For example, if there has been a major writeoff in the first quarter, the SEC will look for warnings in the prior year's MD&A, especially if it is not obvious from the financial statements that the trends are downward.

For the reader of financial statements, MD&A is the place to look for any future uncertainties. For example, if a patent has expired and it has been a major factor in the company's sales, the expiration should be reported in MD&A. Preliminary merger negotiations will often be disclosed here, since such negotiations qualify as a known uncertainty that is likely to have a material effect on the company's future. On the other hand, one may not find a discussion of merger negotiations, since the SEC recognizes that premature disclosure could jeopardize the completion of such a transaction.

The financial statements themselves are neutral. Although they contain a wealth of data to be analyzed, they do not include any analysis. MD&A, which presents the company's point of view, is the starting point for analyzing financial statements. The reader will find analytical tools that can be applied to financial data in Part II. of this book.

(b)   The Content of MD&A

Readers of MD&As will find each report unique. It is hard to generalize about what information a reader will find in MD&A, because companies and transactions are so diverse and complex. Each company is expected to present the information that is most relevant to its circumstances. The SEC allows some flexibility in content and format, but most companies follow conventional categories.

Often, when a company is involved in more than one type of business, it provides information on each segment of its business, but this is not a requirement. A segment-by-segment report is required only if one segment contributes disproportionately to revenues, profits, or capital needs.

The discussion in MD&A generally covers the following topics:

- **Specific information**. MD&A should discuss the company's liquidity, capital resources, and results of operations.

- **Prospective information**. This includes known material events and uncertainties that may cause the financial information not to be indicative of future operations.

- **Explanation of material changes**. MD&A should analyze the cause of changes in line items of the consolidated financial statements, when these items are compared with prior amounts.

- **The impact of inflation and changing prices**. Inflation is not always a major issue, but in times of double-digit inflation, MD&A should discuss its impact on net sales and revenues.

- **Other information**. MD&A should include any other information the company believes will help readers understand its financial condition, changes in financial condition, and results of operations.

This chapter will discuss the typical contents of MD&A: liquidity, capital resources, results of operations, foreign operations, the impact of inflation and changing prices, and other required disclosures.

§4.2   Liquidity

A company's liquidity depends on its ability to generate adequate amounts of cash for current and future needs. These cash needs include paying debt as it matures, maintaining capacity, providing for growth, and planning for a competitive return on investment. This section of MD&A tells where the cash will come from and how the company will pay its dividends, taxes, and debt.

Generally, the discussion of liquidity looks beyond the next 12-month period, focusing mainly on the following items:

- Known trends, demands, events, or uncertainties that will affect the company's liquidity,

- Plans to remedy any deficiency in liquidity, and

- Internal and external sources of cash.

In short, MD&A contains all the considerations the company believes to be important to its liquidity. Since management often uses the statement of cash flows as the basis for this section, it is useful to read it in conjunction with the cash flow statement.

This section of MD&A usually does not reiterate any information that is already in the financial statements. Its intent is to elaborate upon the financial statement information, with an emphasis on future operations. Companies generally include discussion not only of working capital but of a whole spectrum of cash resources: cash flows from expanded operations, plans to sell material assets, and plans to add more debt. An MD&A may discuss, for example, how the company plans to pay off its debt—by issuing stock if the market is right, by setting aside a special fund, or by negotiating a loan or a line of credit.

MD&A should, of course, address any deficiency in liquidity, meaning a critical shortage of either long- or short-term cash resources. For example, if a company is in default on a loan covenant, this default might lead to a material decrease in the company's liquidity. If this decrease would create a critical shortage of cash, the company should explain how it plans to remedy the deficiency.

Companies whose auditors have expressed uncertainty about whether they are a going concern should disclose information about their financial difficulties and how they plan to overcome them. Such companies should add to MD&A a detailed discussion of cash flow during the 12 months after the date of the financial statements.

MD&A may contain information on balances and average interest rates of the company's short-term borrowings. This information is required by Schedule IX of the 10-K form, but companies may opt to put it in the MD&A instead, if such a discussion would help present the information more clearly. In addition, the company should discuss any expected cash outlay for the next three years on income taxes in excess of the income tax expense on the statement. Also, when the notes disclose restrictions on transfers of funds from subsidiaries to a parent company, MD&A should address the nature and extent of the restrictions and their effect on the parent's ability to meet its cash obligations.

§4.3   Capital Resources

It is difficult to separate the discussions of capital resources and liquidity, so a company may combine them under a single heading.

Generally speaking, capital resources refer to material commitments for capital expenditures. For example: If the company is planning to build a new plant, how will it be funded? The discussion usually includes the purpose of these commitments and the company's plans to finance them, as well as any favorable or unfavorable material trends, including any expected changes in the mix and relative costs of these commitments.

Sometimes this section discusses the risks involved in high-yield financing or highly leveraged transactions. The SEC encourages such a discussion, though it stops short of mandating it or defining "highly leveraged" financings. However, the Federal Reserve Board has defined highly leveraged financing as financing by a borrower whose debt to total assets ratio exceeds 75 percent.

§4.4   Results of Operations

This section describes any significant components of revenue or expenses that help the reader to understand the company's operations. Typically, it contains a great deal of analytical data and comparisons with prior periods.

The discussion should illuminate any transactions, unusual events, or significant economic changes that will affect the company's income from its operations. Examples of such transactions include a sale of assets or operations, sale of tax benefits, early debt refunding, and LIFO inventory liquidations. This section is meant to inform the reader not only about the mere fact of such events, but about their impact on future cash flow, profits, and trends. It also should reveal whether a transaction is a one-time event or part of a trend. Any impending changes in accounting methods that affect future results can generally be found here.

This is also the place to discuss whether material increases in net sales or revenues arose out of increased sales volume, new products, or higher prices. And, if the company is aware of any events that will cause a change in the relationship between costs and revenues, this information should appear here.

Finally, if the company has decided to take any facilities out of operation, that announcement would also appear here. The discussion would explain why the facilities are idle and describe the company's plans, if any, for their future use.

§4.5   Foreign Operations

Readers of financial statements will find a wealth of information on a company's foreign operations in this section of MD&A. In addition to reporting on the activities of subsidiaries, this section analyzes the impact of foreign currency transactions on the company. Since no specific disclosures are required, the company has considerable latitude in deciding what information will help users understand the impact of foreign operations and foreign currency transactions.

In this section a reader is likely to find a discussion of the effects of changes in exchange rates. Such changes may have far-reaching implications when comparing recent results with past results. Some examples: A weakening foreign currency may have a depressing effect on sales and operating results. Changes in exchange rates will affect backlog, interest expense, wages, inventory levels, debt to equity ratio, cost of sales, effective tax rate, working capital, the cost of raw material purchased from the parent, and transactions between subsidiaries.

This information can be very complicated. Sales from foreign operations might appear to decline, but the decline may be more apparent than real if it is due to a change in exchange rates. If, for example, the company also has a manufacturing operation in the country where sales declined, the costs incurred in foreign currency might be significantly lower. Thus, the overall effect on profits may be minimal or nonexistent.

§4.6   The Impact of Inflation and Changing Prices

In times of double-digit inflation, this section was important in understanding the inflation-adjusted results of operations. Since this issue has become less central in recent years, a reader of MD&A will find little information here. However, if inflation rates climb again, this section will become more relevant. The SEC requires a brief presentation of management's views on the effects of inflation, in narrative rather than in number form.

§4.7   Other Required Disclosures

The final section of MD&A is a catch-all for any material changes that have not been discussed elsewhere. The SEC requires companies to include any information here that would help users understand the business as a whole. For example, if inventory has risen and has affected cash flow but not profits, the company would explain that situation here.

In this section a reader should also find discussion of any past or contemplated changes in earnings per share. Such changes might be the result of a change in the number of shares outstanding, perhaps because the company has purchased treasury stock. Management should address here the impact of such transactions on items in the balance sheet and income statement, and especially on earnings per share.

Here, too, is the place to explain the effect of any new accounting standards which have been issued but not yet adopted.[3] The discussion should describe the new standard, how the company will apply it, and how it will affect the financial statements and other significant aspects of the business.

---

[3] See Staff Accounting Bulletin No. 74.

The Work of the Outside Auditor

§5.1　Overview

Many users of financial statements confuse auditing with accounting, and indeed, the two overlap. Many accountants are auditors or were auditors at some time in their careers. The discipline of auditing requires a knowledge of accounting, though the work of auditors and accountants differs in significant ways. Simply put, company accountants prepare financial information; auditors examine it.

The auditor's function is to perform an independent examination of financial information and to evaluate accounting procedures, measurements, and presentations. In deciding whether accounting information is properly recorded, auditors base their judgments upon the accounting rules known as "generally accepted accounting principles" (GAAP).

Audits can be performed by both internal and external auditors. Internal audits are conducted by employees of the entity, and their primary purpose is to protect the assets of the entity. External audits are conducted by certified public accountants who are not employees, and their primary purpose is to render an opinion on the financial statements of the entity. Audits by government agencies, quasi-governmental groups, and other organizations are beyond the scope of this book.

Internal auditors consider the operations of the subdivision they are auditing and make suggestions for improving those operations. They focus on the correctness of particular account balances; consequently, their procedures are more detailed than those of external auditors, who focus on the financial statements. Internal auditors may examine transactions that are much less material than those that are reviewed by external examinations. Because of the level of detail they examine, internal auditors are more likely to find errors or fraud.

The weakness of internal audits, however, is that they are not independent, although the degree of their independence varies from company to company. The most independent kind of internal audit department reports directly to the audit committee of the board of directors; but even such an internal audit group is not truly independent.

Over the years, internal auditing has evolved into a highly skilled professional career that attracts talented people. The quality of the work of most of these groups is very high. Attorneys should ask for the workpapers of these groups in discovery and should consider using internal auditors to defend their clients in litigation.

The remainder of this chapter will focus on the work of the external auditor.

§5.2   The Basic Elements of Auditing

Auditing can be defined as the process by which an independent person collects and evaluates evidence regarding financial information about a specific economic entity's business activities. The purpose of an external audit is to determine and report on the fairness of the presentation of the information in the entity's financial statements.

The auditor must be a competent professional who is independent in fact and in appearance. He or she must understand the relevant audit requirements and must know what types of evidence and how much evidence to consider in reaching a reasoned conclusion.

In an audit, evidence is defined as anything used by the auditor to determine whether the information being examined is stated correctly and in accordance with established criteria. Evidence takes many different forms, both oral and written, including representations given and documents prepared by the party being audited, documents supporting transactions, communication and verification from third parties, and observations and tests by the auditor.

Whenever an audit is conducted, the auditor makes the scope of his or her responsibility clear, and defines the economic entity and the time period. In most instances the economic entity is also a legal entity, such as a corporation, partnership, proprietorship, or governmental unit. In some cases, the entity may be a division, a department, or an individual. The auditor's engagement letter identifies the party being audited and the services the auditor will perform.

Audits generally consider one year's financial information for an entity, but there are also audits of a month, a quarter, or several years.

§5.3 Auditing Standards

The American Institute of Certified Public Accountants (AICPA) has established a body of generally accepted auditing standards (GAAS). These standards are general guidelines that promote uniformity in the profession's approach to its major public responsibility—that of examining and reporting on financial statements. Besides addressing reporting requirements and evidence, the standards give guidance on professional competence and independence.

The AICPA's Auditing Standards Board, its senior technical body on auditing standards, dates back to 1939, when the AICPA formed a Committee on Auditing Procedure. In the 1970s, the FASB was established as an independent organization with responsibility for setting accounting rules for the profession. Leaving accounting to the FASB, the AICPA decided to concern itself with auditing standards.

The basic framework of GAAS is built on 10 standards. These standards, approved many years ago, are not sufficiently specific to serve as a checklist of procedures for practitioners. However, they represent a framework within which the auditor can determine which procedures to perform in various situations. Along with the 10 general standards, the AICPA's SAS's, are considered authoritative. Every member of the profession is required to follow them whenever they are applicable. As of March 1992, the AICPA has issued 69 SAS's.

While GAAS represents the authoritative source for the conduct of an audit, they require almost no specific procedures, nor do they offer much help to auditors in making decisions about sample size, selecting sample items from the population for testing, or evaluating results. However, highly specific requirements would limit the audit process rather than enhance it. They could not keep pace with the rate of change in the types and nature of business and financial transactions. The 10 standards appear in their entirety in Exhibit 5-1.

GAAS and the SAS's are not the only authoritative sources for the conduct of independent audits. The AICPA and state societies of CPAs have adopted codes of professional ethics. Several of the rules in these codes pertain to performance of audits. The AICPA also publishes audit guides applying GAAS to specific industries.

Many trade organizations publish their own auditing guides or procedures for their industries. These guides are not as authoritative as GAAS, the SAS's, or other AICPA publications. Industry auditing guides were developed for internal audits, but they contain information that is also helpful to outside auditors who are engaged to examine a company in that industry.

§5.4   Audit Reports

Since 1988, auditors have used a revised report format to give opinions on clients' financial statements. This was the first substantial revision to the opinion format in many years.

Before the 1970s, it was not unusual for accountants and other business people to refer to an auditor's opinion as a "certificate," as in "The accountants certified the financial statements." This implied that the auditors gave assurances about the accuracy of the financial statements.

Exhibit 5-1

General Standards
1. The audit is to be performed by a person or persons having adequate technical training and proficiency as an auditor.

2. In all matters relating to the assignment, an independence in mental attitude is to be maintained by the auditor or auditors.

3. Due professional care is to be exercised in the performance of the audit and the preparation of the report.

Standards of Fieldwork
1. The work is to be adequately planned and assistants, if any, are to be properly supervised.

2. A sufficient understanding of the internal control structure is to be obtained to plan the audit and to determine the nature, timing, and extent of tests to be performed.

3. Sufficient competent evidential matter is to be obtained through inspection, observation, inquiries, and confirmations to afford a reasonable basis for an opinion regarding the financial statements under audit.

Standards of Reporting
1. The report shall state whether the financial statements are presented in accordance with generally accepted accounting principles.

2. The report shall identify those circumstances in which such principles have not been consistently observed in the current period in relation to the preceding period.

3. Informative disclosures in the financial statements are to be regarded as reasonably adequate unless otherwise stated in the report.

4. The report shall either contain an expression of opinion regarding the financial statements, taken as a whole, or an assertion to the effect that an opinion cannot be expressed. When an overall opinion cannot be expressed, the reasons therefore should be stated. In all cases where an auditor's name is associated with financial statements, the report should contain a clear-cut indication of the character of the auditor's audit, if any, and the degree of responsibility he or she is taking.

These implied assurances actually constituted a misconception that, quite frankly, was fostered by CPAs. During the late 1960s and early

1970s, CPAs were faced with malpractice litigation whenever companies failed after receiving a "clean" (unqualified) auditor's opinion. This litigation aroused the concern of CPAs about the expectations of the public regarding the purpose and effectiveness of audits conducted according to GAAS.

GAAS audits are designed to find material errors or fraud. But tests are only tests, and do not involve examinations of every single transaction with completely independent verifications. Consequently, material error or fraud may exist without being detected, although the chance of errors or fraud not being discovered is greatly diminished when a GAAS audit is conducted properly.

Nevertheless, because of the "expectation gap" between what auditors can realistically do and what they were held responsible for, the accounting profession has paid greater attention to educating the public about the capabilities, duties, and responsibilities of CPAs. One step in this education process was taken a few years ago, when the auditor's report was redesigned to specify the responsibilities of the auditor and the company, and the limitations of a GAAS examination.

(a)   The "New" and the "Old" Report

Unless it was qualified, the old report contained only two paragraphs, a scope paragraph and an opinion paragraph. The new report typically contains at least three paragraphs. The additional material is devoted largely to describing the key elements of the audit process, and the company's and CPA's responsibilities in the reporting process. The current version underscores two fundamental postulates:

- Management is responsible for the financial statements; the independent accountant is responsible for the audit, and

- The audit, which forms the basis of the accountants opinion, should provide reasonable assurance that the financial statements are free of material error.

The old report mentioned neither of these ideas, although similar statements have long been made to clients in CPAs' engagement letters.

However, until 1988, these ideas were not communicated to readers and users of financial statements.

(b) The New Standard Unqualified Report

The standard report in the new format comprises three paragraphs—the introduction, the scope, and the opinion.

The introduction to the report is where the auditor distinguishes between the financial statement responsibilities of management and the CPA. The CPA audits the financial statements in a process that the report describes in its "scope" paragraph. However, ultimate responsibility for the content of the financial statements remains with management.

The new report format replaces the statement "we have examined" with "we have audited." This change and some new language about "testing" rather than "verifying" are designed to focus the report on the purposes and limitations of an audit instead of relying on what the reader might construe "examine" to mean.

The new scope paragraph addresses the major characteristics of an audit conducted in accordance with GAAS. The old report simply stated that the examinations were conducted in accordance with GAAS and that they included tests of the accounting records and other auditing procedures that the auditors considered necessary. The new report states that the auditor's purpose in the audit is to be reasonably certain that the financial statements are free of material misstatement. To meet that objective, the auditor samples the evidence that underlies the financial statements ("examining on a test basis") rather than verifying all the information that is presented in the financial statements and the notes.

The scope paragraph makes clear, too, that in evaluating the financial statements, the auditor has examined management's application of accounting principles as well as estimates. This paragraph attempts to make the reader aware of the procedures that are the basis for the auditor's opinion.

With the exception of two major changes, the new opinion paragraph mirrors the opinion paragraph in the old report. The previous report simply stated that the financial statements "present fairly" the financial position and results for the period. The new report adds the qualifying language, "in all material respects." The other change in the opinion paragraph was to remove a reference to consistency in the application of accounting principles.

A fourth paragraph may contain a report on changes in accounting principles, substantial doubt about the entity's going concern status, or other matters. Changes in accounting principles can significantly affect financial statements. When analyzing financial statements, readers should look to see if there is a fourth paragraph in the auditor's opinion. Such a paragraph may indicate a change in accounting practices, and will measure its impact on the statements and on their comparability with statements of prior years and of other companies.

Exhibit 5-2 shows the typical form of an auditor's unqualified report for ABC, Inc.

(c) Departures from the Standard Unqualified Report

Auditing standards permit four other types of opinion: a standard opinion with additional explanatory language, a qualified opinion, an adverse opinion, and a disclaimer of opinion.[1]

Standard Report with Explanatory Language Added. The auditor may add explanatory language to the standard report. Typically, the explanatory language does not affect the auditor's unqualified opinion on the financial statements. One example of such language is in the case of a contingent liability that cannot be quantified as of the date of the financial statement (see § 1.15).

Qualified Opinion. In a qualified opinion the auditor's report reflects the effects of the matter or matters to which the qualification relates. A qualified opinion would be given, for example, when the financial statements do not contain required disclosures. When the auditor gives a qualified opinion, he or she includes all the substantive reasons for the qualification in one or more separate explanatory paragraphs preceding the opinion paragraph. The opinion paragraph also contains appropriate qualifying language and refers to the explanatory paragraph. A qualified opinion includes phrases such as "except for" or "with the exception of."

---

[1] Statement of Auditing Standards No. 58, "Reports on Audited Financial Statements."

Exhibit 5-2

Report of Independent Auditors

The Board of Directors and Shareholders
ABC, Inc.

We have audited the accompanying consolidated balance sheets of ABC, Inc. and subsidiaries as of December 31, 19X5 and 19X4, and the related consolidated statements of income, shareholder's equity, and cash flows for the years then ended. These financial statements are the responsibility of the Company's management. Our responsibility is to express an opinion on these financial statements based on our audits.

We conducted our audits in accordance with generally accepted auditing standards. Those standards require that we plan and perform the audit to obtain reasonable assurance about whether the financial statements are free of material misstatement. An audit includes examining, on a test basis, evidence supporting the amounts and disclosures in the financial statements. An audit also includes assessing the accounting principles used and significant estimates made by management, as well as evaluating the overall financial statement presentation. We believe that our audits provide a reasonable basis for our opinion.

In our opinion, the financial statements referred to above present fairly, in all material respects, the consolidated financial position of ABC, Inc. and subsidiaries at December 31, 19X5 and 19X4, and the consolidated results of their operations and their cash flows for the years then ended in conformity with generally accepted accounting principles.

Ernst & Young

March 31, 19X6

(This exhibit also appears in Appendix B.)

Adverse Opinion. An adverse opinion affirms that the financial statements do *not* present fairly the financial position of the entity in conformity with GAAP. In expressing an adverse opinion, the auditor will precede the opinion paragraph with a paragraph a statement of:

- all substantive reasons for the adverse opinion, and

- if possible, the principal effects of the subject matter of the adverse opinion on the entity's financial position, results of operations, and cash flows. When necessary, the report will state that the effects of the adverse opinion are not reasonably determinable.

When an adverse opinion is given, the opinion paragraph usually includes a direct reference to the separate explanatory paragraph or paragraphs.

Disclaimer of Opinion. A disclaimer of opinion is appropriate when the auditor has not performed an audit whose scope is sufficient to allow expression of an opinion on the financial statements. When disclaiming an opinion because of limited scope, the auditor will state explicitly that the scope of the audit was not sufficient to warrant the expression of an opinion, and will indicate the reasons why the audit did not comply with generally accepted auditing standards.

§5.5   Reviews, Compilations, and Other Reports

Although auditing is the best known service of certified public accountants, audit firms also provide other financial statement services. CPAs perform compilations, reviews, and various other services that culminate in special reports.

(a)   Compilation Services

Compilation services consist merely of presenting financial information in the form of financial statements. This is the lowest level of financial statement services that accountants render. A compilation is management's representation of its financial position and results of operations, and the accountant does not express any assurance whatsoever on the statements.

(b)   Review Services

A review is more involved than a compilation, but far less thorough than an audit. A review can apply in two situations. It is most commonly used to refer to the application of analytical procedures applied to the financial statements of privately held companies. Accountants usually compare current financial data of a privately held company to the same data for prior periods, to see if it appears to be reasonable. Part of a review is a discussion with management to ascertain whether there have been any changes in the business or operating procedures that might give rise to variations in the financial data.

The term "review" is also applied to a series of limited audit procedures performed on the financial statements of a publicly owned company for interim periods that are not being audited. This section addresses only reviews of financial statements of privately owned companies.

Reviews are governed by the AICPA's Statement on Standards for Accounting and Review Services (SSARS) No. 1.[2] After applying review procedures, the accountant's report expresses only very limited assurances that the statements are in conformity with GAAP, or in some cases, with another accounting basis.

(c)   Other Types of Reports

In addition to audits, reviews, and compilations of financial statements, CPAs may issue a variety of so-called "special reports" on such matters as:

- Financial statements presented on some basis other than generally accepted accounting principles—for example, statements prepared on a basis prescribed by a regulatory authority;

- Specific elements of a financial statement, such as one or more accounts or items;

---

[2] Issued in December 1978 by the AICPA Accounting and Review Services Committee. This statement was the first in a series of statements that provide guidance to certified public accountants that perform services in connection with the unaudited financial statements of a non-public entity.

- The company's compliance with contractual agreements or certain regulatory requirements; and

- Financial information presented in prescribed forms or in schedules that require a prescribed form of auditor's report.[3]

When an accountant reports on a basis of accounting other than GAAP, the report includes a scope paragraph stating that the audit was made in accordance with GAAS, a middle paragraph naming the accounting basis, and an opinion paragraph in which the auditor expresses an opinion on the fairness of the statement's presentation.

Other special reports specify the scope of the work done by the auditor and the scope of the auditor's findings, opinion, or disclaimer of opinion. Each situation is different, and the details about various kinds of reports are contained in the literature of the accounting profession.

Part II will focus on various forms of analysis, ranging from reading and interpreting financial information to ratio analysis and the time value of money.

---

[3] Statement on Auditing Standards No. 62, Special Reports, April 1989.

PART II
Analyzing Financial Information

Putting the Pieces Together

§6.1 Overview

Financial statements are like jigsaw puzzles or mosaics. The reader looks at the pieces and puts them together, while continuing to gather more pieces through research, inquiry, and observation. Like jigsaw puzzles, financial statements are not designed to be put together in any particular order, but based on our experience, we will suggest one approach to analyzing financial statements, without implying that this is the only possible approach.

A reader of financial statements should view them in the context of what the company does. Look for the unexpected, and be aware of what would be expected in a particular type of business. The experience of interpreting financial statements resembles seeing a movie after having read the book. The object is to notice what is missing and what has been added, what should and should not be there. For example, if the business is a retailer, the reader would be interested in inventory. If it is a community bank, the reader would be surprised to see it engaged in foreign exchange trading. If the statements of a manufacturing company includes "goods held for resale," this should raise questions, because manufacturing companies do not usually hold goods for resale. One would expect to see raw material, work-in-progress, and finished goods inventory, but the presence of "goods held for resale" is an indication that the company is involved in another line of business. Analysis focuses on things that look unusual or irregular. The object is to raise questions and get more information.

If you look only at one year's data, you will miss the point. Using financial statements in analysis requires comparisons over longer periods of time and against other types of data: this year vs. last year, sales growth vs. the rate of inflation, this company vs. competitors, the industry, or the economy, and many other possible comparisons. Look for trends. Are revenues up, down, or level? Each trend has to be interpreted in context; for example, the trend of revenues could be downward and still be acceptable, if the economy is in a steeper decline.

Economic realities are so multifaceted that readers must beware of jumping to conclusions too quickly. Consider the example of a cash flow statement that shows depreciation far in excess of the cash investment in income-producing assets over a long period of time. This may mean that: the company is taking depreciation deductions very rapidly, much faster than its assets are losing economic value, or that it is not modernizing its plant and equipment and will eventually have a problem, because it is managing for current cash and not for the long term.

The best way to read financial statements is to take notes as you read, setting down the points that need further inquiry. The answers may be found in the financial statements themselves, management's discussion and analysis, the company's Form 10-K, the quarterly financial statements, or even in data about the industry.

Since the statements are mosaic-like, different pieces come into perspective as one reads, and eventually one sees a picture. It is possible that a few pieces will still be missing, especially if the company is not willing to disclose the information. At that point, the analyst may have to surmise, but will probably have some clues for guidance. Any projection of trends to future periods involves some degree of speculation. Limit speculation to a tolerable amount, based on a good understanding of what this entity has done and is currently capable of doing.

Throughout this chapter, we will refer to financial statements of ABC, Inc., which appear in Appendix B.

§6.2 Getting Background Information

Readers of financial statements will be better informed if they begin with some research about the company. To learn about a public company, read the textual sections of the published annual report. Additional information is also included in the company's Form 10-K, which may be obtained from the company itself, from a broker, or from public files of the SEC. (An example of a Form 10-K for ABC, Inc. is included as Appendix C.) The 10-K presents the facts without the gloss and possible distortion of the more public annual report. Lately, many companies have been preparing glossy 10-Ks for distribution to shareholders, in lieu of less informative annual reports. In the front portion of the 10-K, the company describes itself in a section called "Business," which can reveal much about the company's product lines and business, including principal markets, competitive factors, backlogs, availability of raw material, patents, licenses, franchises, number of employees, compliance with environmental laws, and more.

More information is available for public companies than for private companies, for which the amount of available information depends upon how much the company chooses to disclose. The analyst can search the press, or use services like Value Line, Standard and Poor's, Dun and Bradstreet, and others. Do not overlook trade associations, public and private libraries, chambers of commerce, and local historical societies.

§6.3 First Steps: The Auditor's Report and the Income Statement

Suppose that you have just been handed a set of financial statements. What is the first step? If the company is public, a good way to begin is with a quick perusal of the auditor's report. Make sure to check the extent of the auditor's work. Was it an audit, a review, or a compilation? (See Section 5.5.) An auditor's report attests only to the fairness of the company's reporting. An unqualified opinion does not, of course, mean that the company is financially healthy or will be profitable. If the auditors found problems in financial reporting, however, extra explanatory paragraphs will appear in addition to the normal three paragraphs of their report. Qualified opinions can signal a departure from GAAP, a change in accounting principles, a going concern problem, a material uncertainty, and other possible issues.

After perusing the auditor's report, skip the balance sheet and go to the income statement, looking at net income and per share amounts. Net income is the "bottom line," the difference between revenues and expenses. Financial statements are usually comparative. The SEC requires three-year comparisons for income statements, two years for balance sheets, and three on cash flow statements. Non-SEC reports usually contain only two-year financial statements. Most financial data, including earnings and earnings per share, are more meaningful when viewed in terms of trends. Are earnings up, down, or level? Look at five or more years' summaries, if they are available, for a better indication of trends.

Notice the number at the top of the income statement, which may be called "revenue," "net sales," or "net revenue." This figure shows what the company has sold in dollar terms, and like the bottom line, it should be considered comparatively. In looking at sales figures, be aware of the impact of inflation. If sales are up 3 percent and inflation has risen 5 percent, sales really may not have increased. However, even inflation is never black and white, but varies by industry and by region. If prices did not increase and sales are up, unit sales may have increased or the product mix of sales may have changed, favoring bigger ticket items. Why haven't prices increased? Is it because of a positive factor or a negative one?

After revenues, look at cost of goods sold, noticing any increase or decrease. Is cost of goods sold going up faster or slower than revenues? Similarly, note whether selling and administrative expenses are rising or falling, and whether they are moving in tandem with revenues. You may notice that while revenues are going up, selling and administrative expenses are falling. Though this looks like a good sign, it may not indicate a positive trend. The company may have stopped advertising or may have cut down on its sales activities. It may be a mistake to cut costs if that will result in reduced future sales. Perhaps management is trimming down to save shareholders money, or perhaps it anticipates a downturn in sales. At this point, the analyst should make a note of this issue. It poses a question which deserves an answer.

Look next at "other income and expense," reading it in tandem with the "bottom line." Interest income and expense is the cost of money. If this item is up, it could mean that debt is up, or that the company has a floating-rate or short-term debt and interest rates are up. If the analyst knows that interest rates are down, but interest expense has risen, the most logical explanation is more debt. To investigate the debt issue further, look at the long-term debt note to the financial statements. If interest expense has risen, this note will indicate whether it is because of new debt or because of a floating-rate loan in a period of rising interest rates.

The next item, "other income," includes non-operating sources of income. The amount shown is usually net of other non-operating losses. Operating earnings, not other income or expenses, normally drive trends, so consider leaving other income and expense out of a true trend analysis.

In looking at income taxes, ask whether they are in line from year to year, in relation to income before income taxes. There is almost always a note on taxes in which the rates may be analyzed. If the tax rate has gone down, find out whether that is a one-time event or whether the lower tax rate will continue into the future as a result of changes in the law or good tax management. Using the ABC, Inc. financial statements in Appendix B as an example, the income tax expense went up $2.7 million on a $5 million increase in income before income taxes—a 54 percent effective tax rate, compared to an overall rate of 44 percent in the prior year.

This tax rate looks high. Were there tax credits the year before that did not continue this year? The numbers alone will not say much, but the reader should make a note to look at the tax area and see what happened. Perhaps the tax structure has changed or state taxes have risen. Does it mean the company will have to earn more in the future to bring more to the bottom line?

At this point, one might either postpone looking further into the tax issue and jot down a reminder, or turn to the reconcilement of the statutory rate to the effective rate in the note on income taxes. (See Exhibit 6-1.)

This income tax note shows that while the federal tax rate went down from 40 to 34 percent, state taxes and the effect of foreign income tax rates went up 7 percent, and there was an alternative minimum tax imposed this year, which caused a 3.2 percent increase in the effective

Exhibit 6-1

ABC, Inc.
Consolidated Statements of Income

	Year ended December 31	
	19X5	19X4
	(In Thousands)	
Net sales	$150,000	$125,000
Cost of products sold	111,500	90,300
Selling and administrative expenses	19,950	22,100
	18,550	12,600
Other income (expense):		
Interest expense	(5,550)	(4,400)
Other income	1,000	800
Income before income taxes	14,000	9,000
Income taxes (Note 8)	6,700	4,000
Net income	$ 7,300	$ 5,000
Earnings per share:		
Primary	$2.42	$1.69
Fully diluted	$2.32	$1.67

(This exhibit also appears in Appendix B.)

tax rate. Overall, ABC Inc. is paying income taxes at 47.8 percent this year, in comparison with 44.4 percent last year. The major tax problems for ABC Inc. are the effect of foreign income tax and the alternative minimum tax. Payment of an alternative minimum tax could indicate lack of attention to strategic tax planning.

The final item in the income statement is net income, which is up a healthy 46 percent from last year. Comparing earnings per share with net income, notice that earnings per share did not rise proportionally (only 43.2 percent). This means that the company probably issued additional common shares or common stock equivalents during the year. Net income as a percentage of net sales increased from 4 percent to 4.9 percent—a healthy trend.

§6.4   Reading the Balance Sheet

In going through financial statements, it is important to keep asking questions. Think about what caused each of the positive or problematic events, and continually compare the amounts and trends against your knowledge of the industry and the economy. So far, ABC Inc. appears to be doing well, but it could be doing poorly in comparison to the rest of the industry, and thus losing market share.

A glance at the asset side of the balance sheet in Exhibit B shows that receivables are up (from $28 million to $29 million), but sales are up even more (from $125 million to $150 million). This is positive and usually means that collections are faster. The increase in the allowance for losses is small (only $50,000). If receivables were going up but sales were not rising, or if there was a significant, disproportionate increase in the allowance for losses, there may be cause for concern, because accounts receivable are getting old and people are not paying. This would be a normal occurrence in an economic downturn, but could represent a major problem in an economic upswing.

Inventory is up too (from $51 million to $59 million), but that is understandable since we noted in the income statement that sales are up. If sales were up and inventory declined, the company might have a capacity problem or might anticipate a downturn. The inventory seems to be "turning" faster since it increased at a lower rate than sales. (The effect of the inventory method used—LIFO or FIFO—also needs to be considered.) This is a positive sign, but a word of caution is in order. The income statement shows activity over a year's time, like a moving picture. The balance sheet is a snapshot at the very end of that moving picture. A company could have significant sales increases in the early part of the year and a severe downturn in the last quarter, but still show an upward trend for the entire year. The year-end balance sheet could show a downward trend, while the income statement for the same year shows an upward trend.

Do not stop at the annual statements, but obtain and review the quarterly information. Also, trends can be put in better perspective if they are analyzed over longer periods of time than two years. By looking at the company's past performance, you may be able to predict reasonably well how it is likely to be affected by future swings in the economy. How did it react to prior recessions or upturns? But be careful in predicting the

Exhibit 6-2

Current assets:	Dollars in Thousands	Current liabilities:	
Cash and cash		Notes payable to banks	
equivalents	$ 7,500		$ 3,000
Accounts receivable, net	29,000	Commercial paper	3,000
		Accounts payable and	
Inventories:		accrued expenses	23,600
Finished products	17,000	Income taxes	5,000
Products in process	35,000	Deferred income taxes	700
Raw materials and		Current portion of long-	
supplies	7,000	term debt and capital	
Prepaid expenses	500	lease obligations	1,400
Total current assets	$96,000	Total current liabilities	$36,700

(This exhibit also appears in more detail in Appendix B.)

future from analyzing the past. Management may change, which can have a tremendous influence on operations. What is known about management? If they are new, where are they from, and how did they perform elsewhere?

Next, compare current assets with current liabilities. (See Exhibit 6-2.) The difference gives the working capital, an indicator of whether the company is capable of generating enough cash to conduct its current operations. ABC Inc.'s current assets exceed its current liabilities by $59.3 million, an extremely healthy margin over the $36.7 million of current liabilities. Maybe this margin is too healthy. Does ABC Inc. have too much inventory? There is $59 million in inventory (valued at LIFO) against annual sales of $150 million. Not a very rapid turnover in inventory. Are there problems with obsolesence? Is inventory being managed poorly? Some of these issues will be addressed in Chapter 7.

Compare depreciation to property, plant, and equipment (PP&E). More accumulated depreciation on the balance sheet can sometimes show that the company's equipment is getting old. In ABC's case, however, depreciation is falling in relation to the increase in PP&E. From the consolidated statements of cash flow, it is apparent that the company is both replacing its capital assets and has acquired assets through an acquisition. Depreciation under "operating activities" is $9 million, and under "investing activities," purchases of PP&E are $13.8 million. The acquisition of Future Corporation added assets and, since it was a purchase, the addition would have been at fair market value without accumulated depreciation.

Acquisitions bring to mind another precaution. When analyzing trends over a long period, a valid comparison requires having the same business at the end of the period as at the beginning. A former boutique retailer may now be a discount mass marketer, and different businesses react differently to economic events.

Current liabilities show a drop of $4 million in notes payable to banks. From the related note to the statements, it appears that this debt is from revolving credit agreements with a maximum line of $10 million renewed annually. Also, $3 million of the line of credit is assigned to support the outstanding commercial paper. With $3 million of commercial paper outstanding at December 31, 19X5, this leaves a cash cushion of $4 million for use as needed. The decrease in the amount payable under the line of credit from $7 million to $3 million is positive, particularly in light of the increase in cash of $1.5 million.

ABC Inc. long-term debt has risen by $14 million. Note 6 states that the company issued 10 percent notes, due through 19Y6, totaling $15 million. Usually, the ability to get reasonable long-term debt is an advantage, particularly when the debt has an extended maturity. (Notice that "Y" in dates in the example statements refers to the decade after X, so 19Y6 is 11 years after 19X5.) Also in the long-time debt note which is reproduced as Exhibit 6-3, notice the paragraph that refers to maturities of the long-term debt. In three years (19X8), $15.5 million in debt will mature. Analyst may go to the MD&A to see how the company plans to refinance this debt. This note also addresses restrictions under the debt agreements, and it is a positive sign that $32 million of retained earnings is unrestricted and available for paying dividends.

Investigate why the company is borrowing money. Long-term borrowing gives the company more stability, because long-term debt does not have to be paid back immediately. It is a general rule that short-term borrowing should be only for short-term purposes, for example, to carry receivables and inventory. If short-term borrowing has risen, consider its relationship to accounts payable and inventory. If a company is borrowing short-term for investment in long-term assets, that is a warning sign.

Returning to the balance sheet in Appendix B, the next largest long-term liability is "capital lease obligations," which have decreased $0.4 million from the prior year. Capitalized leases are leases of assets that have the characteristics of acquisitions of assets, as when the lease terms

Exhibit 6-3

Maturities of long-term debt for the five years succeeding December 31, 19X5 are $1 million in 19X6, $1 million in 19X7, $15.5 million in 19X8, $5.5 million in 19X9, and $2 million in 19Y0. Through June 30, 19X8, the 7% debentures are convertible into shares of common stock at the rate of one share for each $40 face amount.

The loan agreements for both note issues include, among other things, provisions relative to additional borrowings, maintenance of working capital, and restrictions on the amount of retained earnings available for the payment of dividends. Under the most restrictive of these covenants, retained earnings in the amount of $32 million were free of such limitations at December 31, 19X5.

(This exhibit also appears in Appendix B.)

---

are for substantially the entire economic life of the assets. They have been recorded based on their substance—an acquisition of an asset with the incurrence of debt—rather than their form—a lease. Note 10 on capitalized leases shows the composition and payment schedule for the leases. The future lease payments should be analyzed in the same way as any future payment of debt.

ABC's current debt is down, long-term assets are up, and current assets are up. Long-term assets do not appear to be supported by current debt. The company has gotten stronger. Its current liabilities are up, but so are its current assets.

Turning to the shareholders equity section, total equity has increased by $7.4 million or 10.4 percent, another positive sign.

§6.5   Cash Flow and Notes

Skipping for the moment over the statement of changes in shareholders' equity, consider the cash flow statement. Cash is important to any company. Though accrual earnings can help a company borrow money, eventually these earnings must be turned to cash to pay vendors and creditors, as well as shareholders' dividends. The cash flow statement shows where cash came from and where it went, comparing cash at the beginning and at the end of the year. It includes what the company borrowed, what it invested in, and the dividends it paid.

Look first at the company's cash from operations, which in the example of ABC Inc. was a healthy $14.4 million. This is a positive sign. The company is not only profitable; it is generating cash from its operations. However, if a company shows a negative cash flow from operations, this is not necessarily a problem. An analyst would have to look at the trend over a period of time, and consider the industry. Investing activities show what the company did with the cash that may benefit its future. Chapter 7 will explain cash flow analysis in more depth.

As can be seen from the above analysis, the notes to the financial statements let one look behind the numbers. Many readers go back and forth from the statements to the notes, perhaps looking at the financial statements quickly, then at the notes, then at the statements and the notes together.

Most readers of financial statements are interested in the company's future. In reading the notes, pay attention to any obligations the company has in the future. The note on pension plans is an important indicator of what the company will have to pay out in the future for this one obligation. The long-term debt payment is another example. Often, too, the notes will contain an item called "contingencies," which relates to lawsuits and other uncertainties that could affect future earnings and/or cash flows.

§6.6   Summary and Conclusion

In this chapter's preliminary analysis, we have briefly glanced at the financial statements and begun to piece together a financial picture of the company. Financial statement analysis generates questions as often as answers. Attorneys should be skilled at this analysis, since it is comparable to sifting through mounds of evidence and putting the pieces of an investigation together into a coherent case. You are constructing a mosaic out of many pieces of evidence.

The next chapter will help you analyze the financial data in greater detail, which can often reveal traps and treasures, or hidden assets and liabilities, in the financial statements. The assets on financial statements are recorded at historical cost, which may be less or more than their real value.

A serious reader of financial statements will supplement the information in statements with information from many other sources. In this chapter we have pointed out several alternative sources of information. Another valuable source in comparing financial information to industry standards is the Robert Morris Associates' *Annual Statement Studies*. The studies give "common size" balance sheets and income statements, which are based on a common standard (or percent) for easy comparability. The studies include data by industry and by size of entity. Which sources you choose and how much you decide to explore depends upon the purpose of your analysis.

CHAPTER SEVEN

Introduction to Financial Statement Analysis

§7.1 Overview

In Chapter 6, we briefly discussed some aspects of analyzing a set of
financial statements using the disclosures in the statements and applying
a few ratio analysis techniques. In that chapter, many questions arose.
Some of these will be answered in this chapter, but new questions will
also arise. Pursuing the answers to those remaining questions is where
the real investigative work begins. Some persistent questions may
require answers from a company's management.

Generally speaking, GAAP-based financial statements are addressed
to an external reader who does not have access to the detailed information that the company's management has at its disposal. Such a reader
might be an investor, creditor, financial analyst, or stockholder. In a
lawsuit, an attorney should request the internal financial information
upon which the financial statements are based. For the purposes of this
chapter, however, we will limit our discussion to the public financial
data that may be available.

Financial analysts use a number of conventional techniques that
together form a kind of "financial diagnosis" of a company. The techniques include various types of ratios, comparisons of budgets with
actual results, and analysis of cash flow. Even when considered together,
these analytical tools do not paint an absolutely firm picture of a company, but they do give an impression. Applied with judgment, these
techniques can transform cold, unconnected information into firm data
that is useful in making investment, lending, and business decisions.

The major credit rating agencies use these techniques, among others, to evaluate how creditworthy an organization may be. However, the analysis can be correct only for historical performance; the future is always less certain, and predictions are replete with assumptions, estimates, and trend projections. The analysis differs among industries and according to the local, regional, and national economies.

Attorneys will find these ratios and analyses helpful in understanding the financial warranties and covenants contained in loan agreements, acquisitions and sales of companies, and other agreements. When these agreements are loosely crafted, they often become issues in dispute. Even though financial experts will probably be involved in such litigation, attorneys can make more informed judgments by understanding the basics of financial analysis.

Most of the ratios we will discuss in this chapter apply to manufacturing or retailing enterprises. These companies traditionally invest heavily in plant and equipment, and have fairly straightforward financing. During the last few decades, however, the American economy has been shifting from product-based companies to more service-based entities. Service firms, like consulting and law firms, do not deal in tangible products, so many of the traditional ratios do not apply. For example, service firms may have few tangible assets and no inventory. However, other measures, such as income per employee or billable hours, are relevant to those businesses.

In calculating ratios or performing any other kind of financial analysis, the most important tool is judgment. Service firms are not like manufacturing firms, but there are some similarities. Companies within the same industry are often comparable, and some apparently different industries are similar. Software firms and pharmaceutical companies, for example, have much in common. An analyst would have to find the numbers that may be comparable, such as the relationship between research and development expenditures and sales, or how much the company spends on training.

§7.2   Ratio Analysis

The most common technique used in analyzing the data on financial statements is ratio analysis. Simply defined, ratio analysis is comparing one number to another. Comparing key numbers on financial statements permits users to evaluate how well a company is operating and how profitable it really is. The two numbers could be any numbers the analyst believes are important. For example, comparing the total number of units the company has sold to the entire market gives an idea of market share, or the size of the company's slice of the pie.

Ratio analysis is neither a magical nor a technical process. An analyst simply picks a pair of values from the financial statements, and divides one number into the other. The answer or quotient is a ratio. By itself, the ratio means very little. It takes on significance only when it is compared with norms or ranges found in other businesses in the same or in a similar industry. By observing trends and signals in such ratios within a company over time, or by comparing actual results to planned results, the analyst can determine whether the business is improving according to certain key performance measures.

Certain ratios are commonly used because they are revealing. Financial ratios can be used to analyze the financial strength and operating success of a company from several different points of view. The most commonly used financial ratios measure liquidity, activity, leverage, and profitability. The objective of such analysis is to identify indicators of change. Is the business better or worse off than in the past? How does it compare to others in the same industry?

Different countries tend to have different norms. For example, companies in hyperinflationary economies will generally be less liquid than companies in countries with low inflation rates.

§7.3   Liquidity Ratios and Analysis

Liquidity ratios measure a company's ability to meet its maturing short-term obligations. The following are some frequently used liquidity ratios.

(a)   The Current Ratio

This ratio measures a company's liquidity. It shows the extent to which the claims of short-term creditors are covered by current assets. The equation for calculating the current ratio is:

$$\text{Current ratio} = \frac{\text{Current assets}}{\text{Current liabilities}}$$

A current ratio of less than 1.0 normally evidences a problem. Too high a current ratio, however, is not good either. If a company is keeping too much of its resources in liquid assets, it may not be developing new products or making other investments that are necessary for long-term survival. For example, the company may not be replacing long-lived assets used in the revenue-producing process. A financial institution, however, will generally have a higher proportion of liquid assets than a manufacturing concern.

(b) Quick or Acid Test Ratio

This ratio is similar to the current ratio. It is the "acid test" of a business' ability to pay off its current creditors. The only difference between the acid test and the current ratio is that the acid test eliminates inventories and prepaid expenses from current assets and considers only cash (including cash equivalents), marketable securities, and accounts receivable. The reason is that these are more liquid than inventories and prepaid expenses. The equation for calculating the acid test ratio is:

$$\text{Acid test ratio} = \frac{\text{Cash} + \text{marketable securities} + \text{accounts receivable}}{\text{Current liabilities}}$$

If this ratio falls below 1.0, it may not be cause for concern, if the inventory and other current assets are turning into cash quickly enough to keep the business afloat. The acid test is really a "worst case" analysis, evaluating a company as if it had to shut its doors and could not sell any more product.

(c) Working Capital

A company's liquidity is very closely related to its working capital position. Working capital refers to investment in short-term assets—cash, short-term securities, accounts receivable, and inventories. Working capital management refers to all aspects of the management of both current assets and current liabilities. The importance of working capital management is that current assets typically represent a major portion of the total assets of a business. Current assets require careful attention and management because of their relatively volatile nature. Working capital management includes such actions as accelerating the collection of receivables, reducing inventory levels, and extending the payment of creditors.

The equation for calculating net working capital is:

$$\text{Net working capital} = \text{Current assets} - \text{Current liabilities}$$

If working capital is at zero or slightly higher, the company is generally considered to be operating efficiently. A lender, however, may want to have extra working capital as a cushion against unexpected demands on resources. Management may want to have extra working capital to take advantage of opportunities. Working capital, like other assets, must be financed. If management wants to have one extra dollar on hand, it must raise that dollar from stockholders or from creditors. Since each of these sources demands a return on its money, working capital management becomes a balancing act.

Lawyers should look for possible manipulation of these liquidity measures. For example, if a company had $1.2 million in current assets and $1 million in current liabilities, it would have a current ratio of 1.2. Now assume that a debt covenant requires a 1.25 ratio at the determination date. Just before the determination date, the management—if its liquidity permitted—could pay down $200,000 in current liabilities, leaving current assets of $1 million, current liabilities of $800,000, and a current ratio of 1.25. It may not be in the best interest of the company to use its liquidity in this manner, but the transaction does allow the company to comply with the restrictive covenant.

Management could also sell or borrow long term against long-lived assets to reduce current liabilities. Notice, however, that in our example, net working capital remained the same at $200,000. An attorney who wishes to eliminate some manipulation can set *both* a working capital ratio and a net working capital restriction. If, in our example, there also had been a requirement for net working capital in excess of $300,000, changing only the working capital ratio would not have been sufficient to comply with the covenants. A debt to equity restriction and a restriction on the amount or type of disposal of long-lived assets, in addition to the liquidity restrictions, would really "lock in" the borrower and protect the lender. However, it should be noted that if it is not detrimental to the entity, manipulation of ratios is not necessarily wrong and can, in fact, indicate a sophisticated and effective management strategy.

In financial analysis, the important point is to look at all the available data in an integrated fashion, and not to focus solely on one or two elements in the mosaic.

§7.4 Activity Ratios

Activity ratios measure how effectively the company uses the resources at its command. Several types of activity ratios are used in analysis:

(a) Days Payable Outstanding

This ratio indicates how long a company takes to pay its bills. The equation for calculating days payable outstanding is:

$$\text{Days payable outstanding} = \frac{\text{Payables}}{\text{Cost of sales per day*}}$$

$$\text{*Cost of sales (COS) per day} = \frac{\text{COS (For Period)}}{\text{Number of days}}$$

If the days payable outstanding is beyond normal credit terms (e.g., 30 days), the company may be relying too heavily on its trade creditors, and it may also be missing out on early payment discounts. Missing discounts can be equivalent to paying interest of almost 36 percent in some cases. Hopefully, the company is collecting its receivables faster than it is paying its creditors; otherwise, it is a net lender on trade credits. What constitutes a reasonable period depends on the organization (the federal government, for example, is a notoriously slow payer), the product or service, and the industry. A trend toward higher days payable outstanding could simply indicate better cash management. Alternatively, it could be a harbinger of cash flow problems.

(b) Days Receivable Outstanding

This ratio indicates how long customers take to pay their bills. The higher the number, the greater should be the concern over customers not paying their bills. The lower the number, the better off the company, since its resources are not sitting idly in receivables but are earning interest or otherwise contributing to profitability. The equation for calculating days receivable outstanding is:

$$\text{Days receivable outstanding} = \frac{\text{Accounts receivable}}{\text{Credit sales per day*}}$$

$$*\text{Credit sales per day} = \frac{\text{Credit sales (for period)}}{\text{Number of days in period}}$$

If the days receivable outstanding becomes too high, it could indicate that the company is not enforcing its credit policies. A high ratio could also mean that the company is such a weak competitor that it must offer longer payment periods to move its goods or services. Since receivables are the opposite of "prepays," they offer a key insight into the business as a whole. As with payables outstanding, whether a number is "good" depends on the industry, the size of the company relative to its customers, and many other factors. If a company is too restrictive with its credit terms, it may lose sales; if it is too permissive, it may lose money on sales it never should have made.

(c) Inventory Turnover Ratio

This ratio indicates how long an item sits in inventory before it is sold or "turns over." The equation for calculating inventory turnover is:

$$\text{Inventory turnover} = \frac{\text{Cost of sales}}{\text{Average inventory balance}}$$

If the inventory is turning over too quickly, there may be stock outs and lost sales. An inventory that is not turning at an adequate rate could be evidence of obsolete goods. Obviously, the inventory at a grocery store should turn over faster than that of a jeweler.

The inventory turnover rate usually moves inversely to the gross margin (net sales revenue less cost of sales); the higher the markup, the higher the gross margin and the longer it takes to move an item. Every company would love to sell a high margin product (such as a gold watch) *and* turn the inventory over quickly. To move a high margin product, however, a company usually has to drop the price or incur costs to promote it, either of which depresses the margin. The alternatives are to hold the product and pay higher inventory costs, which are usually interest on borrowings, or to lose interest by tying up the money in inventory. This is a good example of how a reader can discover management's philosophy by analyzing the financial data.

(d) Sales to Employees Ratio

This ratio indicates how many dollars of sales the company produces for each person it employs. The equation for calculating sales to employees is:

$$\text{Sales to employees} = \frac{\text{Total sales}}{\text{Number of employees}}$$

More "capital intensive" firms usually have higher ratios than do service firms. By comparing this ratio for companies in the same industry, the analyst can tell how automated one company is in comparison to another.

(e) Sales to Assets Ratio

This ratio indicates how many dollars of sales are produced for each dollar of assets the company owns. The equation for calculating sales to assets is:

$$\text{Sales to assets} = \frac{\text{Total sales}}{\text{Total assets}}$$

Companies invest in all types of assets to produce income. Whether the company is a manufacturer or a bank, this ratio gives an idea of how many dollars of income the invested dollars are producing. When this ratio is compared to those of a company's peers, it measures how efficient the company is at profitability.

§7.5 Leverage Ratios

Leverage ratios measure the relative claims that owners and creditors have on the companys assets. The term "leverage" is taken from the physical sciences. Like a fulcrum and lever, borrowed money allows one to multiply one's financial force by investing in opportunities that could be profitable. If those investments pay off, the borrower can profit, but if the investments do not pay off, the borrower must still make the payments. Some examples of leverage ratios, sometimes called "solvency ratios," are times interest earned, debt to equity, and debt coverage.

(a) Times Interest Earned

This ratio measures the extent to which earnings can decline before the company is unable to meet its annual interest costs. The equation for calculating "times interest earned" is:

$$\text{Times interest earned} = \frac{\text{Earnings before interest and taxes}}{\text{Interest charges}}$$

Notice that taxes are left out of the numerator, since the interest cost affects taxes. If interest were high enough, there would be no taxes because there would be no income.

For many companies, this ratio has been driven down by a dramatic increase in debt during the 1980s. Whether a ratio is "good" depends on the company and the nature of the business. A lender likes to see a borrower with a "safe" ratio of possibly 5.0. Paradoxically, the most leveraged companies in the country are banks, which borrow tremendous amounts of money and invest it at higher rates. The debt to equity ratio (see §7.5(b)) for many banks exceeds 30 (97¢ of borrowed funds for every 3¢ of equity capital).

The recent history of banks and savings and loan institutions (S&Ls) shows that leverage is a two-edged sword. If it is managed successfully, leverage can be very profitable. If it is not managed successfully, a company will find itself in serious financial difficulty.

(b) Debt to Equity Ratio

This ratio measures the relative position of lenders and investors in a business. The equation for calculating the debt to equity ratio is:

$$\text{Debt to equity ratio} = \frac{\text{Total debt}}{\text{Total equity}}$$

Some analysts use a variation of this ratio called funded debt to equity. Funded debt consists of amounts that have been put into the business by loans or direct financings. It excludes accounts payable for goods put into the business, such as electricity, that are purchased on account.

This is one of the key ratios that indicate how leveraged a company is. There are several variations of this measure, such as debt to assets, debt to total capitalization, and others.

(c) Debt Coverage Ratio

This ratio measures a company's ability to pay its debts. The equation for calculating the debt coverage is:

$$\text{Debt coverage ratio} = \frac{\text{Income before interest and depreciation}}{\text{Principal and interest charges on debt}}$$

Depreciation is added back to income in this equation because it is a non-cash expense. This ratio focuses on actual cash flow available from operations to service debt. This measure is one way to determine whether a company has enough cash to meet its requirements, since both interest and principal must eventually be repaid.

§7.6 Profitability Ratios

While all of the analytical ratios reflect on management, profitability ratios measure more closely how effectively the company is being managed. Frequently-used profitability ratios include the following four measures:

(a) Gross Margin as a Percent of Sales

Gross margin represents the difference between sales and the cost of sales. Therefore, this ratio reflects the profitability of the product itself. The equation for calculating gross margin is:

$$\text{Gross margin as a percent of Sales} = \frac{\text{Gross margin}}{\text{Sales}}$$

A higher margin could indicate that the product enjoys some advantage over its competition by virtue of technology, legal protection (patent or copyright), or perceived value. A commodity such as milk or coal, whose suppliers have little to distinguish themselves from each other, will typically carry a smaller margin.

(b) Net Income as a Percent of Sales

This ratio simply shows the percent of sales dollars that result in net income or profit. Clearly, the higher this percentage, the more efficiently the business is producing and selling its goods and services. Stockholders are, of course, most interested in this ratio. The equation for calculating net income as a percent of sales is:

$$\text{Net income as a percent of sales} = \frac{\text{Net income}}{\text{Sales}}$$

This ratio is a good leveler among companies, since the "bottom line" is how much money the company is making, regardless of the industry it is in. For many years, large publicly-held U.S. companies have kept about 5 cents for each dollar of sales (5 percent). "Good" companies have kept as much as 12 or 13 percent. This ratio is sometimes called return on sales and abbreviated as ROS.

(c) Return on Assets

This ratio assesses the profitability of a business in relation to its assets. Generally speaking, the higher the return on assets, the more skilfully management is using its resources. The figure used for assets can be calculated in a number of ways. The equation for calculating return on assets is:

$$\text{Return on assets} = \frac{\text{Net income}}{\text{Average total assets}}$$

It is important to use an average number for assets rather than a year-end amount, since income is earned over an entire year and not only at one point in time. The average number gives the analyst a better sense of how well the assets were employed throughout the year. However, this ratio is most useful within an industry, not between industries. A service entity such as a law firm with low or no fixed assets on its balance sheet would have a very high return on assets. This ratio is more revealing when it is applied to asset-intensive firms such as manufacturers and financial institutions.

(d)   Return on Investment or Return on Equity

This ratio shows what return the business is producing on the stockholders' investment. Long-term equity investors are most interested in this ratio, since it reflects how well the business is using the stockholders' capital. The equation for calculating return on equity is:

$$\text{Return on Equity} = \frac{\text{Net Income}}{\text{Average Equity}}$$

Like return on assets, this ratio is also better calculated using an average, since some of the earnings are reinvested throughout the year. Some companies—including, surprisingly, banks and S&Ls—have achieved returns on equity exceeding 20 percent in recent years. If managed successfully, the use of other people's money can have an exhilarating effect on earnings.

§7.7   How to Calculate and Interpret Ratios

To get some practice in calculating ratios, let's use the balance sheet (Exhibit 7-1) and income statement (Exhibit 7-2) of a company we'll call "Average Company, Inc.":

Exhibit 7-1

AVERAGE COMPANY, INC.
BALANCE SHEET
DECEMBER 31, 1991 AND 1990

	1991	1990
	($000)	($000)
Assets		
Current assets		
Cash	$17,000	$24,000
Accounts receivable	323,000	231,000
Inventory	688,000	425,000
Total current assets	1,028,000	680,000
Non-current assets		
Building and equipment	477,000	395,000
Less accumulated depreciation	290,000	188,000
Buildings and equipment, net	187,000	207,000
Other assets	6,000	7,000
Total assets	$1,221,000	$894,000
Liabilities and stockholders' equity		
Current liabilities		
Accounts payable	$257,000	$129,000
Accrued liabilities	65,000	48,000
Notes payable	238,000	85,000
Total current liabilities	560,000	262,000
Non-current liabilities		
Mortgage payable	31,000	34,000
Total liabilities	591,000	296,000
Stockholders' equity		
Common stock	306,000	306,000
Retained earnings	324,000	292,000
Total stockholders' equity	630,000	598,000
Total liabilities and stockholders' equity	$1,221,000	$894,000

Exhibit 7-2

AVERAGE COMPANY, INC.
INCOME STATEMENT
FOR THE YEARS ENDED DECEMBER 31, 1991 AND 1990

	1991	1990
	($000)	($000)
Net sales	$2,739,000	$2,495,000
Cost of sales	2,038,000	1,836,000
Gross margin	701,000	659,000
Salaries	325,000	300,000
Payroll taxes	25,000	22,000
Interest	49,000	15,000
Amortization	1,000	1,000
Depreciation	102,000	85,000
Insurance	30,000	25,000
General, administrative, and selling	105,000	96,000
Total expenses	637,000	544,000
Net income before taxes	64,000	115,000
Taxes (50%)	32,000	57,500
Net income	$32,000	$57,500

Here are the calculations and brief interpretations of six ratios for Average Company for 1991.

Current Ratio

$$\text{Current Ratio} = \frac{\text{Current Assets}}{\text{Current Liabilities}}$$

$$= \frac{\$1,028,000}{\$560,000}$$

$$= 1.8$$

This ratio points to a relatively good relationship between current assets and current liabilities. The ratio of 1.8 means that Average Company has more than 1.8 times the value of its current liabilities available in short-term assets that are expected to be converted into cash during the period in which the liabilities are due.

If we performed the same calculation for 1990, the result would be 2.6. This decline should cause the reader to search further to find out why. Was it a result of a downturn in business, poor management, or better management of liquidity? Remember, financial statement analysis is a lengthy, integrative process. There is no single "catch-all" calculation, and judgment is required in the interpretation. For example, it takes judgment to decide what is important and what is not, or to gauge the future implications of current information.

Funded Debt to Equity

$$\text{Funded Debt to Equity} = \frac{\text{Total Funded Debt}}{\text{Total Equity}}$$
$$= \frac{\$269,000}{\$630,000}$$
$$= 43\%$$

The debt portion of this ratio is calculated by combining notes payable and mortgage payable, $238,000 and $31,000, respectively. The equity portion of the ratio is calculated by combining common stock of $306,000 and retained earnings of $324,000. The ratio of 0.43 indicates that Average Company has about 2.5 times as much funding from equity sources as from outside creditors. Overall debt-to-equity is roughly 94 percent ($591,000 ÷ $630,000), showing a fairly conservative capital structure. Calculating the same ratios for 1990 shows that there was a significant shift in 1991 to greater reliance on debt. This should be evaluated in the light of other information. A mosaic of this company's operation is beginning to form.

Return on Equity

$$\text{Return on Equity} = \frac{\text{Net Income}}{\text{Equity}}$$
$$= \frac{\$32,000}{\$614,000^{(1)}}$$
$$= 5.2\%$$

The ratio of net income after taxes to equity measures the rate of return on the stockholders investment. Depending upon the goals of management and stockholders, a 5.2 percent return is generally interpreted as a below-average return. Because common stock is a relatively risky investment, investors typically demand higher rates of return to compensate them for the risk. An investor in Average Company could achieve a return of well over 5.2 percent fairly easily by investing in corporate bonds that carry less risk.

In 1990, the return on equity was 10.1 percent. [1] This decline to an unacceptable level of 5.2 in 1991 should be cause for concern. However, the results should be measured in relation to the performance of the economy and the industry as well.

Return on Assets

$$\text{Return on Assets} = \frac{\text{Net Income}}{\text{Total Assets}}$$

$$= \frac{\$32,000}{\$1,057,500 [2]}$$

$$= 3.0\%$$

The ratio of net income after taxes to total assets measures the return on total investment in the company. A 3.0 percent return is a below-average return.

Gross Margin

$$\text{Gross Margin \%} = \frac{\text{Gross Margin}}{\text{Sales}}$$

$$= \frac{\$701,000}{\$2,739,000}$$

$$= 25.6\%$$

---

[1] The average equity calculation assumes earnings were made equally throughout the year. The only change in equity on the financial statements relates to earnings retained in the business.

[2] Assumes assets were added equally during the year.

This ratio gives a general idea of the profitability of the company's product or service. It is based on the difference between revenues and the direct cost of generating those revenues. The 25.6 percent margin represents what remains available to cover all the indirect costs of doing business. Another way of looking at this ratio is to say that whatever Average Company produces for $1.00 it sells for $1.26.

For Average Company the indirect expenses are shown on the income statement as salaries, payroll taxes, interest, amortization, depreciation, insurance, and general and administrative expenses. The poor return may be due to any of a number of reasons; for example, the product may not be competitive or Average's cost to produce it may be too high.

By contrast, some pharmaceutical and tobacco companies have gross margins in excess of 200 percent. They have higher costs to produce these results (R&D and marketing, respectively), but the contribution from the product sales is there to "feed" the supporting costs. Again, we see this company on a downward trend, since the same calculation for 1990 showed a 26.4 percent gross margin.

Net Income as a Percent of Sales

$$\text{Net Income As a Percent of Sales} = \frac{\text{Net Income}}{\text{Sales}}$$

$$= \frac{\$32,000}{\$2,739,000}$$

$$= 1.2\%$$

This ratio shows that Average Company earned a 1.2 percent profit after taxes on sales of $2,739,000. This is a relatively low return and could be a result of Average Company's prices being too low, its costs of doing business too high, or both. In 1990 this ratio was 2.3 percent. However, interpreting a ratio as "good" or "bad" typically depends upon the industry and environment in which the company operates. For this reason, ratios should be compared to those of other companies in the same or similar industry during the same time periods. More information is needed and other analyses need to be performed.

Exhibit 7-3 contains a summary of how ratios can be used to evaluate a company's performance.

Exhibit 7-3

How to Uncover Vital Facts

Is the company solvent?

$$\frac{\text{CURRENT ASSETS}}{\text{CURRENT LIABILITIES}}$$

A test for solvency. Provides clues to the magnitude of the financial margin of safety. For more stringent test, delete inventory from assets and compute new ratio.

Has it borrowed wisely?

$$\frac{\text{TOTAL DEBT}}{\text{NET WORTH}}$$

Reveals the extent to which the company has borrowed from suppliers and credit grantors. Too much debt may indicate insufficient capital. Could jeopardize purchase discounts and weaken competitive position.

How is company performing?

$$\frac{\text{WORKING CAPITAL}}{\text{SALES}}$$

Shows relationships of working capital to business transacted. Compare with industry average to determine company performance.

Industry averages are obtainable from industry trade groups, or by computing figures from several companies in the industry.

Are the products selling?

$$\frac{\text{COST OF SALES}}{\text{INVENTORY}}$$

Shows number of times inventory turns over. Can be inconclusive because it lumps all items—some products may move faster, others slower. Comparisons with industry averages can be revealing.

How is management doing?

$$\frac{\text{NET PROFIT}}{\text{NET WORTH}}$$

Shows return on invested capital. This measures how well management is doing on earning a return on capital. Compare with industry average, and for further insight, take into account the degree of risk involved.

Is it earning a profit?

$$\frac{\text{NET PROFIT}}{\text{SALES}}$$

This measures profit margins. Again, for real measurement, compare with others in the industry.

Exhibit 7-3 (continued)

Are profits adequate?

$$\frac{\text{COST OF SALES}}{\text{SALES}}$$

If the margin here appears thin, compared to industry averages, it could mean the company is headed for trouble. This ratio is an indicator of what is available, after deducting costs of sales, to defray general and selling expenses, research and development costs.

From "What Else Can Financial Statements Tell You?" published by The American Institute of Certified Public Accountants, Inc. Reprinted with permission.

§7.8   Variance Analysis

Variance analysis is a tool that corporate managers use in analyzing the results of their operations. The essence of this technique is to compare actual results and budgeted amounts, keeping in mind the company's results from previous months or years.

Budgets prepared by an entity are a powerful tool to analyze that entity's operations and management. Even if you do not have a budget, you can compare actual results to public announcements about expected results to determine how well the company is managed. An effective technique for finding problems is to compare actual performance to forecasted, projected, or budgeted amounts, and investigate any differences.

Budgets are not merely estimates of what revenues and expenses will be; they are more in the nature of objectives to be sought. When a budget is properly set, its attainment represents the achievement of a degree of proficiency in operating a business.

The first step in budget variance analysis is to note the frequency and magnitude of the variances or gaps between budgeted and actual results. A financial analyst should consider both favorable and unfavorable variances, attempting to isolate the specific source and cause of each variance.

Exhibit 7-4

FINANCIAL ANALYSIS RATIOS

Liquidity Ratios

The Current Ratio

$$\text{Current Ratio} = \frac{\text{Current Assets}}{\text{Current Liabilities}}$$

Quick or Acid Test Ratio

$$\frac{\text{Acid Test}}{\text{Ratio}} = \frac{\text{Cash + Marketable Securities + A/R*}}{\text{Current Liabilities}}$$

Working Capital

Net Working Capital = Current Assets − Current Liabilities

Activity Ratios

Days Payable Outstanding

$$\frac{\text{Days Payable}}{\text{Outstanding}} = \frac{\text{Payables}}{\text{Cost of Sales per Day}^1}$$

Days Receivables Outstanding

$$\frac{\text{Days Receivable}}{\text{Outstanding}} = \frac{\text{Accounts Receivable}}{\text{Credit Sales per Day}^2}$$

Inventory Turnover Ratio

$$\frac{\text{Inventory}}{\text{Turnover}} = \frac{\text{Cost of Sales}}{\text{Average Inventory Balance}}$$

Sales to Employees Ratio

$$\frac{\text{Sales to}}{\text{Employees}} = \frac{\text{Total Sales}}{\text{Number of Employees}}$$

Sales to Assets Ratio

$$\text{Sales to Assets} = \frac{\text{Total Sales}}{\text{Total Assets}}$$

Leverage Ratios

Times Interest Earned

$$\frac{\text{Times}}{\text{Interest Earned}} = \frac{\text{Earnings Before Interest and Taxes}}{\text{Interest Charges}}$$

Debt to Equity Ratio

$$\text{Debt to Equity Ratio} = \frac{\text{Total Debt}}{\text{Total Equity}}$$

Debt Coverage Ratio

$$\frac{\text{Debt Coverage}}{\text{Ratio}} = \frac{\text{Income Before Interest and Depreciation}}{\text{Principal and Interest Charges on Debt}}$$

Profitability Ratios

Gross Margin as a Percent of Sales

$$\frac{\text{Gross Margin}}{\text{as a \% of Sales}} = \frac{\text{Gross Margin}}{\text{Sales}}$$

Net Income as a Percent of Sales

$$\text{Net Income as a \% of Sales} = \frac{\text{Net Income}}{\text{Sales}}$$

Return on Assets

$$\text{Return on Assets} = \frac{\text{Net Income}}{\text{Average Total Assets}}$$

Return on Investment or Return on Equity

$$\text{Return on Equity} = \frac{\text{Net Income}}{\text{Average Equity}}$$

---

[1] $\text{Cost of Sales (COS) Per Day} = \dfrac{\text{COS (For Period)}}{\text{Number of Days}}$

[2] $\text{Credit Sales Per Day} = \dfrac{\text{Credit Sales (For Period)}}{\text{Number of Days in Period}}$

* AIR—Accounts Receivable

Unfavorable variances can result from variations in revenue, expenses, or both. On the revenue side, there may be shortfalls in volume, capacity, or utilization; or the company may have received a lower than expected price for goods or services provided. Unfavorable variances can also exist between actual and budgeted expenses. Expenses could have been higher than was planned due to such factors as higher cost of supplies, unforeseen repairs, poor cost management, or difficulties encountered in providing goods or services.

§7.9 Trend Analysis

Trend analysis is a useful method of analyzing differences between current and historical results. Unlike single-period ratio analysis, trend analysis enables one to look at operating trends as they develop over several reporting periods. Trends in a company's ratios are tracked and compared with the overall trends of the industry.

This kind of analysis permits a determination about whether a company is suffering from internal problems. One can deduce that there are internal problems if deteriorating trends appear in the company's ratios but not in industry averages. On the other hand, the trend analysis may reveal that the industry as a whole is suffering difficulties, and the analyst may conclude that the problems are not unique to the company.

§7.10 Financial Analysis of Cash Flow

An analysis of an entity would be incomplete if it were based only on the balance sheet and income statement. The balance sheet presents the status of the assets, liabilities, and equities as of a specific date; the income statement presents a summary of the nature and results of transactions affecting net income. While accrual accounting reflects economic activity more properly than cash-basis accounting, the fact remains that bills, dividend payments, and repayments of loans will have to be made with cash. The cash flow statement gives the analyst insight into the actual movement of cash, without the potential disguise of accrual methods.

A GAAP-based statement of cash flows divides the sources and uses of cash into three categories: operating activities, investing activities, and financing activities. This categorization enables the reader to readily see the sources and uses of cash. If a business is generating more of its cash from financing activities than from operating activities, this could be a bad sign. It could mean that the business is relying on borrowings to satisfy current operating needs. On the other hand, if the borrowing is for recapitalization and investment in future production (and, it is hoped, profits), it could be a good sign.

(a)   Background: Cash vs. Accrual Accounting

Let us start this section with a review of cash vs. accrual accounting. Some relatively small firms, especially those engaged in rendering services, may account for their revenues and expenses on a cash basis. This means that expenses and revenues usually are not recorded until cash actually changes hands. For example, services rendered to customers in 1991, for which cash was collected in 1992, would be treated as 1992 revenues and recorded in the 1992 income statement. They would not be included in the revenues reported in the income statement for 1991, even though this was the year in which the actual services were rendered.

By contrast, accrual accounting records transactions when they occur, regardless of when cash is received or paid. Accrual accounting becomes necessary as a business moves away from strictly cash transactions and enters into credit transactions, which bring about the creation of accounts receivable and accounts payable. In accrual accounting, revenues are recognized when sales are made or services rendered, even though cash has not yet been received; expenses are recognized as they are incurred, regardless of whether or not cash has been paid out.

Accrual accounting produces a set of financial statements that show what the business earned in a year, regardless of when the cash was actually received. Cash basis accounting does not allow this. The income statement in Exhibit 7-5 shows the difference between cash and accrual accounting in recording the earnings of a business.

The accrual basis of accounting is favored over the cash basis because it allows proper "matching" of revenues and expenses. Revenue is recorded as it is earned and expenses that produce revenue are recorded when they are incurred.

Exhibit 7-5

CASH VS. ACCRUAL INCOME STATEMENT

	CASH BASIS	ADJUSTMENTS		ACCRUAL BASIS
Revenue	$1,000	$200	(1)	$1,200
Expenses				
Purchases	200	30	(2)	230
Salaries	100	5	(3)	105
Electricity	50	10	(4)	60
Insurance	30	5	(5)	35
Telephone	20	10	(6)	30
	400	60		460
Income	$600	$140		$ 740

(1) Sales made to customers but cash not received yet.
(2) Manufacturing inventory received but not yet paid for.
(3) Salaries due for the last two days of the year but cash not yet paid to employees.
(4) Estimate of electricity consumed but not yet billed by the utility company.
(5) Estimate of insurance premiums due but not yet paid to the insurance company.
(6) Telephone calls made but not yet billed by phone company.

(b) The Statement of Cash Flow

Many financial analysts use the term "cash flow" to mean the total of the net income, minus any component of income that does not generate cash. Of course, net income is only one of many sources of cash because a business can engage in financing activities such as borrowing, issuing stock, or disposing of assets.

Non-cash items, such as depreciation and amortization, arise because of accounting conventions that require recording the fact that a long-term asset decreases in value over time. This decrease in value does not involve any actual cash outlay; the cash outlay occurred when the business purchased the asset. Cash flow from operations is usually shown in a manner similar to the following:

Net income for the year	$30,000
Add back non-cash items:	
Depreciation expense	8,000
Amortization expense	3,000
	11,000
Cash provided by operations	$41,000

The above is not a complete cash flow statement, but it is the part that many analysts focus on, first and foremost. The statement of cash flows included in a full set of GAAP financial statements is more comprehensive and provides a wealth of information for lawyers, investors, creditors, analysts, and others. It indicates whether the enterprise generated positive net cash flows in the past, and can be used to help project cash flow in the future. It can also be made to show whether the enterprise is likely to meet its debt obligations and pay dividends, and whether it may need external financing.

It is important to note that cash flow is only part of the picture. Cash balances may actually decrease even though the company is operating at a profit, or cash flows can increase while the company is operating at a loss. The reason for this apparent contradiction becomes clear from a list of the sources of cash outflows and inflows.

Cash *outflows* result from such transactions as:

- Payments for current operating costs and expenses;

- Payments for raw materials to be used in producing inventory;

- Repayment of short-term debt;

- Acquisition of property, plant, equipment, and other long-term assets;

- Redemption of long-term debt; and

- Payment of dividends.

Cash *inflows* result from such transactions as:

- Sales for cash;

- Collection of accounts receivable;

- Conversion of marketable securities to cash;

- Obtaining short-term financing;

- Sale of property, plant and equipment;

- Issuance of bonds and other long-term obligations; and

- Issuance of stock for cash.

Many heavily capitalized companies can have a net loss but generate significant cash, since depreciation is a non-cash expense and is added back to determine cash flow. However, if a company is continuing to have losses and is not spending to replace long-term assets consumed in operations, it cannot survive in the long run. It is converting its income-producing assets to cash, and in essence is liquidating. Like every other aspect of financial analysis, cash flow analysis is only one piece of the mosaic. Do not be fooled by looking only at one part of the picture.

(c)   A Sample Statement of Cash Flows

Exhibit 7-6 is the Statement of Cash Flows for a hypothetical company, Clayton Manufacturing, Inc.

Initially, note that the net income of $30,000 does not equal the net cash flow (net increase in cash) from operations ("net cash provided by operating activities") of $47,000. Depreciation and amortization are non-cash expense items, so they are added back to net income for cash flow purposes. Next, a reserve for doubtful accounts is not a cash loss but an accrual for losses anticipated in the accounts receivable portfolio. It, too, is added back. Nor is a loss on the sale of a non-current asset a cash loss. The outflow occurred when the asset was purchased, so it is added back. These are just a few of the types of adjustments one may encounter when reading a cash flow analysis.

Another adjustment is in the area of cash received for sales. Sales volume in a given period is not the same as cash received for sales. In

Exhibit 7-6

CLAYTON MANUFACTURING, INC.
STATEMENT OF CASH FLOWS
FOR THE YEAR ENDED DECEMBER 31, 1990

Operating Activities

Net income for the year		$30,000
Adjustments to reconcile net income to net cash provided by operating activities:		
Depreciation expense	$8,000	
Amortization expense	3,000	
Reserve for doubtful receivables	2,000	
Loss on sale of non-current assets	1,000	
		14,000
Changes in working capital:		
Increase in accounts receivable	(2,000)	
Decrease in inventories	3,000	
Increase in accounts payable	2,000	
		3,000
Net cash provided by operating activities		47,000
Investing Activities		
Purchase of equipment	(4,500)	
Proceeds from non-current assets sale	3,000	
Net cash used in investing activities		(1,500)
Financing Activities		
Proceeds from long-term borrowings	10,000	
Payments of long-term borrowings	(3,000)	
Dividends paid	(5,000)	
Net cash provided by financing activities		2,000
Increase in cash		47,500
Cash at beginning of year		5,000
Cash at end of year		$52,500

---

most companies, sales are made on credit and the cash is not received for some days or months. Clayton Manufacturing's Statement of Cash Flows makes an adjustment for this in the "Operating Activities" section called "increase in accounts receivable." There has been an increase in accounts receivable during the year of $2,000, which means that $2,000 more in sales were made on credit than cash was received for sales (this year's and last year's unpaid receivables).

The following illustration demonstrates how this works:

	Accrual Basis	Cash Basis
Accounts receivable January 1	$ 60,000	
Sales	300,000(A)	
	360,000	
Cash received for accounts receivable (cash for sales) 12/31	298,000	$298,000(B)
Accounts receivable December 31	$ 62,000	
Accrual Less Cash Sales		
Sales included in accrual income	300,000(A)	
Cash received from sales	(298,000)(B)	
Increase in accounts receivable	$ 2,000	

Returning to the Operating Activities section, the next amount is an increase in cash flow of $3,000 resulting from a decrease in inventory. This means that $3,000 more in inventory items was sold than was purchased during the year. Consequently, the inventory balance at the end of the year was $3,000 less than at the beginning of the year.

The last item in the Operating Activities is an adjustment for cash flow caused by a $2,000 increase in accounts payable. When a company incurs expenses, it rarely pays in cash. Usually, the company waits 30, 60, or 90 days before paying. The increase in accounts payable represents $2,000 more in expenses than was paid in cash during the year. This is similar to the accounts receivable example, except that it is for a liability account related to expenses rather than for an asset account related to revenue.

Looking at the investing activities of Clayton, it appears that the company is purchasing equipment for $4,500. Relating this fact to the company's consumption of $8,000 in equipment (depreciation of original cost) in operations, there could well be concern that the company is not replacing its income-producing assets. To put this concern in proper perspective, however, the reader must analyze activity for a number of years. Equipment could have been purchased in earlier years, or funds could be accumulating to purchase new equipment in later years. The point is to look further and ask questions until any given concern is resolved. Part of the mosaic of analysis is comparison over time.

The other item in the Investing Activities section is the amount of cash received when long-lived assets were sold. Determine the book value of the asset sold (cost less depreciation) by adding the loss on the sale shown under "Operating Activities" to the net proceeds (which were received in cash):

Loss	$1,000		Book value	$4,000
Proceeds	3,000	or	Loss	1,000
Book value	$4,000		Proceeds	$3,000

This calculation demonstrates how, with a bit of diligence, analysis can determine other facts about a company's transactions, even though not explicitly disclosed.

Turning to the Financing Activities section, we see that the company borrowed $10,000 long-term and made principal payments on long-term debt of $3,000. Net long-term borrowing increased $7,000. Also, the company paid $5,000 in dividends. Since cash from operations ($47,000) would have been sufficient to cover all of the company's cash needs, the reader should ask, "Why borrow long term? Is there an identifiable future need for the cash?"

This example deals with thousands of dollars, but it could just as easily involve millions. Why is the company building up a cash balance and borrowing long-term? Are they considering an acquisition? Are they planning to purchase significant assets or to expand? Long-term borrowing is often done to acquire long-term assets. The point here is to look at other data and ask questions. If this is a public company, look at MD&A in the Form 10-K. Look at the historical data to determine whether they need the cash. Was the opening balance of $5,000 too low, or is this a cyclical business that needs a cash cushion? The analyst may have to ask management why they are building the balance.

The key to any business is cash—to pay bills, to expand, to pay dividends, to pay debt. Ultimately, all transactions must end with cash changing hands. A successful business receives more than it gives out. However, cash is only one section of the mosaic. The results of any analysis must be interpreted in light of the following factors:

- Historical activity and norms;

- Industry and geographic norms;

- Regional, national, and international economic conditions;

- Other analysis of different but related data; and

- Management's comments on its operations and business activities.

Virtually every business experiences periods of cash shortages and temporary excess idle cash because of seasonal fluctuations in the level of its activities. The more severe these fluctuations, the greater the need for careful planning and management of cash needs and investments. When the demands for cash during a given period are expected to exceed available cash, plans must be made to obtain cash from some other source, such as through the conversion of short-term securities or through short-term credit from a bank or other financial institution. During periods when cash inflow is expected to exceed cash outflow, the plans should provide for a reduction of short-term debt, an increase in temporary investments, or both.

(d)   Cash Flow Analysis and Cash Planning

Exhibit 7-7 is an extract from the statement of cash flows for Jenny Peterson, Inc. for the six months from January to June, 1989. Jenny Peterson is a former world champion surfer who now manufactures and sells surfboards. Jenny's business is very seasonal and most of her customers do not start buying surfboards until May—just in time for summer. This means that she will not receive cash from her customers until May or even later.

Jenny competes in the "Golden Oldies" circuit. She needs to make most of the surfboards by April so she can have the summer off to surf. Because she runs a small company, her suppliers demand that she pay cash for her supplies. Jenny needs enough cash from January to April to pay her suppliers.

Now look at Exhibit 7-8, the monthly cash flow statement of Jenny Peterson, Inc. Keep in mind that the company's net income for the six months was $17,500 and its cash flow from operations was $19,500.

Exhibit 7-7

JENNY PETERSON, INC.
STATEMENT OF CASH FLOWS
JANUARY TO JUNE 1989

Net income	$17,500
Add back non-cash items	2,000
Depreciation expense	
Cash provided by operations	<u>$19,500</u>

The statement shows that Jenny needs to borrow money in March and April if her business is to survive. If you simply looked at the $17,500 net income or even the $19,500 cash from operations that the company made by the end of May, you would not be able to tell that Jenny needed to borrow money. Only a detailed cash flow analysis brings these things to light. (In case you are wondering, the difference between the $19,500 cash from operations and the ending cash balance of $29,500 results because the company started January with $10,000 in the bank—as you can see from the "opening cash" in the January column.)

Jenny's situation illustrates the fact that management needs a more detailed cash flow analysis than the one that appears in the financial statements if it is to effectively manage the cash resources of a business. Attorneys should be aware that this type of cash analysis is available at many large and medium-sized companies that have a treasury function. Knowledge of the existence of cash management documents may also give a better understanding about what to ask for from an adversary in litigation.

Exhibit 7-8

JENNY PETERSON, INC.
MONTHLY CASH FLOWS
JANUARY TO MAY 1989

	1/89	2/89	3/89	4/89	5/89
Revenue	$0	$0	$0	$12,000	$22,500
Cash Expenses	(4,000)	(4,000)	(4,000)	(2,000)	(1,000)
Opening Cash	<u>10,000</u>	<u>6,000</u>	<u>2,000</u>	<u>(2,000)</u>	<u>8,000</u>
Closing Cash	<u>$6,000</u>	<u>$2,000</u>	<u>($2,000)</u>	<u>$8,000</u>	<u>$29,500</u>

Exhibit 7-9

MANUFACTURING COMPANY, INC.
Common Size Balance Sheet
12/31/91

Assets		Liabilities and Equity	
Cash	0.2	Notes payable to bank	1.6
Marketable securities, at cost which		Accounts payable	10.2
approximates market	1.8		
		Accrued liabilities	5.6
Accounts receivable, less		Income taxes payable	0.5
allowance of $5,000 for			
doubtful accounts	15.8		
		Dividend payable	2.2
Inventories	8.8	Long-term debt due within	
		one year	3.4
Total current assets	26.6	*Total current liabilities*	23.5
Investments, at cost	1.8	*Long-term debt due after one year:*	
Property, plant, and equipment, at cost		8% note payable, due $4,000 monthly	22.5
		10% note payable	12.6
Land	22.8	Total long-term debt	35.1
Buildings	49.2		
Machinery and equipment	25.3	*Shareholders' Equity*	
	97.3	Common stock, $10 par	
Less accumulated		5,500,000 authorized,	
depreciation	29.8	3,100,000 issued	2.2
Net property, plant, and equipment	67.5	Capital in excess of par value	20.4
		Retained earnings	18.8
Other assets	4.2	*Total shareholders' equity*	41.4
		Total liabilities and	
Total assets	100.0	equity	100.0

If a business client calls in desperation, seeking assistance with negotiating a loan or drafting a lending agreement, counsel might well suggest that the client do some cash management planning. This would give the client more time to negotiate a better rate, terms, or restrictive covenants. The client would benefit by being able to schedule cash needs well in advance of actual shortfalls.

§7.11   Common Size Financial Statements

An effective, yet simple analytical technique to apply to the balance sheet and income statement is the use of common size statements. The term "common size" means that all companies' financial statements, regardless of company size, are placed on a level playing field. The mechanism to accomplish this is simple. For the balance sheet, total assets are made to equal 100 and every component of the balance sheet is expressed as a percentage of total assets. For example, a balance sheet may show millions of dollars in different asset and liability account categories, but all of these numbers can be reduced to percentages of total assets. The result is a common size balance sheet that may look like Exhibit 7-9. Manufacturing Company, Inc.'s actual balance sheet appears at Exhibit 7-10.

An income statement, on the other hand, uses sales or revenue as its basis of 100. With the statement in common size form, the analyst can compare different companies very easily, because the components of sales and income are based on percentages rather than dollar amounts.

Relationships within the statements themselves become more apparent when common size statements are used. For example, in Manufacturing Company Inc.'s common size balance sheet (Exhibit 7-9), it is easy to see that the current ratio is slightly higher than 1 (current assets of 26.6 and current liabilities of 23.5).

An example of a common size income statement is shown in Exhibit 7-11. The common size balance sheet in one exhibit is based on the income statement in Exhibit 7-12. From the common size income statement one can also clearly see the gross margin (gross profit) percentage is 28 and that return on sales is 5.6%. However, the best use of the common size statement is for comparison with peer companies to highlight variances for further investigation.

Exhibit 7-10

MANUFACTURING COMPANY, INC.
Balance Sheet 12/31/91
(dollars in thousands)

Assets		Liabilities and Equity	
Current Assets		*Current Liabilities*	
Cash	$3,000	Notes payable to bank	$23,000
Marketable securities, at cost which		Accounts payable	145,000
approximates market	25,000		
		Accrued liabilities	80,000
		Income taxes payable	7,000
Accounts receivable,		Dividend payable	31,000
less allowance of			
$5,000 for doubtful			
accounts	225,000		
		Long-term debt due	
		within one year	48,000
Inventories	125,000	Total current liabilities	334,000
Total current assets	378,000		
		Long-term debt due after	
		one year:	
Investments, at cost	25,000	8% note payable, due	
		$4,000 monthly	320,000
Property, plant, and		10% note payable	180,000
equipment, at cost			
Land	325,000	*Total long-term debt*	500,000
Buildings	700,000		
Machinery and		*Shareholder's Equity*	
equipment	360,000		
	1,385,000	Common stock, $10 par	
Less accumulated		5,500,000 authorized,	
depreciation		3,100,000 issued	31,000
Net property, plant, and		Capital in excess of par	
equipment	960,000	value	290,000
		Retained earnings	268,000
Other assets	60,000	Total shareholders	
		equity	589,000
		Total liabilities and	
Total assets	**$1,423,000**	**equity**	**$1,423,000**

When comparing common size statements with other companies, one can easily identify the unusual. For example, one can tell whether cash of 0.2% of assets is the norm and not too low, and whether an inventory of 8.8% of assets is within the expected range. Differences between the

Exhibit 7-11

Another Company Inc.
Common Size Income Statement
For the Year Ended December 31, 1990

Net sales	100.0
Cost of goods sold	72.0
Gross profit	28.0
Selling, general and administrative expense	17.5
Total operating income	10.5
Interest expense	(2.3)
Other income and expense (net)	0.9
Income before income taxes	9.1
Federal and state income taxes	3.5
Net income	5.6

Exhibit 7-12

Another Company, Inc.
Income Statement
For the Year Ended December 31, 1990
(dollars in thousands)

Net Sales	$101,347
Cost of Goods Sold	72,972
Gross Profit	28,375
Selling, General and Administrative Expenses	17,736
Total Operating Income	10,639
Interest Expense	(2,350)
Other Income and Expense (net)	899
Income Before Income Taxes	9,188
Federal and State Income Taxes	3,550
Net Income	$5,638

composition of the entity's statements and its ratios and those of its peers can be investigated, since they offer red flags or warnings of problems brewing under the surface of the statements. Many times, however, the differences may only indicate differences among business sectors and management styles.

A good source for comparable common size statements is Robert Morris Associates' *Annual Statement Studies*. The studies include data by industry and by size of entity. This source also gives ratios and other data that can be used to compare each entity with its peers.

§7.12 Summary and Conclusion

Broadly defined, financial analysis is the attempt to understand the operations and profitability of a company by considering relevant financial data. Reading all the financial data available and not being limited to the basic financial statements is the logical first step. The next step is to analyze ratios, trends, and cash flows. The analyst's best tools, however, are judgment and an interest in looking behind the numbers.

The Time Value of Money

§8.1   Introduction

In negotiating a settlement in litigation, in drafting provisions for business contracts and agreements, and in collecting your own fees and payments, you are no doubt aware that dollars today are worth more than the same number of dollars in a year or two. Receiving the money today allows you or your client to invest it in whatever financial instrument or business is desired and to earn a return, typically in direct relationship to the business risk taken.

When settling disputes, lawyers often need to compare the value of a lump sum amount with the value of a stream of payments. Is $350,000 today equal to, less than, or greater than $2,500 per month for twenty years? The answer depends on the interest rate charged for an annuity that would pay a beneficiary $2,500 per month for 20 years. If the going rate is seven percent, the annuity would cost approximately $322,500 in today's dollars.

Present and future value concepts arise in many business situations including valuing assets and liabilities, negotiating acquisitions, accounting for pensions and other postretirement benefits, and valuing certain receivables and payables.

To understand financial statements requires an understanding of present and future value concepts and the pitfalls inherent in many assumptions about interest rates. People who frequently have to perform present and future value calculations have developed some standard approaches. No one, except perhaps the most technically-oriented mathematicians and actuaries, bothers to go through the formula manually and compute the results. To perform these calculations, it is easiest to use a good financial calculator, which costs between $75 and $130. An alternative is to use annuity and present value tables similar to those contained in Tables 1 through 4 at the end of this chapter.

More complex calculations are easier to perform on an electronic spreadsheet, and all the major spreadsheet software programs contain present value functions. Using a spreadsheet makes the task much easier if there are a number of cash flows (say 10 or more), if you change the variables often, or if you do the same kind of calculation repeatedly.

§8.2   Definitions

(a)   Present value

Present value is the value in today's dollars of a payment or a stream of payments expected to be received in the future. Present value is always the value today, expressed as "time 0." A present value calculation is a computation of the lump-sum equivalent today of the future payment or payments, discounted back to a single amount.

The current market price of a zero coupon bond (one that pays no current interest, such as a U.S. Savings Bond) is an example of the present value of the expected future payment of the bond. The market price of the bond is based on the equivalent in todays dollars of what someone will give up to get the promised payoff in the future.

For example, an investor seeking a 10 percent return might pay $386 today for a $1,000 bond to be redeemed in 10 years. The $386 purchase price is the present value of the future payoff, discounted at 10 percent. As interest rates change, the current market value will also change; a decline in interest rates will increase the value of the bond, and an increase will decrease its value. Generally, the market value increases as the bond approaches its maturity date, since the bond holder has less time to wait to get the money back. Zero-coupon bonds are one way to guarantee a set return on the $386 for ten years. The holder of a zero-coupon bond will earn 10 percent on the principal and 10 percent on the interest earned each year (compounded). If one were to invest the $386 for 10 years at l0 percent paid annually, there would be no assurance of getting the 10 percent interest rate on each annual interest payment.

(b)   Future value

Future value is the value to be received at a point of time in the future. The future value of a bond, for example, is its redemption value. The future value of the bond mentioned above is $1,000 in year 10, when it is redeemed. If the buyer wanted to sell the bond before that date, for example, in year 5, the future value would depend on many factors, including the interest rates at the time of redemption, time to maturity, and others.

Consider the $10 million prize in a magazine subscription solicitor's marketing contest. If you believe that the winner is getting a prize worth $10 million on the day it is awarded, you need to read the fine print and study this chapter. The fine print will tell you the award is paid out in annual installments over 30 years, with a "balloon" payment in the thirtieth year. A practical way to solve for the true value is to determine what you would need to invest today (at today's interest rates) to receive a 30-year annuity for the annual payment amount, and what to invest today (again at today's interest rates) to receive the lump sum payment in thirty years. The answer will be substantially less than $10 million. In fact, it could be less than $3.3 million, depending on the vehicle used for the investment and on the interest rate.

(c) Payments

Payments mean periodic payments (or receipts) of cash occurring between the first and last payments. Most people are familiar with these in the forms of loan payments, dividend payments, and bond payments.

Let us return to the example of a bond. Some bonds pay interest throughout their lives. If the $1,000 bond described above also paid $100 interest per year for 10 years, it would have a present value of $1,000 because the periodic (in this case, annual) payments of $100 compensate the bond buyer at a rate of 10 percent for the use of the money until it is paid back in 10 years.

In the case of debt payments, each payment usually reduces the principal balance due on the loan, while also paying interest on the balance. For example, most automobile loans have payments that pay off interest and principal over three to five years. Payment amounts are affected by the length of time, the interest rate, and the principal balance.

A payment that remains constant for a specified period is sometimes called an annuity. A true annuity is a contract between a buyer (an investor) and an institution such as a bank or insurance company, in which the buyer invests a single lump sum, and the seller pays it off in a stream of payments that are fixed in amount.

(d) Discount rate

Discount rate is a rate which is used to calculate payments, future values, and present values. In the bond example (i.e., a $1,000 bond purchased for $386, to be redeemed in 10 years), the discount rate is 10 percent. Using that discount rate lets the bond buyer calculate the price (present value) he or she would pay for a bond with a future value of $1,000 in 10 years.

(e)   Internal rate of return (IRR)

Simply stated, Internal Rate of Return is the interest rate that the project earns. An internal rate of return assumes that all cash flows are reinvested at the same rate (the calculated rate) until the end of the project. This tends to overstate the true yield on a project, unless the cash generated from the project can actually be reinvested elsewhere at the same interest rate for exactly the same amount of time as the project.

In some cases, such as that of a zero-coupon bond held to maturity, the internal rate of return may be equal to the yield. However, in most cases, a modified internal rate of return is more accurate. A modified internal rate of return is a "blended rate" of the internal rate and a secondary, "safe" rate for the cash coming out of the project. For example, if a speculative investment succeeds and begins generating cash at rate of $20 annually per $100 invested, the internal rate is theoretically 20 percent, but that calculation assumes that all the $20 payouts are *also* reinvested in something yielding 20 percent. If the $20 cash payout can only be reinvested at less than 20 percent, the modified rate for the investment will be less.

(f)   Compounding

Compounding, in a simple sense, is "interest on interest." For example, a $10,000 savings account with simple interest at 12 percent a year would earn $1,200 in a year. If the rate were 12 percent compounded monthly (effectively one percent per month), the account would earn $1,268, with the difference due to compounding of the interest rate. With compounding, the first months earnings would be $100, the second months $101, and the final months interest nearly $112, as each successive month's earnings are calculated on a growing or compounded balance.

Increasing the frequency of compounding increases the effective yield. By compounding a 12 percent annual yield monthly, the effective yield is 12.68 percent, or $1,268 of interest on a $10,000 investment. If the rate had been compounded weekly instead of monthly, the effective rate would have been 12.73 percent, yielding $1,273 of earnings.

(g) Summary

Each type of problem related to the time value of money is based on the interest formula:

Interest = Principal × Rate × Time

In future value determinations, you know the amount of cash (principal) to be invested and want to calculate the amount of principal plus interest that will be available at some future date. In present value determinations, you know the amount that will be available at some future date (principal plus interest) and are asked to calculate the current cash equivalent of that amount.

The Future Value of a Single Amount. The future value is the sum to which an amount will increase at I interest rate for N periods. The future sum will be the principal plus compound interest.

The Present Value of a Single Amount. The present value of a single amount is the value now of an amount to be received at some date in the future. It can be said to be the inverse of the future value concept. To compute the present value of a sum to be received in the future, you subject the future sum to compound discounting at I interest rate for N periods. In compound discounting, the interest is subtracted, as opposed to compounding, in which the interest is added.

The Future Value of an Annuity. Basically, the future value of an annuity is the same as the future value of a single amount, except for the fact that it is an annuity. The term annuity refers to a series of periodic payments characterized by:

(1) an equal amount each period (for two or more future consecutive periods),

(2) equal length of each consecutive period, and

(3) equal interest rate each period.

The future value of an annuity consists of the principal plus compound interest on each amount during each period.

The Present Value of an Annuity. The present value of an annuity is the value now of a series of equal amounts (for example, rents) to be received each period for some specified number of periods in the future. The present value of an annuity can be said to be the inverse of the future value of an annuity, and it involves compound discounting of each of the equal periodic amounts.

§8.3 Conventional Terminology and Equations

Most financial calculators—and analysts applying present value techniques and principles—typically use a shorthand for describing the various elements of cash flow:

- **P** or **PV** for present value or the value of something right now;

- **F** or **FV** for value received at some date in the future;

- **N** or **n** for the number of periods (which can be in months, years, etc.);

- **I** or **i** for the discount, interest, or growth rate per period of time; and

- **PMT** or **r** for the payment, an amount to be paid in (or out) in a series, sometimes called "rents."

The four most common equations are:

1. $FV = PV (1+i)^n$

2. $PV = \dfrac{FV}{(1+i)^n}$

3. $PV\ Annuity = Payment\ Amount \times \left(\dfrac{1 - \dfrac{1}{(1+i)^n}}{i} \right)$

4. $FV\ Annuity = Payment\ Amount \times \left(\dfrac{(1+i)^n - 1}{i} \right)$

This last formula is for an ordinary annuity (annuity in arrears). It presupposes that each payment is made at the end of the period. This is the formula you will find in annuity tables. If you want to determine the annuity values when payments are made at the beginning of the period (annuity in advance), add 1 to n and subtract one payment from the result. To develop an annuity table factor, add 1 to n, and then subtract 1.00 from the factor in the table. Finding the factor for $n+1$ and subtracting 1.00 from it results in a factor that only includes the compound interest rate for the additional period.

§8.4   Diagramming and Solving Problems

Many novices find it helpful to diagram the cash flows to make sure that they understand them and that they are doing the calculation correctly. The diagram is usually a simple time line denoting when the cash flows, which direction it goes, and the amount. The diagram can then serve as a blueprint for entering the cash flows into a financial calculator or spreadsheet. A simple example appears below.

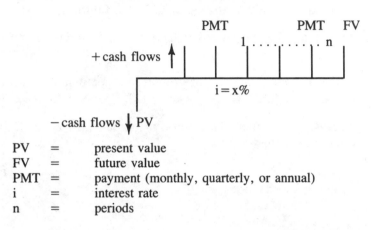

PV	=	present value
FV	=	future value
PMT	=	payment (monthly, quarterly, or annual)
i	=	interest rate
n	=	periods

Below the line are those payments, present value, or future value entries that represent cash outlays. Above the line are the amounts that represent cash inflows. By filling in the known value, one can figure out the value needed to be solved for.

The examples that follow calculate the result mathematically and also refer to Tables 1, 2, 3, and 4, which can be found at the end of this chapter for the calculation factor.

(a)   Example: The Future Value of a Single Amount

This type of transaction reveals the value of a single sum of money invested at a given rate for a specific period of time. It also shows what amount to invest now if you want to produce a given value in the future.

Assume that we plan to invest $1,000 at 8 percent for four years, and we want to know what it will be worth at the end of the four-year period. The time line below shows the formula, how the values are assigned, and what we are solving for.

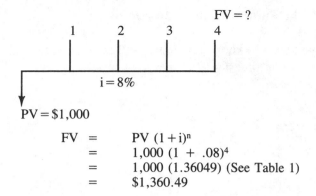

$$
\begin{aligned}
FV &=& PV\,(1+i)^n \\
&=& 1{,}000\,(1\ +\ .08)^4 \\
&=& 1{,}000\,(1.36049)\ \text{(See Table 1)} \\
&=& \$1{,}360.49
\end{aligned}
$$

The value for $(1+i)^n$ can be retrieved from Table 1 by looking under the 8 percent column for four periods. This example illustrates how a present value grows into a future value. It also shows the effects of compounding.

(b)   Example: The Present Value of a Single Amount

Assume that you have a payment of exactly $1,469.32 that is due in five years, and you want to know how much you must invest today so that you will have the money when the payment is due. The market rate of interest is eight percent. The time line and the formula are:

$$
FV = \$1{,}469.32
$$

| 1 | 2 | 3 | 4 | 5 |

$i = 8\%$

$PV = ?$

$$
\begin{aligned}
PV &= \frac{FV}{(1+i)^n} \\[2mm]
&= \frac{1{,}469.32}{(1+.08)^5} \\[2mm]
&= \frac{1{,}469.32}{1.46932} \\[2mm]
&= \$1{,}000 \quad (.06806 \times \$1{,}469.32.\ \text{See Table 2.})
\end{aligned}
$$

This illustrates discounting, which is the opposite of compounding. It shows how much must be invested now to return a specific future value.

(c) Example: The Future Value of an Annuity

Assume now that you want to know how much will be in your savings account in three years if you invest $1,000 per year at 10 percent.

$$
\begin{array}{ccc}
1 & 2 & 3
\end{array}
\qquad FV = ?
$$

i = 10%

PMT = $1,000

$$FV \text{ Annuity} = \text{Payment Amount} \times \left(\frac{(1+i)^n - 1}{i}\right)$$

$$FV \text{ Annuity} = \frac{PMT(1+i)^n - PMT}{i}$$

$$= \frac{1,000(1+.10)^3 - 1,000}{.10}$$

$$= \frac{1,331 - 1,000}{.10}$$

$$= \frac{331}{.10}$$

$$= \$3,310$$

The future value (FV) of an annuity of $1 can be obtained from Table 3. Multiply that number (3.31) by the $1,000 present value, and the result is $3,310.

The $3,000 in deposits will have grown to $3,310. The $310 represents the time value of money, or interest earned. Because this is an ordinary annuity, the payment is considered to be made at the end of the period. The $3,310 represents the initial $2,000 investment (at the end of years 1 and 2), the interest earned on that amount, and the additional $1,000 invested at the end of year 3. If you want to determine the amount when payments are made at the beginning of the period (annuity in advance), add 1 to n and subtract one payment from the result. To develop an annuity table factor, add 1 to n, and then subtract 1.00 from the factor in the table. Finding the factor for n + 1 and subtracting 1.00 from it results in a factor that only includes the compound interest rate for the additional period.

(d)   Example: The Present Value of an Annuity

You will receive $1,000 per year for two years at 10 percent. What is the investment's value today if you wished to sell it to someone?

$$PMT = \$1,000$$

$$i = 10\%$$

$$PV = ?$$

$$PV\ Annuity = Payment\ Amount \times \left(\frac{1 - \frac{1}{(1+i)^n}}{i} \right)$$

$$PV = \frac{PMT - \left(\frac{PMT}{(1+i)^n} \right)}{i}$$

$$= \frac{1000 - \left(\frac{1000}{(1+.10)^2} \right)}{.10}$$

$$= \frac{173.55}{.10}$$

$$= \$1,735.55$$

Once again, the present value (PV) of an annuity of $1 can be obtained from Table 4. That number (1.7355) multiplied by the $1,000 payment is $1,735.55. The difference (discount) between $2,000 of payments and $1,736 is the time value of money, or $264 in interest earned.

(e)   Example: Whether to Finance or Pay Cash

As another example of the present value of an annuity, assume that you are in the process of buying a car and can either finance the purchase or pay cash. The salesperson suggests that you finance it and let your money earn interest in your money market fund at the bank. Ignoring the fact that the finance charges are no longer deductible for tax purposes, let us look at the time value of money and decide what to do.

Assume the following facts:

Car price:	$15,000
Finance rate:	11%
Term:	4 years
Monthly payment:	unknown

Money market fund balance: $15,000
Money market fund rate: 8% compounded monthly

The diagram and calculations are as follows:

Determine the dollar value of the interest that would be lost if the $15,000 certificate of deposit were used to pay for the car. First determine what the $15,000 would be worth in four years.

$$FV = ?$$

| 1 | 2 | 3.. | 48 Monthly periods |

$i = 8\%$ (per year)

$PV = \$15,000$

$$
\begin{aligned}
FV &= PV\,(1+i)^n \\
&= 15,000\,(1 + .00667)^{48} \\
&= 15,000\,(1.375885) \\
&= 20,638
\end{aligned}
$$

Next, deduct the $15,000 investment from the future value

$$
\begin{aligned}
&= 20,638 - 15,000 \\
&= \$5,638 \text{ (interest that would be earned over four years)}
\end{aligned}
$$

Total interest paid on the car loan four years, assuming monthly payments, is calculated as follows:

$PV = \$15,000$

$PMT = ?$

$i = 11\%$ (per year)

| 1 | 2 | 3.. | 48 |

$$PV\ Annuity = Payment\ Amount \times \left(\dfrac{1 - \dfrac{1}{(1+i)^n}}{i} \right)$$

$$\$15,000 = PMT \times \left(\dfrac{1 - \dfrac{1}{(1 + .0091666)^{48}}}{.0091666} \right)$$

$$\begin{aligned}
\text{PMT} &= \$387.68 \\
\text{Total payments} &= \$18,609 \ (\$387.68 \times 48) \\
\text{Amount financed} &= \$15,000 \\
\text{Interest paid} &= \$3,609
\end{aligned}$$

Thus, if we pay cash, we lose $5,638 of interest on our savings. If we finance the loan, we pay $3,609 in interest. Apparently, we save $2,029 ($5,638 − 3,609) by financing the car. But do we? Present value calculations by themselves do not give a complete answer. The question arises: Where do the monthly payments come from?

If the payments are taken from savings, the loan payoff will absorb $15,000 plus $3,609 in interest costs. So the $5,638 in interest that we expected to earn will be dramatically lower. If, on the other hand, the payments are taken from income, the amount would be diverted from possible savings and we would lose potential income of approximately $3,200, calculated as follows:

FV = ?

```
FV = ?
  ┌─────────────────┐ ↑
  ↓1  ↓2  ↓3..       ↓ 48
PMT = $387.68
```

PMT = $387.68

$$\text{FV Annuity} = \frac{\text{PMT}(1+i)n - \text{PMT}}{i}$$

$$= \frac{387.68(1 + .00667)^{48} - 387.68}{.00667}$$

$$\begin{aligned}
\text{FV} &= 21,846 \\
\text{Interest lost} &= 21,846 - 18,609 \ [21{,}846 \text{ minus the principal invested in} \\
&\qquad\qquad\qquad\qquad\quad \text{savings } (387.68 \times 48)] \\
&= \$3,237
\end{aligned}$$

In summary, the table below depicts the net interest cost of financing the automobile or paying cash. It assumes that in financing the car you will pay for the car from your monthly income, and in paying cash for the car, you will put into savings what you would have paid on the loan:

	Finance	*Pay Cash*
Interest paid on the auto loan	$(3,609)	$ 0
Interest earned on the savings account	5,638	3,237
Net interest income	$2,029	$3,237

The point is that when you borrow at 11 percent and save at eight percent, you cannot come out ahead. In this example, you would lose $1,209.

We ignored the tax effect for simplicity's sake, but including taxes makes the calculation much different. With taxes, paying cash is worth approximately $2,000 more to us than borrowing, not $1,209 as shown above. We would have to pay tax on the interest income, but would not be allowed a deduction for the interest expense. At present, some borrowers use home equity loans to get the interest expense deduction for tax purposes.

§8.5 Advantages and Disadvantages of Present Value Tools

Present value formulas are a set of tools that should be applied with judgment. Like the tools of an artist or carpenter, they require an understanding, trained hand. Working with present value calculations is sometimes considered to be an exercise in precision but not accuracy. This means that although the equations yield very specific, exact numbers, the answers are not necessarily correct.

Although the arithmetic is very precise, the equations require estimates, and, as we have seen in the example of the car loan, the final answers are only as good as the assumptions they contain. Interest rates, inflation rates, tax deductibility, and tax rates—these factors often need to be estimated when they enter into calculations that concern future periods.

§8.6 Tips for Using Present Value Tools

It is not necessary to do the calculation by hand, and it is better not to do so. While financial calculators are fine for simple present value calculations, more sophisticated calculations are usually better handled by personal computers. Like financial calculators, most commercial spreadsheets for personal computers have built-in present value functions. (If yours does not, you can easily duplicate the present value formulas shown in §8.3.) When using established formulas in a spreadsheet, review the user's manual to make sure that the formulas are structured as you wish. Assumptions can vary; for example, payments may occur at the beginning or the end of each period.

CPAs and other experienced analysts advise several rules of thumb for performing present value calculations: First, run the numbers more than once. This will eliminate input errors. Then vary one of the inputs and do the calculation a few times. This is called sensitivity analysis, and it gives the analyst a "feel" for how the calculation responds to slight changes in the variables. Many novice analysts are surprised by the impact of apparently minor changes in discount or interest rates. Finally, give the calculation a smell test. Step back from the details and ask whether the whole thing makes sense. The unwinding of many leveraged buy-outs in the late 1980s shows that even sophisticated analysts can overstate projections and assume unreasonable events in their forecasts.

§8.7   Presentation and Testimony Using Present Value Concepts

Present value is often a difficult concept for jurors and other lay persons to understand. Using charts, graphs, and other visual devices often helps. It is also useful to draw analogies that the listeners are familiar with, such as comparisons to an individuals savings accounts, loans, or earnings. In personal injury cases, for example, it is not difficult to explain why it would be inequitable to award a worklife's worth of gross earnings in one lump sum, instead of spacing it out over many years (as it would be earned). Similarly, examples help someone who is unfamiliar with present value to see the value of discounting. Any stream of income can be compared to an individual's earnings. The key to successful testimony is keeping it short and simple (KISS) and, where possible, using visual aids.

The Time Value of Money

Table 1—Future value of $1, $FV = \$1(1+i)^n$

Periods	2%	3%	3.75%	4%	4.25%	5%	6%	7%	8%
0	1.0000	1.0000	1.0000	1.0000	1.0000	1.0000	1.0000	1.0000	1.0000
1	1.0200	1.0300	1.0375	1.0400	1.0425	1.0500	1.0600	1.0700	1.0800
2	1.0404	1.0609	1.0764	1.0816	1.0868	1.1025	1.1236	1.1449	1.1664
3	1.0612	1.0927	1.1168	1.1249	1.1330	1.1576	1.1910	1.2250	1.2597
4	1.0824	1.1255	1.1587	1.1699	1.1811	1.2155	1.2625	1.3108	1.3605
5	1.1041	1.1593	1.2021	1.2167	1.2313	1.2763	1.3382	1.4026	1.4693
6	1.1262	1.1941	1.2472	1.2653	1.2837	1.3401	1.4185	1.5007	1.5869
7	1.1487	1.2299	1.2939	1.3159	1.3382	1.4071	1.5036	1.6058	1.7138
8	1.1717	1.2668	1.3425	1.3686	1.3951	1.4775	1.5938	1.7182	1.8509
9	1.1951	1.3048	1.3928	1.4233	1.4544	1.5513	1.6895	1.8385	1.9990
10	1.2190	1.3439	1.4450	1.4802	1.5162	1.6289	1.7908	1.9672	2.1589
20	1.4859	1.8061	2.0882	2.1911	2.2989	5.6533	3.2071	3.8697	4.6610

Periods	9%	10%	11%	12%	13%	14%	15%	20%	25%
0	1.0000	1.0000	1.0000	1.0000	1.0000	1.0000	1.0000	1.0000	1.0000
1	1.0900	1.1000	1.1100	1.1200	1.1300	1.1400	1.1500	1.2000	1.2500
2	1.1881	1.2100	1.2321	1.2544	1.2769	1.2996	1.3225	1.4400	1.5625
3	1.2950	1.3310	1.3676	1.4049	1.4429	1.4815	1.5209	1.7280	1.9531
4	1.4116	1.4641	1.5181	1.5735	1.6305	1.6890	1.7490	2.0736	2.4414
5	1.5386	1.6105	1.6851	1.7623	1.8424	1.9254	2.0114	2.4883	3.0518
6	1.6771	1.7716	1.8704	1.9738	2.0820	2.1950	2.3131	2.9860	3.8147
7	1.8280	1.9487	2.0762	2.2107	2.3526	2.5023	2.6600	3.5832	4.7684
8	1.9926	2.1436	2.3045	2.4760	2.6584	2.8526	3.0590	4.2998	5.9605
9	2.1719	2.3579	2.5580	2.7731	3.0040	3.2519	3.5179	5.1598	7.4506
10	2.3674	2.5937	2.8394	3.1058	3.3946	3.7072	4.0456	6.1917	9.3132
20	5.6044	6.7275	8.0623	9.6463	11.523	13.7435	16.3665	38.3376	86.7362

Table 2—Present Value of $1, $PV = \dfrac{FV}{(1+i)^n}$

Periods	2%	3%	3.75%	4%	4.25%	5%	6%	7%	8%
1	0.9804	0.9709	0.9639	0.9615	0.9592	0.9524	0.9434	0.9346	0.9259
2	0.9612	0.9426	0.9290	0.9246	0.9201	0.9070	0.8900	0.8734	0.8573
3	0.9423	0.9151	0.8954	0.8890	0.8826	0.8638	0.8396	0.8163	0.7938
4	0.9238	0.8885	0.8631	0.8548	0.8466	0.8227	0.7921	0.7629	0.7350
5	0.9057	0.8626	0.8319	0.8219	0.8121	0.7835	0.7473	0.7130	0.6806
6	0.8880	0.8375	0.8018	0.7903	0.7790	0.7462	0.7050	0.6663	0.6302
7	0.8706	0.8131	0.7728	0.7599	0.7473	0.7107	0.6651	0.6227	0.5835
8	0.8535	0.7894	0.7449	0.7307	0.7168	0.6768	0.6274	0.5820	0.5403
9	0.8368	0.7664	0.7180	0.7026	0.6876	0.6446	0.5919	0.5439	0.5002
10	0.8203	0.7441	0.6920	0.6756	0.6595	0.6139	0.5584	0.5083	0.4632
20	0.6730	0.5534	0.4789	0.4564	0.4350	0.3769	0.3118	0.2584	0.2145

Periods	9%	10%	11%	12%	13%	14%	15%	20%	25%
1	0.9174	0.9091	0.9009	0.8929	0.8850	0.8772	0.8696	0.8333	0.8000
2	0.8417	0.8264	0.8116	0.7972	0.7831	0.7695	0.7561	0.6944	0.6400
3	0.7722	0.7513	0.7312	0.7118	0.6931	0.6750	0.6575	0.5787	0.5120
4	0.7084	0.6830	0.6587	0.6355	0.6133	0.5921	0.5718	0.4823	0.4096
5	0.6499	0.6209	0.5935	0.5674	0.5428	0.5194	0.4972	0.4019	0.3277
6	0.5963	0.5645	0.5346	0.5066	0.4803	0.4556	0.4323	0.3349	0.2621
7	0.5470	0.5132	0.4817	0.4523	0.4251	0.3996	0.3759	0.2791	0.2097
8	0.5019	0.4665	0.4339	0.4039	0.3762	0.3506	0.3269	0.2326	0.1678
9	0.4604	0.4241	0.3909	0.3606	0.3329	0.3075	0.2843	0.1938	0.1342
10	0.4224	0.3855	0.3522	0.3220	0.2946	0.2697	0.2472	0.1615	0.1074
20	0.1784	0.1486	0.1240	0.1037	0.0868	0.0728	0.0611	0.0261	0.0115

Table 3—Future value of annuity of $1 (ordinary), $FV = PMT \dfrac{(1+i)^{n}-1}{i}$

Period pmts	2%	3%	3.75%	4%	4.25%	5%	6%	7%	8%
1	1.0000	1.0000	1.0000	1.0000	1.0000	1.0000	1.0000	1.0000	1.0000
2	2.0200	2.0300	2.0375	2.0400	2.0425	2.0500	2.0600	2.0700	2.0800
3	3.0604	3.0909	3.1139	3.1216	3.1293	3.1525	3.1836	3.2149	3.2464
4	4.1216	4.1836	4.2307	4.2465	4.2623	4.3101	4.3746	4.4399	4.5061
5	5.2040	5.3091	5.3893	5.4163	5.4434	5.5256	5.6371	5.7507	5.8666
6	6.3081	6.4684	6.5914	6.6330	6.6748	6.8019	6.9753	7.1533	7.3359
7	7.4343	7.6625	7.8386	7.8983	7.9585	8.1420	8.3938	8.6540	8.9228
8	8.5830	8.8923	9.1326	9.2142	9.2967	9.5491	9.8975	10.2598	10.6366
9	9.7546	10.1591	10.475	10.5828	10.691	11.0266	11.4913	11.9780	12.4876
10	10.949	11.4639	11.867	12.0061	12.146	12.5779	13.1808	13.8164	14.4866
20	24.2974	26.8704	29.0174	29.7781	30.5625	33.0660	36.7856	40.9955	45.7620

Period pmts	9%	10%	11%	12%	13%	14%	15%	20%	25%
1	1.0000	1.0000	1.0000	1.0000	1.0000	1.0000	1.0000	1.0000	1.0000
2	2.09	2.1000	2.1100	2.1200	2.1300	2.1400	2.1500	2.2000	2.2500
3	3.2781	3.3100	3.3421	3.3744	3.4069	3.4396	3.4725	3.6400	3.8125
4	4.5731	4.6410	4.7097	4.7793	4.8498	4.9211	4.9934	5.3680	5.7656
5	5.9847	6.1051	6.2278	6.3528	6.4803	6.6101	6.7424	7.4416	8.2070
6	7.5233	7.7156	7.9129	8.1152	8.3227	8.5355	8.7537	9.9299	11.2588
7	9.2004	9.4872	9.7833	10.0890	10.404	10.7305	11.0668	12.9159	15.0735
8	11.028	11.4359	11.859	12.2997	12.7573	13.2328	13.7268	16.4991	19.8419
9	13.021	13.5795	14.164	14.7757	15.415	16.0853	16.7858	20.7989	25.8023
10	15.192	15.9374	16.7220	17.5487	18.419	19.3373	20.3037	25.9587	33.2529
20	51.160	57.2750	64.2028	72.0524	80.946	91.0249	102.443	186.688	342.944

There is one payment each period.

Table 4—Present value of annuity of $1 (ordinary) $PV = PMT \dfrac{1-\dfrac{1}{(1+i)^{n}}}{i}$

Period pmts	2%	3%	3.75%	4%	4.25%	5%	6%	7%	8%
1	0.9804	0.9709	0.9639	0.9615	0.9592	0.9524	0.9434	0.9346	0.9259
2	1.9416	1.9135	1.8929	1.8861	1.8794	1.8594	1.8334	1.8080	1.7833
3	2.8839	2.8286	2.7883	2.7751	2.7620	2.7232	2.6730	2.6243	2.5771
4	3.8077	3.7171	3.6514	3.6299	3.6086	3.5460	3.4651	3.3872	3.3121
5	4.7135	4.5797	4.4833	4.4518	4.4207	4.3295	4.2124	4.1002	3.9927
6	5.6014	5.4172	5.2851	5.2421	5.1997	5.0757	4.9173	4.7665	4.6229
7	6.4720	6.2303	6.0579	6.0021	5.9470	5.7864	5.5824	5.3893	5.2064
8	7.3255	7.0197	6.8028	6.7327	6.6638	6.4632	6.2098	5.9713	5.7466
9	8.1622	7.7861	7.5208	7.4353	7.3513	7.1078	6.8017	6.5152	6.2469
10	8.9826	8.5302	8.2128	8.1109	8.0109	7.7217	7.3601	7.0236	6.7101
20	16.351	14.8775	13.896	13.5903	13.294	12.4622	11.4699	10.5940	9.8181

Period pmts	9%	10%	11%	12%	13%	14%	15%	20%	25%
1	0.9174	0.9091	0.9009	0.8929	0.8850	0.8772	0.8696	0.8333	0.8000
2	1.7591	1.7355	1.7125	1.6901	1.6681	1.6467	1.6257	1.5278	1.4400
3	2.5313	2.4869	2.4437	2.4018	2.3612	2.3216	2.2832	2.1065	1.9520
4	3.2397	3.1699	3.1024	3.0373	2.9745	2.9137	2.8550	2.5887	2.3616
5	3.8897	3.7908	3.6959	3.6048	3.5172	3.4331	3.3522	2.9906	2.6893
6	4.4859	4.3553	4.2305	4.1114	3.9975	3.8887	3.7845	3.3255	2.9514
7	5.0330	4.8684	4.7122	4.5638	4.4226	4.2883	4.1604	3.6046	3.1611
8	5.5348	5.3349	5.1461	4.9676	4.7988	4.6389	4.4873	3.8372	3.3289
9	5.9952	5.7590	5.5370	5.3282	5.1317	4.9464	4.7716	4.0310	3.4631
10	6.4177	6.1446	5.8892	5.6502	5.4262	5.2161	5.0188	4.1925	3.5705
20	9.1285	8.5136	7.9633	7.4694	7.0248	6.6231	6.2593	4.8696	3.9539

There is one payment each period.

PART THREE

Specific Applications for Lawyers

CHAPTER NINE

Financial Language in Legal Documents

§9.1 Introduction

Virtually all attorneys must, at some point in their careers, draft agreements or advise clients on legal matters that hinge on accounting concepts. The examples are many: An employee incentive program may be based upon a company's net profit. An acquisition agreement may be contingent on a companys net worth or future profitability. A loan agreement may require the borrower to maintain specific financial statement ratios. A royalty or license agreement may be based on sales or net profits.

Since most lawyers are not accountants, they must be especially careful when using accounting terminology in legal documents. Too often, terms chosen in haste or ignorance come back to haunt the drafters, either by making them unwilling participants in their own clients' undoing, or by drawing them into unwanted disputes and litigation. When accounting concepts are involved, therefore, it is best to consult a competent accountant, perhaps the clients accountant. Preventive action at the beginning of a transaction is less expensive than litigation at the end.

The major reason why accounting information can be difficult to handle is well known: financial data can be manipulated, even within the boundaries of GAAP and good accounting practice. Practitioners of this art call it "window dressing." Such ratios as a current ratio, for example (see §7.3(a)), can be changed by last-minute transactions that may, in the long run, damage the entity, while providing a short term "fix" to comply with a restrictive covenant. In drafting legal documents, attorneys should be aware that the party in control of financial decisions can manage the financial data for its own purposes.

Accounting language can also be problematic because many of the items in financial statements are based on judgments and estimates. Disagreements can arise over the adequacy of reserves or the acceptability under GAAP of different methods of computing those reserves. Does "unencumbered cash" include certificates of deposit? If so, does it include certificates due in 30 days, 90 days, or both?

§9.2 Dealing with GAAP and Changing Accounting Principles

Many attorneys believe that it is sufficient to say in a contract that the financial statements or data "shall be prepared in accordance with generally accepted accounting principles." This is not true, for at least three reasons. First, ambiguities and problems can arise, since GAAP allows for choices in methods of depreciation, inventory valuation, and other items. Second, GAAP is not static, but changes to adapt to changing business conditions and practices. Finally, following GAAP may not necessarily be in the clients best interest.

The best general principle to follow in drafting documents is to take time to shape the accounting provisions to the needs of the individual client. This may require knowledge that is beyond the scope of the attorney's training. Some understanding of GAAP, however, can help the attorney draft better agreements and avoid unwanted results.

Perhaps the best way to deal with the many alternative ways GAAP allows companies to account for certain items is to state in the document that choices among methods should be consistent with prior periods and throughout the period that the agreement covers. However, if your client will not have control of the records, you may want to include a list of significant accounting policies and practices in the agreement.

Changes in GAAP have had dramatic effects on all kinds of legal agreements. In recent years, for example, preparers of financial statements have had to account for liabilities for pension plans and for other postretirement benefits. This often sizable increase in recorded liabilities has sometimes had a dramatic effect on loan covenants that specify certain debt-related ratios and relationships. Because of this change in GAAP, many banks suddenly had the power to dictate that, due to the violation of a debt-related restrictive covenant, certain loans were due immediately. This put the bank in a position to extract more favorable terms, waive the violation, or amend the agreement. Nothing had changed in the financial situation of the companies—only GAAP had changed. The solution is to refer to GAAP "as of the date of the agreement."

It is worth noting that GAAP may not offer the best guidelines to follow for your client's proposed transaction. You may want to write in specific exceptions to the parties' reliance on GAAP. For example, GAAP follows the principle of "conservatism," which leads financial statement preparers to understate assets. GAAP calls for using historical cost rather than current or fair market value. Thus, the value of assets on a balance sheet may be well below (or above) fair market value. There are other instances in which it may not be in the clients interest to follow GAAP.

§9.3   The Importance of Accounting Terminology

Unless they are defined, some accounting terms may lead to later disagreements and possibly to litigation. Examples of such terms are "consistently applied" and "material."

Simply because an accounting policy or procedure has been consistently applied in the past, it is not necessarily in accordance with GAAP.

A reserve for bad debts may be computed using a method that applies a specific percent to each receivable category. For example: zero percent for current receivables, two percent for receivables over 30 days old, five percent for receivables over 60 days old, 25 percent for receivables over 90 days old, and 100 percent for receivables over 180 days old. In the past, the reserve that was calculated may have been adequate to comply with GAAP, which requires that receivables be valued at the amount that will be collected.

The method may simply be an expedient technique, but as long as it properly values the receivable balance, it is an appropriate way to determine the reserve. If economic or business conditions change, the method used to calculate the reserve (which was acceptable in the past) may not adequately value the receivables at the current date, so the current statements may not be in accordance with GAAP. Unlike methods of depreciation, which are recognized in GAAP, mechanical formulas for reserves for bad debt are only a means to the end of assuring an adequate reserve.

GAAP issues frequently make a big difference in acquisition agreements. For example, a seller of a business had historically over-reserved for uncollectible receivables. The company had always used a mechanical, percentage-driven formula to determine its reserve. However, an account-by-account analysis of collectibility was prepared for the closing date balance sheet and the reserve was substantially reduced, increasing the company's net worth (and the purchase price, which was adjusted for increases in net worth over a stipulated amount). The buyer objected, but in vain. The closing date balance sheet was on a GAAP basis.

The buyer should have asked for a list of GAAP and methods used to determine reserves, depreciation and amortization, and then clarified the language in the agreement to require those same methods to be used in determining the closing amounts. A little accounting "due diligence" can go a long way.

"Materiality" is a term that has been the bane of the accounting profession since its earliest days. Despite millions of words in both legal and accounting literature seeking a universal meaning for the word, there is none. Materiality of financial data has been defined as "the magnitude of an omission or misstatement of accounting information that, in light of surrounding circumstances, makes it probable that the judgment of a reasonable person relying on the information would have been changed or influenced by the omission or misstatement.''[1]

In financial statements, materiality is determined in relation to earnings, net worth, and other relevant financial statement balances. Often, the materiality of data on financial statements can be measured in the millions of dollars. When purchase prices of businesses are tied to closing date balance sheets, does the buyer really want to pay millions of dollars more for the business because the exceptions were ''immaterial''? Should materiality be based on the purchase price rather than on financial statements' criteria, since the statements were prepared to determine the purchase price?

Many problems could be solved with a statement that defines materiality as an absolute number for each individual exception and in the aggregate, totalling all exceptions. For example, any individual exception under $25,000 will be considered immaterial for purposes of determining the purchase price, unless the total of all exceptions under $25,000 exceeds $100,000. Alternatively, an agreement could specify materiality based on financial statement amounts, or materiality based on the purchase price. For example, materiality used in convenants and warranties related to the closing date financial statement is defined as 2% of the purchase price and applies to the aggregate of all exceptions.

§9.4   General Principles of Drafting

Often, attorneys draft agreements by adapting a previously used agreement to a new transaction. Some precautions are in order, however, when financial language is involved. The following is a list of guidelines to follow when legal documents contain accounting concepts:

Use proper accounting terminology.

Some lawyers like to use such phrases as ''good accounting practices'' or ''true and correct.'' Unfortunately, these phrases are not defined in accounting literature, and a lawyer who uses them will be at a distinct disadvantage if the document is brought to litigation. ''True and correct'' implies absolute precision, and the meaning of ''good accounting practices'' is open to many interpretations. The correct terms, of

---

[1] Financial Accounting Concepts Statement No. 2, ''Qualitative Characteristics of Accounting Information.''

course, are "generally accepted accounting principles" and "present fairly in conformity with GAAP." In any agreement or contract, it is important to use precise accounting terminology.

Clear the documents with the client's accountants.

Legal documents can have both accounting and tax ramifications, and it pays to check on these with an accountant. Many attorneys know the tax implications of contractual terms, but fewer understand how transactions are treated on financial statements.

Mutual documents are not necessarily fair.

Many attorneys believe that all the terms in an agreement should apply equally to all parties. The fallacy in this thinking was pointed out long ago by a social commentator: "The law, in its majestic equality, prohibits the rich as well as the poor from sleeping under the bridges of Paris." A purely parallel contract may not serve "rich" and "poor" clients equally. An agreement that gives both parties the right of first refusal to buy the other's interest may be meaningless to the party who owns 20 percent of the entity and cannot afford to buy the remaining 80 percent. Furthermore, the 80 percent represents control, so it may be worth a higher price per share to a third party.

Work out the mechanics of the calculations.

When financial data appears in a document, it is advisable to "run the numbers" with the company's accountant. For example, if a proposed loan agreement has restrictive covenants based on certain ratios or calculations, have the accountant calculate the ratios and balances, and look at the company's projected budgets and forecasts. Can the company meet the criteria based on a current evaluation of future events?

Such a review can avoid embarrassing situations. In one actual buyout agreement, purchase price installment payments were equal in the aggregate to book value plus interest. The payments were at a specific annual rate, and they would apply first toward accrued interest and then toward the unpaid principal. However, the annual interest charges exceeded the annual payments, and consequently, the agreement resulted in perpetual payments!

Use a percent of the bottom line if your client is in control and a percent of the top line if the other party is in control.

This is the single most important piece of advice an accountant can offer an attorney or business person. We have seen that financial results can be manipulated. Judgments and options can alter such items as useful lives of depreciable assets, bad debt reserves, and obsolescence reserves for inventory. These manipulations affect the bottom line earnings and net worth, but the top line revenues are not affected. Consequently, if your client is in control of the accounting judgments, negotiate for an agreement keyed to the bottom-line. If you represent the opposing party, key the agreement to the top line.

For example, Hollywood studios frequently offer artists a percent of the net profit. Because the studio is in control of the accounting, it can allocate more costs to a successful movie, thus reducing the bottom line or creating "paper losses." A recent instance of this manipulation resulted in columnist Art Buchwald's suit against Paramount Pictures over the royalty for *Coming to America*. Although the film grossed $300 million, the studio claimed it made virtually no profit, leaving Buchwald with a small royalty.

The moral: Never allow a bottom line percent in a contract unless you can control the bottom line.

Control of the accounting is less important for long term agreements.

The longer the term of the agreement, the less impact the people who control the accounting can have. It is easier to manipulate numbers in the short term or for one discrete project among many. For example, a company may forego bottom line earnings and write off assets in the first year. But sooner or later, if the company takes expenses now, it will generate more profit in the future, unless its accounting is dishonest. Thus, one way of dealing with a party that controls the accounting is to use a long measuring period.

§9.5   Agreements that Contain Balance Sheet Items

Many agreements are based on such balance sheet items as total assets, current assets, tangible assets, net worth, and working capital. Here are some examples of typical provisions that use balance sheet items:

- Acquisitions whose purchase price is based on book value, net worth, or total assets;

- Provisions in commercial agreements that give either party the right to terminate if the other party becomes "insolvent";

- Loan agreements that carry covenants requiring a borrower to maintain specific working capital, current ratio, tangible assets, or net worth; and

- In a borrowing agreement, funding limits based on the book value of inventory, machinery and equipment, and/or accounts receivable.

An attorney drafting an agreement based on the company's balance sheet should try to make the underlying accounting principles work for and not against his or her client.

The key question in drafting agreements that are based on balance sheet items is "Who is in control of the accounting?" Accounting judgments have a major impact on the balance sheet. Those in control have latitude in computing such items as the useful lives of assets, and allowances for bad debts and obsolete inventory. The net worth of a business may also be significantly affected by the method used to calculate inventory.

Similar control problems exist for either side if there is a contingent payout of old receivables. Sometimes, an acquisition agreement states that the purchase price (usually when tied to working capital or net worth) will be reduced by the book value of all receivables over 90, 120, or 180 days old. Any collections on these amounts will be for the benefit of the seller. If the seller retains control of the disallowed receivables for collection he may harass a continuing customer of the company (now owned by the buyer) with collection efforts. On the flip side, the customer may not respond to pressure to liquidate the receivable since the seller may no longer have a product the customer wants to buy.

If, on the other hand, the collection of receivables is left with the buyer, the buyer may not pursue the collection for fear of annoying a customer. Nor does the buyer gain by collecting the balance. Thus, before drafting provisions that relate to future activities or events, the attorney should focus on which party has control and what can happen in the future.

A variation of the "Who's in control?" question is whether it is in the opposing party's best interest to take advantage of such control. For example, it is usually risky for a seller to receive payment based upon the net worth of the business three years after the date of the acquisition. The acquiring party will then be in control and can manipulate the accounting or the operational decisions of the business.

GAAP can sometimes have unexpected effects on an agreement. Consider a multi-year bank loan that specifies a current ratio of at least 2:1. Under GAAP, the outstanding balance of the loan becomes a current liability in the loan's final year. By following GAAP, the borrower's attorney may unknowingly negotiate a one year shorter term for the loan. If the loan is shown as a current asset, it may cause a violation of the current ratio restriction and accelerate the required liquidation of the amount owed. To avoid this outcome, the attorney can negotiate a special provision, which might be worded as follows: "The outstanding balance of the loan shall always be deemed a long-term liability for the purposes of computing the borrower's current ratio."

Following are several additional specific accounting concerns an attorney should consider when drafting agreements based on balance sheet items:

Consider how your client should value the entity's assets and liabilities.

Sometimes it is to the clients advantage to accord full value to both tangible and intangible assets, and at other times a client's interest will favor "hard" or realizable assets.

If you represent a seller of a business or a borrower, you will want the agreement to allow full value (or more than book value) to all intangible assets, such as trademarks, patents, and goodwill. However, if you are drafting a loan agreement for a lender, your client may not be protected if a large portion of the borrowers net worth is represented by goodwill. If the company is later unable to repay the debt, its goodwill may be worthless. There are three ways to pay back a loan: with cash generated from operations, with cash received in refinancing, and with cash generated by selling assets. What will the goodwill be worth if cash from operations or refinancing is not available?

Consider whether the company is a single entity or part of a consolidated group of companies.

In a parent's relationship to a subsidiary, the important aspect to focus on is the element of control. Often the parent company can move assets around, put cash in, or take it out. For example, in an acquisition, the parent can take the cash out and not pay the liabilities, leaving the acquirer of the subsidiary with liabilities and little cash.

It is helpful to understand the activity between the parent company and the subsidiary, especially as it pertains to cash. Covenants, warranties, and conditions need to be designed with the impact of parent-subsidiary transactions in mind.

If you represent a lesser party within a consolidated group, you might want to use the consolidated balance sheet rather than the borrowing subsidiary's unconsolidated financial statements. On the other hand, if you represent a bank considering a loan to a subsidiary, the borrower's ability to pay will depend on its own statement, not that of the parent, unless the parent has guaranteed the loan.

It is often advisable to specify how certain balance sheet items should be treated.

Sometimes, a special treatment of a specific balance sheet item will be beneficial to the client. The attorney may find it helpful to review the balance sheet for items that should receive unusual treatment.

For example, in an acquisition, it may be advantageous to base a purchase price on the companys net worth, with the exception that fixed assets are to be valued at replacement rather than actual cost. Or, if you are representing a lender, you may want to put a cap on the loan amount that can be based upon the borrowers receivables. In this situation, it is often useful to draft a provision that counts only receivables no older than 90 days.

Be aware of the value distortions of fixed assets on balance sheets.

Under GAAP, fixed assets are recorded at cost, which is often less than their current value. Similarly, common stocks and other equity investments may also be recorded at cost. A seller might prefer to value such assets at their current or fair market value.

If you are representing a lender, remember that asset book value (and even appraised value) may never be recovered in insolvency, nor for specialized equipment in place in one location. A road grader may be appraised at $125,000, but if no one is building a road, it has little real value.

Consider treating certain contingent liabilities as actual liabilities for purposes of the agreement.

Examples of important contingent obligations to consider include obligations to fund environmental cleanups (whose existence often is unknown), or liabilities resulting from threatened or pending litigation.

§9.6   Agreements that Contain Income Statement Items

Many agreements are based on a company's revenues or earnings. In such situations, attorneys need to protect their clients against accounting choices that will deprive them of compensation. Typically, revenue or earnings formulas appear in acquisitions, employment and consulting agreements, license and franchise agreements, partnership agreements, preferred stock provisions, and pension plans.

The first question to consider in drafting such a formula is whether earnings or revenue is more appropriate. Generally speaking, a revenue formula is best in situations in which the client makes a contribution to revenues but has little or no control over the enterprise's overall operations. Sales and marketing people, independent contractors, and franchisors are typically paid on the basis of revenues.

Another relevant question concerns the nature of the revenues or earnings. Are they those of a single company or of a consolidated group? How are common and headquarters expenses allocated among entities in a group managed or controlled by another entity, where your client has rights in only one or some of the controlled entities? Are earnings before or after income taxes? Are earnings determined on a cash or an accrual basis? Are the applicable earnings (or losses) and the resulting payment based on monthly, quarterly, or annual earnings? Is the calculation based on cumulative results, so that prior losses reduce current earnings? Will the formula include or exclude extraordinary items? The answer to each of these questions may have a material effect on the amount of revenues or earnings.

GAAP favors consolidated statements, so that if the agreement is silent on the subject, consolidated results will govern. In some cases, however, consolidated data may not apply, as, for example, in a bonus agreement for the manager of a subsidiary company who has no responsibility for the operations of the parent company or other subsidiaries. However, even though nonconsolidated statements may be appropriate, they pose many problems in allocating costs, income, and taxes.

Earnings are normally computed after taxes, except in certain situations. For example, after-tax earnings may not fairly represent the results of operations if the company is part of a consolidated group that includes companies that generated losses.

Another consideration in drafting documents with revenue or earnings formulas is the treatment of "extraordinary items," which are unusual revenues or expenses, such as those arising from purchasing or selling operations. Since the GAAP definition of "extraordinary" is somewhat restrictive and excludes many items that might be viewed by lay persons as extraordinary, attorneys drafting earnings formulas may want to define "extraordinary" differently.

In some cases, too, an attorney may want to specify earnings on a cash instead of an accrual basis. For example, cash accounting may be more appropriate in both real estate and professional partnerships.

Generally speaking, earnings and revenue formulas merely follow GAAP. However, as we have seen, following GAAP allows the preparer of financial statements much room to maneuver and to manipulate the numbers by choosing accounting methods and by making operational decisions that materially affect the statements. For this reason, it is wise for the attorney to be aware of accounting options and to choose those that best serve the client. Here are examples of choices an attorney should consider:

- *Computing revenues.* A variety of issues may complicate the computation of revenues, notably the reliability of the company's accounting system, especially if the company engages in cash transactions. One approach to this problem is a clause allowing the payee the right to inspect the company's books and records. However, in the case of an inadequate accounting system, inspection may not be enough. The attorney might want to impose record keeping and internal control requirements.

  Discounts, such as those for prompt payment or bulk purchases, may pose a problem, and the attorney may decide to specify a maximum dollar or percentage limitation. A company can also distort its revenues for a particular product by incorporating it into a larger product, or by using the product as a "loss leader." In each of these situations, the revenues may not reflect the true value of the product.

  If your client's royalty is for sales of the subcomponent or loss leader, you may want a flat rate royalty for each product manufactured rather than a percent of sales revenue attributed to the product. It can become extremely complicated when royalty or license payments are tied to net income from one or some of many products produced and sold by the licensee.

- *Changes in accounting methods and estimates.* The typical provision is that GAAP must be applied in a way that is consistent with the past. However, many items that are estimates are not restricted by GAAP. Changes in such estimates as cost allocations and useful lives of assets, as long as they are reasonable and justified by changing events, can have a material effect on earnings. The consistency clause should therefore specify methods and assumptions used for estimates as well as GAAP.

- *Depreciation.* A single enterprise may use several different methods for computing depreciation for financial reporting and tax purposes. It may be helpful, therefore, for the attorney to set guidelines for computing depreciation.

- *Treatment of contingent payouts.* In anything that is contingent, one party is at risk because the other party is in control and may be able to manipulate the payment in numerous ways. Generally speaking, contingent payouts should be avoided, but if they cannot be, the attorney for the party that is at risk should require warranties to protect the client against operational and accounting changes.

  With contingent payment, many precautions need to be taken to protect a buyer or a seller from a variety of financial and operational manipulations. The party in control can expand or contract the operations at will, delay needed repairs and maintenance, accelerate scheduled repairs and maintenance, or manipulate related-party transactions (pricing of purchases, allocation of costs, and more). All such actions distort the financial results.

§9.7 Documents that Call for Financial Statements

Many kinds of documents require a party to provide financial statements periodically, or contain warranties that refer to financial statements. An attorney whose client is working with such documents must consider a number of issues. Which financial statements should be required? Should the statements be those of the company alone, or should the agreement also require statements of the parent and affiliated companies? Should the statements be annual, quarterly, or monthly? Should they be audited, reviewed, or compiled by a CPA? (See §5.5 for a discussion of the different levels of work a CPA performs for audits, reviews, and compilations.)

A CPA can be involved at many levels. An attorney representing a client who is entitled to receive financial statements should consider requiring the following options:

- That any opinion or report of an independent accountant be addressed to the attorney's client as well as to the company employing the accountant;

- That the company supplying statements also subject these statements and the books and records to a review by another independent accountant; and

- That the auditors report be unqualified.

When large sums of money are in question, the document may stipulate that statements prepared by one independent CPA may be challenged by a second CPA, with final authority vested in a third independent CPA. This stipulation, of course, is very expensive.

§9.8 Summary and Conclusion

Attorneys should take all possible precautions when using accounting principles and terms. If this is not done, the language used may come back to haunt you by working to your client's disadvantage, or by drawing you into unwanted litigation.

Dealing with GAAP can be problematic for several reasons: GAAP allows for choices in methods; it is not static but changes with time; and in some cases, it may not be in the client's interest to follow GAAP. The best course to follow is to shape the accounting provisions of each document to the needs of the client and to consult an accountant when you need help.

Perhaps the key question in drafting documents is "Who is in control of the accounting?" The single most important rule of thumb to remember is to use a percent of the bottom line if your client is in control and a percent of the top line if the other party is in control.

In addition to this rule, the following broad guidelines apply to legal documents that contain accounting concepts:

- Use proper accounting terminology.

- Clear the documents with the client's accountants.

- Mutual documents are not necessarily fair.

- Work out the mechanics of the calculations.

- Control of the accounting is less important for longer-term documents.

CHAPTER TEN

Using Accountants and Financial Information in Litigation

§10.1 Introduction

Numbers are an inevitable part of every commercial lawsuit, since businesses conventionally measure their performance in monetary terms. The role of accountants is to track and organize the raw data and to summarize the transactions of the entity in annual, quarterly, or monthly financial statements. Because the financial statements are summaries, there is typically a great deal of recorded monetary, economic, or transactional detail behind each number. Accountants are familiar with this "paper trail," which can vary widely from company to company and from industry to industry.

Today, of course, the paper trail is no longer primarily on paper, but in computerized information systems. Because their job is to assemble and examine the computerized data, accountants and auditors have extensive knowledge of the information systems that particular industries conventionally use.

In addition to understanding the numbers, accountants—and auditors in particular—understand the operational dynamics of various businesses. In today's complex business environment, many accountants specialize in a particular industry. The books and records of a bank, for example, while quite similar in many respects to those of a manufacturing enterprise or an oil and gas company, are very different in other ways.

In commercial litigation, an accountant can be invaluable to an attorney in a number of ways. An accountant who knows the systems and documents supporting a company's books and records can sift through the numbers, ferreting out the information that is relevant to the case. Being thoroughly familiar with the recordkeeping systems that businesses use, an accountant knows what records will be kept and where to look for them.

Litigators tend to think of accountants primarily as expert witnesses and number crunchers for damage calculations, but this overlooks the importance of the accountant as a business consultant during earlier phases of litigation. Actually, the earlier an accounting expert is brought into a case, the more the accountant can do to help the attorney. While the attorney looks at the facts of the case from a legal standpoint, the accountant can assess the situation from a business perspective.

In one case, for example, the plaintiff was a manufacturer claiming millions of dollars in lost profits. The accounting consultant questioned the capacity of the plant to produce the number of units the plaintiff claimed it could have produced. Upon investigation, it became clear that the "plant" was nothing more than a garage and was incapable of producing the volume of product that the plaintiff had alleged it could produce.

This is one example of how the accountant can help an attorney as a consultant during the earliest stages of a lawsuit. Not only can the accountant assess the amount of damages, but accountants' skills can also be helpful during the discovery process. This chapter will outline an accountants perspective on the business and financial aspects of discovery and damage strategies. It will also treat the special problems involved in presenting numbers to juries and discuss the characteristics of a good expert.

§10.2 Selecting an Expert Financial Consultant and Witness

A number of years ago, Ernst & Young conducted a survey on the characteristics and qualities attorneys seek in expert financial consultants and witnesses. We used a statistically valid sample of attorneys in a number of major cities. First, we asked them how they used their experts. Each attorney made several replies. 82 percent said they used experts to do damage analysis and calculations. 75 percent used them to objectively review their client's financial data and position. Also scoring high on the attorneys' list were using financial experts to assist in deposition and with cross-examination at trial, to analyze the opposition's testimony, to assist with document production, and to testify as an expert witness at trial.

We next asked the attorneys for the characteristics they sought when hiring a financial expert for consulting and pretrial work. The most important characteristics they looked for were:

- Timeliness of work and availability;

- A good instinct for finding data that is important to the case;

- Being a good educator for the attorney;

- Telling the truth, even though it may be detrimental to the case;

- Paying great attention to detail; and

- Following directions carefully and discussing courses of action with the attorney before taking them.

When looking for expert witnesses, attorneys said that the most important characteristics they sought were:

- Truthfulness;

- Ability to justify a position precisely and decisively;

- Understanding the objectives and direction of the case;

- Following directions;

- Speaking simply and clearly;

- Ability to stand up to cross-examination;

- Having special expertise; and

- Answering only the questions asked and not giving rambling answers.

Knowing what other attorneys want and seek in experts, how can you determine what you need? A little planning, although it may seem to take too much time, will save time and anguish in the long run. First, list what you believe the issues are in the case, and next to each issue, list what you want to prove and what you will need to prove it. In most civil litigation, damages will have to be proven, or refuted, with reasonable certainty.

A financial expert is usually needed in all but the simplest of cases. In large cases involving antitrust, patent infringement, and similar complex disputes, an economist as well as a financial expert may be required. Do not try to use an accountant when an economist is needed i.e., when the case involves economic indicators and market share analysis. Similarly, do not use an economist when an accountant is needed, i.e., when practical knowledge of business operations and financial matters are important. Of course, the size of the case will also be an important factor.

Consider using your client's staff whenever possible. They generally know the most about the business and, from a review of recent significant cases, appear to be as credible or more credible than independent experts, at least in bench trials. There are, of course, drawbacks. For internal accountants, the case will be secondary to their regular responsibilities, and they may not be as objective or as truthful with you as an independent expert would be. Some attorneys say that using a client's staff is cheaper, but if you lose the case or a part of the damage claim because of a purely financial decision, the savings may be lost many times over. The deciding factor should be the requirements of the case.

In addition to their function as damage specialists, financial experts are also often retained to value land, property, and equipment, to analyze transactions, to investigate fraud, and for a multitude of other purposes dictated by the particulars of each case.

Where do you find these experts? Here are a number of ways to find an expert, going from the best to the least desirable:

- Experts you have used in the past and have developed confidence in;

- Recommendations of experts you have used in the past;

- Experts your partners, associates, or friends have used in the past;

- Experts you have seen in action;

- Experts your client recommends (this may be the first choice);

- Professionals you meet through other professional activities;

- Professors you had in school who impressed you;

- Experts you have read about in articles or in legal filings or court decisions;

- Professionals with credentials at service organizations, such as accounting firms, with which you are familiar;

- Writers whose articles or books you have read;

- Professionals whom you have met socially and who impressed you;

- Professionals listed as members of local and national associations; and

- When desperate—names of people from advertisements in legal publications.

One thing is essential: No matter how you select your potential expert, meet and interview him or her. Do this even if you have used the expert before, because issues change from case to case. Be sure your "tried and true expert" is not overstating credentials to suit the needs of the particular case. Question experts whom you do not know. You are the expert at cross-examination. Use that skill here.

Ask hard, pointed questions and analyze the expert's responses. Does he stand up well under vigorous questioning? Does he ramble on and on? Does she have a grasp of the subject matter? Does she understand what you need? Is he familiar with the role of an expert in litigation? Is he honest and up front with you, or does he hedge? Does she speak simply and concisely, or do you hear a lot of technical jargon? Is she a good educator? Does he look professional? Does he appear arrogant? These are a few of the questions you will want to answer for yourself. Just as you scrutinize your opponent's expert, do so with your potential expert.

Get a resume or curriculum vitae. Ask for prior testimony and any published articles.

You must have confidence in your expert. You will be working long, hard hours with him or her. There must be some "chemistry" between you. And, if this is your testifying expert, he or she will be up on the witness stand all alone, with your case riding on the testimony.

§10.3   Discovery of Financial Information

An accountant can be helpful with all phases of the discovery process: drafting precise requests for production of documents, helping the attorney frame interrogatories, and participating in depositions as a technical consultant to the attorney.

In document production requests, attorneys sometimes ask opposing parties to produce everything that is even remotely related to a lawsuit, because the attorneys are uncomfortable with financial documents and related records, and do not know exactly which documents they may eventually need. However, there are typically many more documents available than many lawyers realize, and once they receive a mass of documents, they are faced with the formidable task of sorting them. There is a real danger that, by getting everything, the attorney could miss a critical document. Furthermore, spending hours sifting through documents takes valuable time away from lawyering activities that are vital to the client. Often the desire to seek all possible documents has its roots in the fear that an important document will be missed if the request is too specific.

Another danger is that a lawyer who is unfamiliar with business records will ask for the wrong documents, or request the information in the wrong way. In one instance, a request was made for all sales files. The defendant sent separate files of names and addresses, account numbers, and transactions. What the attorney received was the separate files as they existed on the computer, but without the program that integrated the information and generated a report by location, account, and product sales and amounts. There was no "file" of the end report, since it was maintained on the computer in a relational database. A relational database maintains related but separate files for different categories of information. To generate different reports, the database program matches and formats the information in the separate files.

Instead of asking for the "computer files," the attorney should have requested a hard copy of the report, or the data files in machine readable form and the information needed to read the files and prepare a report. Instead, the attorney had to retain accountants to act like a computer, searching for, matching, and manually preparing line items in the report.

With the help of a financial consultant, an attorney can reduce the amount of discovery significantly, gaining much in efficiency and saving the client money and time. The way to do this is to engage in planning early in the case, in which the attorney determines the issues and the type of evidence that is needed to support the client's position. At this stage, a financial consultant can help specify what documents are available and what documents will be helpful in making the case.

Many general types of financial documents are available to an attorney for discovery. (See Exhibit 10-1, Financial Document Chart, starting at the bottom left-hand side of the chart and reading up.) The initiation of an economic event and receipt of supporting documentation generates an entry into the accounting records. Examples of supporting documentation for accounting entries include agreements, sales invoices, receiving reports, purchase invoices, workpapers supporting reserve estimates, and any other documents, whether prepared internally or externally, which evidence an economic event. Such documents will initiate a transaction entry ticket or journal entry. Often, some or all of these documents and entries will be prepared, transmitted, and stored electronically on computers. Companies on the leading edge in computer technology keep little written supporting documentation, but use a data link to make entries on the books of both the supplier and purchaser.

After the entry is prepared, if it is done manually, it is entered in the subsidiary or general ledgers. Subsidiary ledgers contain the details of various accounts that need to be maintained for business purposes. For example, to collect amounts owed, the company needs to know who owes how much and from how long ago. The accounts receivable subsidiary ledger will contain these details by customer. The total of the individual account balances in the subsidiary ledger should agree with the accounts receivable balance in a general ledger. Subsidiary ledgers are usually maintained for inventory, accounts receivable, accounts payable, and other high-activity accounts where access to detail is important.

Journals are chronological records of all entries with a common source, such as cash receipts. Periodically, the journal is totalled and

Exhibit 10-1

Financial Documentation Chart

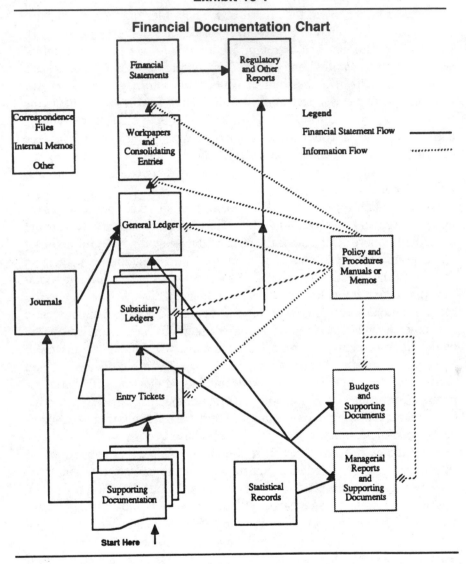

entries are made in the general ledger. The general ledger includes the summary of activity from the subsidiary ledgers and the activity from all other accounts.

Accountants summarize, consolidate, and adjust the information in the general ledger. They use this information as a basis for preparing the financial statements. Using an electronic spreadsheet, accountants can link all the individual corporations in a consolidated group, eliminating intercompany accounts and activity. They also use the information in financial statements, general ledger, and subsidiary ledgers to prepare regulatory or other reports.

At each step along the way, documents usually are prepared and filed. To summarize data coming from all these different sources, accountants normally prepare a document that shows the source and amount of each component. This can be done electronically on a computer or with manually prepared worksheets. It is normal business practice to maintain a file of these reports.

Managers use the information in the general ledger and the subsidiary ledgers, along with information from statistical records, to develop budgets and managerial reports. Budgets are projections of revenue and expenses, and they are used to monitor operations through an operating cycle. They normally are prepared for the ensuing year and include revenue and expenses, separated in great detail into departments, projects, or groups. Budgets are also prepared for each subsidiary in a consolidated entity. The subsidiary budgets can be consolidated to prepare an overall budget for the consolidated company. Management tracks the company's actual results and compares them with the budgeted amounts, investigating and evaluating any variances between the two.

Departments throughout a company often keep statistical records in a variety of management reports. For example, the manufacturing floor may keep statistics for such items as inventory and supplies. Even service companies may keep statistical records on the number of employees, number of engagements, or other data. These statistical records can also be used in more sophisticated budgets that include, for example, labor planning or operating capacity results.

In addition to financial data, the typical finance department keeps correspondence, internal memos, and other documents such as job descriptions, authorizations for general ledger entries related to contingencies, and much more. These types of files can normally be found in almost every type of company, and they are more familiar to more attorneys than are accounting and statistical records and files. Also, there are usually policy and procedure manuals or memoranda which can help a lawyer understand the financial statements and know what documents the company prepares and maintains. Finally, there may also be operating and personnel manuals. Typically, the larger the company, the more written procedures, manuals, and memoranda exists.

Companies which use computers keep extensive documentation of the systems and files in their data processing centers. With the advent of personal computers, however, much of the documentation that should exist does not. An important point to remember when dealing with personal computers is that when someone deletes a file, the deletion does not necessarily erase the information from the data disk. Although the title of the file has been removed from the disk's directory, the information can be recovered until the time when it is replaced by other entries. (Removing the title from the directory tells the computer that it has that space available for other purposes. Eventually, it will write new files in the location where the old files previously existed.)

Quite often, the best data for litigation is not in the books and records but in ancillary documents, such as internal auditors' workpapers, or in tax documents from the tax department. Financial records, or records that have a bearing on financial matters, may not even be in the controller's office. Better information may be in internal audit or in division headquarters' files.

In a fraud case, you may want to look at the policy manuals and internal audit workpapers. If lost sales are at issue, some of the necessary documents and statistics may be in the marketing department. Among the first things to look at in such a case are the sales forecasts the company made before the alleged damage took place. Also relevant to lost sales are prior years' budgets. An attorney would certainly want to investigate the company's track record in forecasting its sales.

The structure and the management of a company play a role in determining what documents it will maintain. Smaller companies, for example, usually have less sophisticated systems and less backup documentation. Larger companies generally have document retention policies, because of the volume of transactions and the need to report to the SEC and to manage the business.

Like document requests, interrogatories which address financial matters can be structured rigorously to preclude objections and irrelevant answers. Much of the advice given in Chapter 9 on legal language in financial documents is applicable here. Use the right terms and be specific. With the help of a financial consultant, an attorney can draft pointed questions which the other side will have a hard time objecting to.

Similarly, it is helpful to have the financial expert present to help in deposing the other sides financial expert, or its financial employees. The financial expert will know whether the financial employee is explaining the events plausibly, and may be able to show that another expert's opinion is based on speculation, not on the facts of the case. A financial expert can also help prepare friendly witnesses and clarify their testimony.

To sum up, the reader can see that companies maintain vast quantities of financial information in different departments and areas. A wise attorney will sit down with an accountant, explain what data is needed, and get the accountant's advice on the documents that will be available and how to best describe them in a request for production. It is to the attorney's advantage to enlist the participation of a financial expert during the discovery process. Well-targeted document requests, interrogatories, and depositions may have the salutary side effect of impressing or even frightening the other side. The opposition will quickly become alert to the presence of strong financial expertise in interpreting the facts and issues in the case.

§10.4 Damage Strategies and Calculations

Most attorneys use financial consultants or economists as experts in constructing or destroying damage claims in civil litigation. While the attorney is typically an advocate, the expert's proper role is to bring an objective view of the actual damages. To get the most out of an expert's advice, the attorney should look for one who has special knowledge of the particular type of business involved, or who has a strong background in general business operations.

A good accounting expert also needs to know something about the legal aspects of damages—at the very least, causation, certainty, and remoteness. It is critical that the attorney make these and other relevant legal concepts clear to the accountant. The expert should know the differences between liability and causation, and between precision and reasonable certainty. The expert should also know when a claimed damage element is overreaching.

For example, if a defendant's advertising was false and the defendant is liable, the liability does not mean that all the losses the plaintiff incurred were caused by the false advertising. In fact, the defendant's case might well rest upon other reasons why the plaintiff lost market share. The plaintiff may have been losing market share before the false advertising occurred. It may also have cut back on people to save money, leaving insufficient staff to operate effectively and service its customers. Four good places to look for admissions of other reasons for losses are management's discussion and analysis of the financial statements (MD&A), reports to security analysts, lenders' loan files, and internal auditors' workpapers.

This example illustrates the context in which a skilled accounting expert should operate. The best damage strategies are not constructed in a vacuum. They call for a knowledge of facts in a number of spheres: the case, the law, the economy, the industry, and the business. It is up to the lawyer to educate the accountant on the issues of the case, the relevant law of damages in the particular jurisdiction, and the laws related to the type of claim, such as the Panduit test for patent infringement.

The accountant should bring to bear a reasonable knowledge of the economic climate nationally, regionally, and within the particular industry. A company that forecasts an increase in sales during a national recession might be suspect unless the industry, the region, or some other factor produced a countercyclical effect.

Some a knowledge of the industry can be even more crucial than a knowledge of the economic circumstances. In one damage projection, a toy retailer used quarterly financial statements that showed a relatively level but upward trend of sales throughout the year. This calculation was immediately suspect, because retailing is a seasonal business, with most of the profits being made in the holiday season during the last quarter.

In addition to the characteristics of the industry, a damage strategy must consider the details of the particular business situation. Without these details, the damage calculation is likely to be inadequate. The case of the manufacturing plant that was located in a garage illustrates the importance of one business factor, that of capacity. Without an actual visit to the factory, the financial consultant could not have ascertained this crucial detail.

Other capacity issues are not as obvious, e.g., a large plant is assumed to operate 16 hours a day, six days a week, 52 weeks a year. Does the plant need to close down for maintenance? Is qualified labor available?

Are the necessary raw materials available? Will there be substantially increased costs for operating the plant at this capacity? Will productivity go down? Will accidents go up? Will there be an increase in product defects? The answers to all these questions and others will bear on the reliability of the damage calculation.

Each business is different and the facts and circumstances of each case are unique. Consequently, there can be no set formula for calculating damages. Ultimately, constructing a damage claim is a problem-solving process in which creativity is the critical element. However, there are typical approaches which are common to many damage calculations.

In commercial cases, the easiest calculations are those used in determining general damages, since these are usually actual out-of-pocket losses that flow from the substantive wrong done by the defendant. Special, or consequential, damages are more difficult to calculate because they are peculiar to the specific plaintiff.

For example, assume that a supplier to a manufacturer fails to deliver materials as contracted for, and the manufacturer sues the supplier and prevails on liability. The general damages, or value of the promised performance, would be the difference between the contract price for the materials and the cost of obtaining the materials from an alternative supplier, or if they are not available elsewhere, the market cost of the materials at the contract delivery date. The financial data for this calculation is generally available: The contract price is in the agreement, the price of the alternative source is on the invoice from the supplier, and the market value is usually public information. (Trade associations and commodity exchanges are good sources for raw material prices.)

Special damages present added problems. Did the interruption in supply cause disruption and additional costs in the manufacturing process? Did it cause sales to be lost? Would those sales have been profitable, and if so, in what amount? Did the manufacturer lose a good customer because of a directly related delay? Assumptions and estimates come into play. Information about capacity must also be reviewed, along with manufacturing cost data and sales information. If there was no disruption in the plaintiff's manufacturing process and its plant was working at full capacity, there would likely be no special damages. Nor would there be special damages if the product normally sold at a loss because of an inefficient manufacturing process. What are the manufacturing costs for this company and what is the sales price of the product? The answers to these questions are unique to the plaintiff and its operations. That is what makes them special and require a greater degree of scrutiny. Different businesses may face different circumstances, costs, and sales prices. Only plaintiff-specific data can show special damages.

This information is often hard to obtain, as it must come from various sources—manufacturing cost sheets, plant statistics, overhead cost records, and plant and home office records. The process of determining future lost profits, or "but for" lost profits when false advertising or antitrust claims are made, adds additional hurdles to overcome in determining special damages. Causation becomes more difficult to isolate, since the business environment is an integrated global marketplace, and numerous other factors affect sales and market share. Estimates of future lost sales must be within the limits of reasonable certainty, and inflation and discount rates must be established.

Some degree of certainty can be obtained if estimates and trends can be anchored to historical performance, budgets, and projections developed prior to the litigation. A decent track record for achieving budgets and projections in the past is always helpful.

Different measurements of loss, such as lost profits, increased costs, and decrease in value of an investment, are computed in different ways:

- *Lost profits.* This is the difference between what the plaintiff actually earned and what it would have earned but for the defendants actions. Lost profits can be computed using three methods: the "before and after" method, the yardstick method, and the market share method. "Before and after" compares the profits of the plaintiffs own business before and after the event in question. The yardstick method uses another company or group of companies as a comparative standard. The market share method calculates market share by the number of items the plaintiff would have sold, subtracts what the plaintiff actually sold, and multiplies the result by the profit the plaintiff could have expected.

- *Increased costs.* This calculation usually applies to breach of contract and price fixing cases, in which the defendants actions allegedly raised the price the plaintiff paid for goods. Increased costs are simply the difference between actual and "but for" costs. The result is multiplied by the number of items the plaintiff purchased.

- *Decrease in value of an investment.* These calculations, which are typically performed by accountants, appraisers, or investment bankers, are based on the "going concern" value of the business, or the price a willing buyer would pay and a willing seller would accept. Damages can be measured by the difference between the "going concern" value before and after the events in question.

§ 10.5   Explaining Numbers to Juries

Whichever method an expert uses in calculating damages, the results must be presented to a trier of fact. There are two basic principles in presenting damages to a court. The first one is to keep it simple. Technical precision will not dazzle a judge or jury, especially if the information is presented in language they do not understand. Perhaps the most important aspect of the experts task is to present complex information in simple terms that lay persons can easily comprehend.

The second principle is reasonableness. Though attorneys are often tempted to ask for the whole pie when they really want only a piece, judges and juries are rarely favorably disposed to inflated claims.

Devising suitable damage strategies and calculating damages are tasks which draw upon the experts technical skills. Explaining the calculations to the jury is another matter, and requires a different set of skills. It is intrinsically a difficult task. A great many people have an automatic aversion to numbers, tuning out whenever anyone talks about them. Thus, whether the attorney or the expert is presenting the numbers to a jury, this resistance must be overcome. Capturing and holding the jury's attention is certain to be a struggle against many obstacles.

Despite their good will and desire to do their job well, the fact remains that jurors have been enlisted to participate in an alien environment in which they are unfamiliar with the rules. They must absorb new information, most of which they are unlikely ever to use again. As active adults, they are unaccustomed to the passivity inherent in their situation, and that passivity places a strain on their attention span.

Add to this the fact that it requires only 15 percent of the mind to understand English, if it is ones native language. That leaves 85 percent of the jurors mind free to wander.[1] An additional strain on the attention of any audience is the natural gap between the rates at which people speak and listen. Research shows that the average listener can understand

---

[1] Hamlin, What Makes Juries Listen, 10 (1985).

words two to four times as quickly as the average speaker can talk. Most people speak at a rate of 125 to 140 words per minute, while people can understand between 275 and 600 words per minute. The result: a universal tendency of listeners to appear to be paying attention when their minds are drifting to other concerns. [2]

The most subtle and powerful impediment lawyers face in presenting numbers to juries is the pervasive influence of television on the way people get information. Gone are the days when audiences were inspired by great orators such as Daniel Webster, William Jennings Bryan and Franklin D. Roosevelt. Today's audiences are virtually incapable of paying sustained attention to a single speaker's words, no matter how well those words are chosen and delivered. Television has accustomed us to ingesting information in bite-size pieces of only a few minutes duration, punctuated with appealing visuals. We have learned to listen with only half an ear and both of our eyes.

The habits bred by television do not change when people are in the somewhat analogous situations of courtrooms and classrooms. Like many students today, jurors need to be cajoled, entertained, and titillated to keep their attention. Rather than bemoan this state of affairs, it is more productive to study how television works and to use that knowledge to advantage. Litigation is quickly becoming a multimedia production, and the field of battle will ultimately belong to the advocate who directs the best presentation.

Since the jury requires small bits of information, the attorney should break the testimony into small pieces and spoon-feed it to them, sweetened and reinforced by visual presentations. The average attention span is very short, estimated at 15 to 20 minutes at most. The lawyer or expert should present the most important or the most complex information first, because the jury's attention will be greatest at the beginning of the presentation.

The information must be made simple, keeping details to a minimum. Computations and other minutiae should be available for cross-examination, but they should not be discussed at great length. The attorney or witness should boil the numbers down to no more than three or four amounts. This focuses the jury's mind on the damage amount while, at the same time, increasing credibility by referring to details. Sometimes it

---

[2] Apple, *Is the Jury Listening?*, 13 Am. J. Trial Advocacy 858 (1989).

is useful to use layered presentations, flipping from the amount of the damages to the details of the calculation and back to the damages.

Numbers become clearer if large sums can be converted into numbers which people can readily understand and connect with their everyday experience. If the amounts are in the millions of dollars, for example, it is helpful to break them down into per household amounts. Suppose the sales of a product were forecast at 5 million units per year, and the geographical area has 2.5 million households. To fulfill the projection of 5 million units a year, each household would have to buy two products of that specific brand a year. People find it easier to think in terms of two units a year than in terms of 5 million units.

The tried and true basic outline of an effective presentation works well for presentations that involve numbers: Tell them what you are going to say, say it, then tell them what you said. All of this must be accomplished simply and quickly.

Rather than inundate jurors with abstract or technical ideas, find a way to translate the material into concrete examples they can visualize. Suppose you need to explain the dynamics of pricing the acquisition of an entity with a number of subsidiaries, including some which do not do well financially but still have a significant book value, and others which do extremely well but have a low book value. Your client backed out of a deal to acquire the company at a price equal to the consolidated book value. The company later sold its losing operations at a loss and retained the profitable subsidiaries. The company sued your client for breach of contract and claimed damages equal to the difference between the price they received and the book value of the sold subsidiaries. The book value of the subsidiaries was, of course, significantly higher than the price received.

A good way to help jurors understand the price of the consolidated entity in comparison to prices of the individual companies would be to use the analogy of purchasing chicken at the supermarket. When they buy a whole chicken, they may pay $1.15 per pound. If they buy just the breast, they may pay $2.10 per pound. If they buy the necks, they may pay only $.25 per pound. How can the plaintiff charge your client for chicken breast when it sold only the necks?

Analogies work very well because they tend to stay in the mind of the jury, especially if they use images drawn from everyday experience. The presentation also becomes more memorable from use and repetition of memorable phrases. Think of the phrases you remember and carry with you, such as "I have a dream," or "Where's the beef?"

Many attorneys are surprised at the limited vocabulary of jurors. Judges have found that more than half of a jury did not understand such words as "prior" and "subsequent." Some jurors have reported puzzlement over the terms "plaintiff" and "defendant." So why use prior and subsequent when you can say "before" and "after"? Strunk and White's famous dictum about writing holds equally true for oral presentations: "Never use a long word where a short one will do."

Here are five principles of making an effective presentation:

1. *KISS, or keep it short and simple.* This is the cardinal rule.
2. *Plan the presentation, focusing on the message, the audience and the medium.* Scrap the trivia, and crystallize the important points.
3. *Be aware of body language and tone of voice.* Most studies show that words are less important than demeanor and tone. We judge people by behavior, eye contact, and tone.
4. *Pick key words ahead of time, but do not overdo them.*
5. *Be visual and stimulate the eye.* Using visuals is indeed a must. Yet, even when you physically move around the room, you add visual interest and tired listeners will perk up.

Finally, it is worth mentioning that many jurors have gotten their legal education from movies and television, especially from "L.A. Law." The arguments on "L.A. Law" are very short and clear, and they appeal to the emotions. As one attorney has said, "In the age of L.A. Law, it is terribly important to do things well."

Graphics are a must, especially when presenting numbers to juries. Television producers are very conscious of the deadening effect which "talking heads" have on their audiences. They avoid focusing the camera on someone who is talking for any length of time. In the age of television, visuals are of central importance, and they must be slick and polished. The purpose of exhibits should be to clarify the major themes of the case. Here again, the task is to shorten and simplify, especially when numbers are involved. No one, not even an accountant, likes to look at too many numbers at once.

Research has shown that we derive up to 90 percent of our knowledge from visual sources, and many studies substantiate the effectiveness of visuals. McGraw-Hills Laboratory of Advertising Performance finds that an advertiser's effectiveness in stimulating readers increases 26 percent with the use of visuals. And a Wharton study found that 79 percent of an audience will say yes when visuals are used, compared to 58 percent without visuals.[3]

Good visuals have the effect of clarifying and focusing the discussion. In addition, they interrupt the monotony of a voice talking, by raising the energy level of the testimony. Visuals draw the expert out of the witness chair and involve him or her in a more active way. And if the visuals are focused and clear, they force the speaker to be clear and to speak to the point.[4]

The author personally finds talk boards to be the most useful graphic display for presenting damages and financial testimony in a courtroom setting. Slide and overhead projectors tend to break down—or worse, the dim lights can put the jury to sleep. Graphics using numbers must be kept simple, and they are best if they take the form of easy-to-read diagrams, graphs, or pictures. A series of charts or exhibits should proceed from the simple to the complex and back again.

The effect of a graphic should be like that of a billboard, easily read and understood at a glance. The print has to be large enough to be seen easily by the jury and the judge. The witness or the lawyer should approach the board when explaining it, but must avoid the common error of talking to the board instead of to the audience.

Timing is crucial when making a presentation that includes graphics. Each visual should be added only when the speaker is ready to talk about it. If a visual is displayed before you are ready to address it, your audience will try to understand the visual instead of listening to you.

Here are four rules for visual presentations:

1. *Be simple and appealing.* The cardinal error in presentation is putting too much information on a board or slide.

---

[3] *Supra* 1, at 275. *See also* "Illustrations in Advertising Play a Significant Role in Leading a Reader/Prospect Up the Five Steps to a Sale," Report No. 5, McGraw-Hill Research Library of Advertising Performance, number 3170.1, pg. 3; and Oppenheim, "A Study of the Effectiveness of the Use of Overhead Transparencies on Business Meetings," unpublished paper, Wharton Center for Applied Research (1981).

[4] *Supra* 1, at 283.

2. *Each item must be clear and understandable.* Use themes and conclusions, not pure data.

3. *Appeal to jurors' experience.* Use pictures and phrases they will recognize, and avoid technical jargon.

4. *Reinforce the information with repetition.* Research shows that people learn through repetition.

In choosing an expert, an attorney should be mindful of what plays well to a jury. An expert may not be a good communicator, and experts who use numbers can be especially technical and boring. No matter how much the expert knows, he or she will not succeed on the stand without an ability to present the information clearly and simply. Above all, the expert must avoid technical jargon. Studies show that fancy language does not impress; instead, it detracts from the presentation and loses the audience.

Juries do not like "hired guns," but prefer experts who are perceived as independent. There is evidence that professional witnesses sometimes even prejudice jurors against the party the witness is testifying for. The witnesses who are most successful with juries have an independent connection with the subject matter of the case, take time to learn about the case, and present testimony in terms which the jury can understand.

Jurors do more than listen to witnesses' testimony. They scrutinize witnesses and assess their personalities and characters. In doing so, they pay attention to demeanor, dress, tone of voice, and much more. Experience shows that a person with a polished presentation style comes across more successfully than one who has superior technical knowledge.

We have stressed the importance of presenting numbers simply and clearly, using visual aids. Such a presentation has the best chance of reaching the jury. When a jury deliberates, however, it often does not reach a decision by mathematical or logical means, but may average or compromise conflicting amounts presented by the two sides. These averages are reached by intuition, not by calculation.

Some decisions, unfortunately, are based on wildly irrelevant data. In one actual case, the jury calculated damages by multiplying the winning attorney's fees by ten![5] Generally speaking, however, juries try to be fair and reasonable and to base their decisions on common sense.

---

[5] Goodman, *et. al.*, *Runaway Verdicts or Reasoned Determinations: Mock Juror Strategies in Awarding Damages*, Jurimetrics J. (Spring 1989): 285-309. *See also* Kalven, *The Dignity of the Civil Jury*, Va.L.R. 1055 (1964).

To sum up, presenting numbers to juries is like presenting any other evidence, except that it is harder. ''Keeping it short and simple'' is the cardinal rule in presenting numbers to juries. But it certainly helps to coat the pill with such sweeteners as graphics, analogies, down-to-earth examples, and dramatic devices. The attorney and the witness must overcome widespread prejudices and fears. Few disagree that numbers taken by themselves lack intrinsic interest. Getting them across to a resistant audience, therefore, requires all the ingenuity the attorney and the witness can muster.

Glossary of Accounting and Financial Terms

Accelerated depreciation. Depreciation methods that write off the cost of an asset at a faster rate than the **straight-line method**. The two principal methods of accelerated depreciation are **sum-of-the-years' digits**, and **double declining balance.**

Accrual basis of accounting. Using this method, items of income or expense are entered in the books when they are incurred, not necessarily when the payment or receipt of cash takes place. Most financial statements are based on accrual, not cash accounting. Using this method, receivables and payables are established to record the amounts owed and owing to the entity.

Accrued expense or revenue. Expense or revenue that has been incurred or earned but is not recorded in the books. Accrual entries are made to record these items at the time financial statements are prepared.

Acid test ratio. See **quick ratio**.

AICPA. The American Institute of Certified Public Accountants, the major national professional organization of public accountants.

Amortization. Paying off debt with periodic payments. Also, the equivalent of depreciation for intangible assets such as patents and copyrights.

Annuity. A series of periodic payments, not necessarily annual. Usually they are of equal magnitude and paid at identically spaced time intervals.

APB opinions. The opinions expressed by the Accounting Principles Board of the AICPA.

ARB. Accounting research bulletins issued by the AICPA's Committee on Accounting Procedure, which was founded in 1938. In 1959, this committee was reorganized as the Accounting Principles Board and the opinions of this body are called **APB opinions**.

Assessed value. The value placed on a piece of property or other business asset for purposes of establishing property taxes.

Assets. Items which a person or business owns and which have probable future economic benefits. They may be classified as current assets (cash, savings and investments) or long-term assets ("fixed assets") such as real estate, automobiles, etc.

Balance sheet. A key financial statement that presents assets, liabilities, and net worth, each measured at a specified point in time.

Balance sheet equation. This equation states that assets equal liabilities plus capital (net worth.) This is usually expressed as $A = L + C$ or $A - L = C$.

Bond. A certificate indicating that a corporation has borrowed a certain amount of money which it has agreed to repay in the future.

Bond discount. The amount by which a bond sells below its face value. Bonds sell at a discount when bonds with similar risk carry higher stated interest rates.

Bond premium. The amount by which a bond's market price exceeds its face value.

Book value. The value of a firm measured by subtracting its **liabilities** from its **assets**, both of which have been recorded using **GAAP**.

Breakeven analysis. A mathematical technique for comparing various levels of income and expense. Breakeven is the point at which all revenues equal all expenses. This analysis is often done with a graph to show the relationship between costs and revenues.

Budget. A tool for planning short-term income and expenditures in order to achieve long-term financial goals. Budgets show expected expenses and income within a specific future period of time.

Capital budget. The process for evaluating and scheduling various investment alternatives. Previously, this method described the acquisition of physical plant and equipment, but is now applied to a wide variety of investments.

Capital structure. In financial analysis this term refers to long-term debt, preferred stock, and **net worth**. Net worth consists of capital, capital surplus, and retained earnings. Capital structure is distinguished from "financial structure," which includes short-term debt plus all reserve accounts.

Capitalized costs. Costs which result from expenditures that will carry value into the future. These include many assets, and contrast with expenditures that are consumed in operations. Examples of capitalized costs include real estate, equipment, and intangibles such as patents and copyrights.

Capital leases. Leases of assets that have the characteristics of acquisitions of assets. Based on their substance, they are recorded on the balance sheet as acquisitions of assets with the incurrence of debt, not as leases. Also called capitalized leases.

Capitalize. To record as an asset a cost that has an economic life in excess of one year. For example, to capitalize interest costs on long-term projects would mean that interest incurred on the debt to finance the project is included in the book value of the project, rather than shown as a deduction from the company's revenue.

Carry-back; carry-forward. For income tax purposes, losses that can be carried backward or forward in time, in order to reduce federal income taxes.

Cash basis of accounting. The recording of transactions only when cash is received or paid. Personal financial statements are normally prepared on this basis.

Cash budget. A schedule projecting cash flows (receipts, disbursements, and net cash) for a company over a specified future period.

Cash flow. A general term describing the nature of how actual money flows into and out of an organization.

Charge. A debit entry to an account. To expense or write off a balance. See expense.

Common size financial statements. Statements in which all elements are expressed as a percent of total assets. This allows for easy comparisons among companies.

Common stock. The basic form of corporate ownership. Purchasers of common stock expect to receive dividends and/or capital gains in return for their investment.

Compensating balance. A minimum checking account balance which a firm is required to maintain with a commercial bank. The required balance is generally 10 to 20 percent of the amount of loans outstanding. Compensating balances can raise the effective rate of interest on bank loans due to the "opportunity cost" associated with the idle cash balance (loss of the opportunity to invest the sum elsewhere and earn interest).

Compilation. The lowest level of financial statement services which an accountant performs. Compilation is simply the presenting of financial information in the form of financial statements.

Conservatism. A guiding principle of **GAAP** which requires accountants to anticipate and record losses, even while these may be somewhat uncertain. By the same token, gains are not recorded until they are certain to occur.

Consistency. A basic principle of accounting which requires that transactions be recorded in a consistent manner. While this is an objective of **GAAP**, differences do occur. If an entity changes its accounting methods, it must disclose the change in the notes to its financial statements.

Contingent liabilities or gains. Possible gains or losses to an enterprise that may result if one or more future events occur. Lawsuits are a good example of contingencies.

Contribution margin. The difference between the sales price and the *variable costs* of production (as opposed to fixed costs, or costs such as rent which do not change.) Variable costs are costs that change in direct proportion to the volume that is being produced.

Cost-benefit analysis. The evaluation of the costs against the benefits of pursuing a project or activity. Many costs and benefits are difficult to forecast and many (such as goodwill created) do not lend themselves to easy translation into monetary terms.

Cost center. A unit in an organization which is not responsible for producing revenue or income. These are typically areas like security, maintenance, etc.

Credit entries. Entries that are conventionally on the right side of a ledger. These are revenues, debts, or equity additions. A credit entry must be equal in amount to a debit entry. For example, a company selling goods would credit the account "Sales" and debit the account "Cash" or "Accounts Receivable" when a sale is made.

Cumulative stock. Stock requiring that all dividends not paid in previous periods accumulate. A company must pay these accumulated dividends before paying any dividends to the common stockholders. Cumulative stock usually ranks ahead of common stock in the event of a business liquidation. See **preferred stock**.

Current assets. Assets on a balance sheet which are expected to be used or converted into something else within one year. **Long-term assets** are those which will not be completely converted within one year.

Current liabilities. Liabilities or obligations that are payable in the current year. They usually include short-term loans, accounts and notes payable, accrued expenses, currently maturing portions of long-term debt; and dividends and taxes payable.

Current ratio. The extent to which the claims of short-term creditors are covered by assets that are expected to be converted to cash in the corresponding period. This ratio is calculated by dividing current assets by current liabilities.

Days payable outstanding. A ratio that indicates how long a company takes to pay its bills. It is calculated by dividing payables by cost of sales per day.

Days receivable outstanding. This ratio indicates how long customers take to pay their bills. It is computed by dividing accounts receivable by credit sales per day.

Debit entries. Entries on the left side of the ledger. These are entries for the acquisition of assets, or payment of dividends and expenses. A debit entry must be equal in amount to a credit entry.

Debt to equity ratio. This measures the relative positions of lenders and investors in a business. It is computed by dividing total debt by total equity. Some analysts use a variation of this ratio called **funded debt to equity**.

Debt coverage ratio. This measures a company's ability to pay its debts. It is calculated by dividing income before interest and depreciation by principal and interest charges on debt.

Default. The failure of a borrower—whether it be an individual, a corporation, or a government—to pay interest or principal on a bond or any type of loan when it is due.

Deferred income and expenses. Deferred income is a claim against the company by a prepayer. An attorney's retainer is one example. Deferred expenses are costs normally recorded as expenses that benefit a future period.

Depreciation costs. The amount by which the value of an asset declines and is written down over a given period of ownership.

Dilution (decreased earnings per share). Dilution occurs when net income stays the same while the number of common shares or common stock equivalents outstanding increases.

Discount (interest) method. A method by which the finance charges are calculated and then subtracted from the amount of the loan. The net difference between the full face amount of the loan and the finance charges is then lent to the borrower.

Discounted cash flow. Future cash flows expressed in current dollars. Techniques for determining the amount include the **internal rate of return method** and the **net present value method**.

Dividends. The distribution of earnings to the stockholders or owners of a corporation.

Dividend yield. The percentage return provided in dividends paid on common stock. The dividend yield is calculated on an annual basis by dividing the cash dividends paid during the year by the current market price of the stock.

Double declining balance method. The systematic write-off of a balance over a period of time at twice the **straight-line method's** rate. This method is applied to the balance remaining after deduction of the prior years' write-offs. For example, an asset that cost $10 with a 10 year useful life would be written off on the straight-line method at $1 per year (10%), but under the double declining balance method, the first year's depreciation would be $2 (20%). In the second year the

20% would be applied to the remaining book value of $8 ($10 less $2) for a write-off of $1.60, and so forth.

Earnings per share (EPS). The return earned on behalf of each share of common stock for a certain period of time. It is calculated by dividing all earnings remaining after paying preferred stockholders by the number of shares of common stock and common stock equivalents outstanding.

Effective rate of interest. The true rate of interest, or the rate paid over the period of time when the funds are actually being used.

Effective tax rate. The average rate at which each dollar of a taxpayer's taxable income is taxed. It is calculated by dividing tax liability by taxable income.

Equity. What is left after subtracting a company's **GAAP**-basis **liabilities** from its **assets**. It is also called **net worth**.

Equity capital. Ownership funds invested in a business either through direct investment or by leaving the business's earnings in the business.

Equity method. The accounting method used for calculating an investor's interest of 20% or more in an unconsolidated company. It is equal to the initial cost of the investment, adjusted for the investor's proportionate share of the investee's earnings and dividends since acquisition.

Expense. The accounting process of deducting a cost from revenue on the books of a company. Mechanically, it is simply the placing of the amount in an expense account on a general ledger. The aggregate of all entries into that account is combined with similar expense accounts, and eventually becomes part of one of the expense categories on an income statement.

Extraordinary items. A line item on the balance sheet which denotes economic events that are material and significantly different from the entity's typical business activities.

Factoring. A method of financing accounts receivable by which a firm sells its receivables to a financial institution (the "factor") at an amount below their face value.

Fair market value. The price that a knowledgeable, willing buyer would pay for an asset and that a knowledgeable, willing seller would accept for the asset.

Federal Insurance Contributions Act (FICA). The law which established the tax sometimes referred to as the Social Security tax, which is levied on both employer and employee.

Financial Accounting Standards Board (FASB). The independent standard-setting body for **Generally Accepted Accounting Principles**. This body is a forum composed of users, preparers, and auditors of financial statements.

First-in, first-out (FIFO). An accounting method which assumes that the first goods sold are the first that were available for sale. This method reflects the flow of goods for most businesses, in which left-over inventory consists of the last items the company purchased in the period. In a time of rising prices, however, this method can overstate earnings. Compare **Last-in, first-out (LIFO)**.

Fixed costs. Expenses that remain relatively constant over an extended period of time and a considerable range of activity. Some examples are rent, fire insurance, and property taxes.

Fixed interest rate. A rate of interest that is fixed at the time a loan is negotiated.

Form 10-K. The annual filing with the Securities and Exchange Commission. This filing includes the financial statements, management's discussion and analysis, a description of the business and other disclosures concerning the business, and selected schedules.

Form 10-Q. The quarterly filing with the Securities and Exchange Commission.

Future value. The amount of money which an investor can expect to receive in the future for money invested today. For example, if $1,000 is invested in a 10% certificate of deposit today, the future value in one year would be $1,100.

Generally Accepted Accounting Principles (GAAP). These accounting rules are primarily the pronouncements of the **Financial Accounting Standards Board**. The pronouncements are called Statements of Financial Accounting Standards (SFAS). Other bodies, such as the Emerging Issues Task Force, establish temporary GAAP rules until the full FASB deals with new transactions or instruments.

Generally Accepted Auditing Standards (GAAS). Standards established by the **AICPA** to help promote uniformity in audits.

Going concern. A basic assumption underlying financial statements that the entity is able to survive and continue its operations.

Graduated mortgage. A mortgage which has low interest rates in the first few years and higher rates thereafter.

Gross margin or **gross profit.** The amount by which sales exceed the direct costs of the product or service sold (i.e., material, labor, and overhead).

Gross margin as a percent of sales. This ratio reflects the profitability of the product. It is calculated by dividing gross margin by sales.

Historical cost principle. An accounting convention which reflects business transactions at the cost at the date of the original transaction, rather than at current (or "fair") value.

Income statement. A key financial statement, which presents a company's income, expenses, and net income for a stated period of time (usually a year). Also called the "statement of operations" or "operating statement."

Incremental tax rate. The tax rate on each new (added) dollar of a taxpayer's taxable income. This will differ from the **effective tax rate** when additional taxable income is assessed at a higher rate, or when credits that are not available to offset the tax rate on the incremental dollars are used to reduce the rate on taxable income below the incremental level.

Installment loan. A loan that is repaid in a series of fixed, scheduled payments rather than in a lump sum.

Intangible assets. Nonphysical assets such as patents, copyrights, and goodwill.

Internal rate of return (IRR). The rate of return on an investment, which is calculated by finding the discount rate that causes the present value of future cash flows to equal the initial cost of the investment.

Inventory. Goods which a company has manufactured for sale, including raw materials for production on hand, production in progress, and goods purchased for resale. This term in service companies is usually used for unbilled time.

Inventory turnover ratio. The ratio that indicates how long an item sits in the inventory before it "turns over." It is computed by dividing cost of sales by average inventory balance.

Last-in, first-out (LIFO). An accounting method which assumes that the first items sold were the last ones acquired and that any remaining inventory consists of the first items purchased. This method is an accounting technique that goes contrary to the flow of goods in most businesses. Its principal benefit is in reducing reported earnings—and taxes—in a period of rising prices. Compare **First-in, first-out (FIFO).**

Leverage. The use of debt financing, as opposed to financing a business completely with the owners' capital (equity). Leverage can increase the return on the equity invested. However, it can also become destructive if the investments do not generate enough income to cover the interest payments.

Liabilities. Money that a person or a business owes for goods or services purchased.

Limited partnership. A type of partnership in which the limited partner is legally liable only for the amount of his or her investment.

Line of credit. The total amount which a customer is allowed to borrow from a bank under a loan agreement that usually specifies a period of time and the maximum amount of credit.

Liquidity. The degree to which current or fixed assets are convertible into cash.

Loan origination fee. A fee paid to a lender for granting a loan.

Long-term assets. Assets that will not be converted into cash within one year. (**Current assets** are those assets that will be converted into cash within a year.)

Management's discussion and analysis (MD&A). Part of the annual 10-K filing of SEC-registered companies, MD&A is often included in annual reports. This is management's explanation of why things happened, what the trends are, and why changes occurred in the company's financial condition.

Market rate of interest. The rate of interest paid on instruments that carry similar risks in the marketplace.

Marketable securities. Short-term investments that can be converted into cash within a few days. These include U.S. government and corporate securities, and are shown at the lower of cost or market in most companies' financial statements.

Matching. An accounting concept which requires an entity to recognize (record) revenue and all related costs in the same time period. Because of this concept, costs that will generate future revenue are deferred.

Materiality. An accounting principle that is relative, and thus, to some degree, a judgment issue. A material item on a financial statement is one that would cause a reasonable reader of the statement to change his or her decision.

Mortgage insurance. An insurance policy on the life of the borrower, naming the mortgage lender as the beneficiary, so that if the borrower dies, the mortgage is automatically paid off.

Net income as a percent of sales. A ratio that tells what percent of sales dollars results in net income or profit. The higher this percentage, the more efficiently the business is producing and selling its goods and services. The ratio is calculated by dividing net income by sales.

Net present value (NPV) method. A method of evaluating and ranking different investment proposals, using a common basis of comparison. The net present value is an estimate of what a stream of future income is worth today. NPV is equal to the present value of future returns, discounted at an appropriate cost of capital, less the present value of the cost of the investment.

Net worth (personal). Often considered the amount of personal or family wealth, it is determined by subtracting all liabilities from all assets.

Net worth (business). The capital accounts of a firm, its capital stock, capital surplus (paid-in capital), earned surplus (retained earnings), and occasionally, certain reserves. For some purposes, preferred stock is included, but net worth generally refers only to the common stockholders' position.

Notes payable. Note obligations with more than a year to go before the principal must be repaid.

NOW account. A negotiable order of withdrawal. This can be viewed as an interest-earning checking account or as a savings account against which checks can be issued. It is similar in appearance and behavior to a checking account, except that it often requires advance notice for a withdrawal.

Operating lease. A right to use an asset in return for a periodic payment, similar to a rent. The rights of ownership, based on the economic substance of the transaction, remain with the lessee.

Opportunity cost. The rate of return on the best "alternative" investment that is available. It is the highest return that will not be earned if the funds are invested in a particular project. For example, the opportunity cost of not investing in Bond A yielding 8 percent might be 7.99 percent, which could be earned on Bond B.

Overdraft. A check written against an account for more money than is in the account.

Par value. The stated value sometimes placed on stock certificates and assigned to the stock. It reflects the minimum price at which the stock could sell without causing the shareholder to assume any liability for the firms actions.

Payback period. The length of time required for the net revenues of an investment to return the cost of the investment.

Point. A fee, equal to one percent of the borrowed amount, charged to raise the annual percentage rate of the loan or to pay the lender for making the loan.

Preferred stock. A form of equity stock having preferential treatment over common stock, usually in relation to dividends and liquidation rights. See **cumulative stock**.

Prepaid expense. An expense paid in advance of the actual use of the goods or services paid for. It is classified as an asset on the balance sheet.

Prepayment clause. A clause which allows for payment of a loan prior to its maturity date. This clause often contains a penalty charge for prepayment to prevent the borrower from refinancing with another lender.

Present value (PV). The value today of a future payment, or stream of payments, discounted at the appropriate discount rate.

Price-earnings ratio (P/E). A ratio calculated by dividing the prevailing market price per share by the earnings per share. This ratio is viewed as an indicator of investor confidence in a given security.

Principal. The face value of a debt instrument, which represents the amount the holder would receive at the instruments maturity.

Pro forma financial statement. A financial statement that shows how the actual statement will look if certain specified assumptions are realized. Pro forma statements may be either future or past projections. (The Latin words "pro forma" mean "as if.")

Property, plant and equipment. Assets that are expected to be used in the business for more than one year after the date they were purchased. This balance sheet item includes land, buildings, machinery, equipment, tools, furniture, and other assets.

Quick ratio or **acid test ratio.** Similar to the current ratio, this is the "acid test" of a business's ability to pay its current creditors. It is calculated by dividing cash, marketable securities, and accounts receivable by current liabilities.

Rate of return. The yield obtainable on a project, investment, or other asset that produces income.

Realize. To convert into actual money; to bring or get by sale, investment, or effort as in "to realize a gain." Often used with reference to investments. Realized gains or losses are those actually incurred through a sale of the investment and recorded in income or expense accounts. Unrealized gains or losses would be the difference, in this example, between the cost of investments still held (and not sold) and their current market value.

Reinvestment rate. The rate of return at which cash flows from an investment are reinvested. The reinvestment rate may or may not be constant from year to year.

Related party transactions. Transactions between affiliated companies, or between the company and its employees, officers, or shareholders.

Replacement cost. The amount necessary to repair, rebuild, or replace an asset at today's prices.

Required rate of return. The rate of return which stockholders expect to receive on common stock investments.

Retained earnings. The portion of earnings that is not paid out in dividends. The figure that appears on the balance sheet is the sum of the retained earnings for each year throughout the company's history.

Return on assets. This ratio assesses the profitability of a business in relation to its assets. The higher the return on assets, the more effi-

ciently management is using its resources. Return on assets is calculated by dividing net income by average total assets.

Return on investment or **return on equity.** Of interest to long-term
investors, this ratio shows what return a business is producing on the
stockholders' investment. It is calculated by dividing net income by
average equity.

Revenue. Also called "net sales" or "net revenue," this line on the
income statement shows what the company has sold in dollar terms.

Selling, general, and administrative expenses (SG&A). A line item
on the income statement which contains all costs other than interest
and cost of goods sold.

Sales to assets ratio. A ratio that shows how many dollars of sales are
produced for each dollar of assets the company owns. It is computed
by dividing total sales by total assets.

Sales to employees ratio. A ratio that shows how many dollars of sales
the company produces for each person it employs. This is computed
by dividing total sales by number of employees.

Sale and leaseback. A transaction in which a firm sells land, buildings,
or equipment to a financial institution and simultaneously makes an
agreement to lease the property back for a specified period under specific terms.

Salvage value. The estimated trade-in value of a tangible asset when it
is disposed of.

Securities and Exchange Commission (SEC). The agency of the federal government which regulates the disclosure of information about
securities, as well as the operation of the securities exchanges and
capital markets. The SEC is responsible for enforcing the Securities
Exchange Acts of 1933 and 1934.

Securities, junior and senior. Junior securities have lower priority in
claims on assets and income than senior securities. For example, preferred stock is junior to debentures, but debentures are junior to mortgage or collateralized bonds. Common stock is the most junior of all
corporate securities; mortgage bonds or collateralized bonds are the
most senior.

Segment data. A note to the financial statements of a company that
describes its various segments, or lines of business.

Simple interest method. The method by which interest is charged only on the actual outstanding principal loan balance.

Statements on Auditing Standards (SAS). The pronouncements of the **AICPA's** Auditing Standards Board, its senior technical body on auditing standards.

Stock dividend. A dividend paid in additional shares of stock rather than in cash. Stock dividends are limited by the amount of retained earnings because they involve a transfer or reclassification from retained earnings to the capital stock account.

Stock split. An increase in the number of shares outstanding by issuing new shares in exchange for current shares outstanding in a ratio greater than 1 to 1; for example, in a 3-for-1 split, shares outstanding would be tripled and each stockholder would receive three new shares for each one formerly held.

Straight-line method. The systematic write-off in equal amounts over a period of time of a balance, usually associated with depreciation and amortization of assets. For example, an asset having a cost of $10 would be written off over 10 years at $1 per year.

Subordinated debentures. Bonds having a claim in liquidation of assets only after senior debt has been satisfied. The subordination agreement that accompanies the bonds specifies what debt is considered senior to the debentures.

Subsequent events. Events that occur after the balance sheet date but before the financial statements and the auditor's report are issued. These events are usually recorded in a note to the financial statements.

Substance over form. The accounting principle which states that a transaction must be recorded based on its substance, regardless of its form.

Sum-of-the-years' digits method. The systematic write-off of an amount over a period of time using a factor created by the number of years remaining to the end of the period as the numerator and the sum of the individual years in the period as the denominator. This method is usually associated with accelerated depreciation or amortization. For example, $\frac{1}{3}$ of the balance would be written off in the first year of a five-year asset's life ($\frac{5}{1+2+3+4+5} = \frac{5}{15} = \frac{1}{3}$) and $\frac{4}{15}$ in the second year, etc.

Tangible assets. Physical assets, as opposed to intangible assets such as goodwill and the stated value of patents.

Tangible property. Tangible items of real and personal property which generally have a long life, such as real estate, vehicles, and buildings.

Tax-exempt securities. Bonds paying interest that is not taxed as income. These securities are issued by various state and local governments and are often called "municipals."

Term loan. A loan generally obtained from a bank or an insurance company payable at a fixed time, usually greater than one year.

Times interest earned. The extent to which earnings can decline before a company is unable to meet its annual interest costs. This ratio is calculated by dividing earnings before interest and taxes by interest charges.

Trade accounts payable. Short-term borrowing for goods purchased in the normal course of business. Such goods and services might include raw material, inventory, utilities, and professional fees.

Treasury bill. Noninterest-bearing short-term (91- to 360-day) debt instruments issued by the federal government at a discount from their face value. These are considered to be safe investments.

Unearned revenues. Payments received before the end of the year for goods or services that have not yet been provided. Examples of such revenues include subscriptions and insurance premiums.

Unlimited liability. Liability that can extend beyond the amount of money which an investor has put into a business (e.g., the liability of a sole proprietorship or partnership).

Variable costs. Expenses that change in direct proportion to activity. Some examples are raw materials, labor used in production, heat, light, and power costs.

Variable rate mortgage. A mortgage that allows the mortgage rate to change over the life of the loan in response to market conditions.

Vesting. The rights of employees to benefits in a retirement plan. These rights are based upon their own and their employers contributions.

Working capital. A firm's investment in short-term assets: its cash, short-term securities, accounts receivable, and inventories. "Gross working capital" is defined as a firm's total current assets. "Net working capital" is defined as current assets minus current liabilities.

If the term ''working capital'' is used without further qualification, it often refers to net working capital.

Yield. The rate of return on an investment.

Financial Statements

ABC, Inc.

Consolidated Financial Statements
and Other Financial Information

Years ended December 31, 19X5 and 19X4

Contents

Report of Independent Auditors

The Board of Directors and Shareholders
ABC, Inc.

We have audited the accompanying consolidated balance sheets of ABC, Inc. and subsidiaries as of December 31, 19X5 and 19X4, and the related consolidated statements of income, shareholders' equity, and cash flows for the years then ended. These financial statements are the responsibility of the Company's management. Our responsibility is to express an opinion on these financial statements based on our audits.

We conducted our audits in accordance with generally accepted auditing standards. Those standards require that we plan and perform the audit to obtain reasonable assurance about whether the financial statements are free of material misstatement. An audit includes examining, on a test basis, evidence supporting the amounts and disclosures in the financial statements. An audit also includes assessing the accounting principles used and significant estimates made by management, as well as evaluating the overall financial statement presentation. We believe that our audits provide a reasonable basis for our opinion.

In our opinion, the financial statements referred to above present fairly, in all material respects, the consolidated financial position of ABC, Inc. and subsidiaries at December 31, 19X5 and 19X4, and the consolidated results of their operations and their cash flows for the years then ended in conformity with generally accepted accounting principles.

* Our audits were conducted for the purpose of forming an opinion on the financial statements taken as a whole. The accompanying consolidating balance sheet at December 31, 19X5 is presented for purposes of additional analysis and is not a required part of the financial statements. Such information has been subjected to the

---

Note: Alternatively, the report on Other Financial Information could be presented as a separate opinion. In this example, the opinion page would precede the Consolidating Balance Sheet.

auditing procedures applied in our audit of the financial statements and, in our opinion, is fairly stated in all material respects in relation to the financial statements taken as a whole.

[Signature]

March 31, 19X6

ABC, Inc.

Consolidated Balance Sheets

	December 31	
	19X5	19X4
	(In Thousands)	
Assets		
Current assets:		
Cash and cash equivalents *(Note 5)*	$ 7,500	$ 6,000
Accounts receivable, less allowance of		
$300,000 in 19X5 and $250,000 in 19X4	29,000	28,000
Inventories *(Note 3)*		
Finished products	17,000	16,000
Products in process	35,000	29,000
Raw materials and supplies	7,000	6,000
	59,000	51,000
Prepaid expenses	500	500
Total current assets	96,000	85,500
Investment in affiliated company	4,200	4,100
Property, plant, and equipment *(Note 10)*		
Land	6,000	5,000
Buildings	38,350	30,850
Machinery and equipment	59,700	47,200
	104,050	83,050
Accumulated depreciation and amortization	35,550	30,550
	68,500	52,500
Other assets	800	1,400
Total assets	**$169,500**	$143,500

	December 31	
	19X5	**19X4**
	(In Thousands)	
Liabilities and shareholders' equity		
Current liabilities:		
Notes payable to banks *(Note 5)*	$ **3,000**	$ 7,000
Commercial paper *(Note 5)*	**3,000**	2,000
Accounts payable and accrued expenses	**23,600**	20,200
Income taxes	**5,000**	2,000
Deferred income taxes	**700**	—
Current portion of long-term debt and		
capital lease obligations	**1,400**	1,350
Total current liabilities	**36,700**	32,550
Long-term debt, less current portion *(Note 6)*	**35,000**	21,000
Capital lease obligations, less current portion		
(Note 10)	**14,500**	14,900
Accrued pension cost *(Note 9)*	**2,000**	2,100
Deferred income taxes *(Note 8)*	**3,000**	2,000
Lease commitments *(Note 10)*		
Shareholders' equity *(Notes 6 and 7)*		
Common stock, $1 par value:		
Authorized shares - 5,000,000		
Issued and outstanding shares -		
3,000,000 in 19X5 and		
2,900,000 in 19X4	**3,000**	2,900
Additional paid-in capital	**15,000**	14,100
Retained earnings	**59,300**	54,950
Currency translation adjustments	**1,000**	(1,000)
Total shareholders' equity	**78,300**	70,950
Total liabilities and shareholders' equity	**$169,500**	$143,500

See accompanying notes.

ABC, Inc.

Consolidated Statements of Income

	December 31	
	19X5	19X4
	(In Thousands)	
Net sales	**$150,000**	$125,000
Cost of products sold	**111,500**	90,300
Selling and administrative expenses	**19,950**	22,100
	18,550	12,600
Other income (expense)		
Interest expense	**(5,550)**	(4,400)
Other income	**1,000**	800
Income before income taxes	**14,000**	9,000
Income taxes *(Note 8)*	**6,700**	4,000
Net income	**$ 7,300**	$ 5,000
*Earnings per share		
Primary	**$2.42**	$1.69
Fully diluted	**$2.32**	$1.67

See accompanying notes.

Note: Earnings per share is not required for nonpublic enterprises (FASB Statement No. 21).

ABC, Inc.

*Consolidated Statements of
Shareholder's Equity

	Common Stock	Additional Paid-In Capital	Retained Earnings	Currency Translation Adjustments	Total
			(In Thousands)		
Balance at December 31, 19X3	$2,900	$14,100	$52,850	$ 500	$70,350
Net income for 19X4	—	—	5,000	—	5,000
Currency translation adjustments	—	—	—	(1,500)	(1,500)
**Cash dividends ($1.00 per share)	—	—	(2,900)	—	(2,900)
Balance at December 31, 19X4	2,900	14,100	54,950	(1,000)	70,950
Proceeds from issuance of 100,000 shares of common stock	100	900	—	—	1,000
Net income for 19X5	—	—	7,300	—	7,300
Currency translation adjustments	—	—	—	2,000	2,000
**Cash dividends ($1.00 per share)	—	—	(2,950)	—	(2,950)
Balance at December 31, 19X5	$3,000	$15,000	$59,300	$1,000	$78,300

See accompanying notes.

---

*Note: It is also acceptable to present "Statements of Retained Earnings" or "Statements of Income and Retained Earnings," particularly when there are few transactions affecting shareholders' equity during the years presented.

** Note: Disclosure of dividends per share is optional for nonpublic enterprises.

ABC, Inc.

Consolidated Statements of Cash Flows

	Year ended December 31	
	19X5	19X4
	(In Thousands)	
Operating activities		
Net income	**$7,300**	$5,000
Adjustments to reconcile net income to net cash provided by operating activities:		
Depreciation and amortization	**9,000**	8,000
Deferred income taxes	**1,700**	850
Undistributed earnings of affiliates	**(1,000)**	(500)
Changes in operating assets and liabilities:		
Accounts receivable	**(1,000)**	(1,000)
Inventories	**(8,000)**	(5,000)
Accounts payable and accrued expenses	**3,400**	1,300
Income taxes payable	**3,000**	(350)
Net cash provided by operating activities	**14,400**	8,300
Investing activities		
Purchases of property, plant, and equipment	**(13,800)**	(5,900)
Acquisition of Future Corp.	**(10,000)**	—
Proceeds from disposal of property, plant, and equipment	**1,000**	200
Net cash used in investing activities	**(22,800)**	(5,700)
Financing activities		
Proceeds from issuance of 10% debentures	**15,000**	—
Proceeds from issuance of common stock	**1,000**	—
Payments of long-term debt	**(1,200)**	(860)
Payments of capital lease obligations	**(350)**	(300)
Net decrease in short-term borrowings	**(3,000)**	(1,000)
Dividends paid	**(2,950)**	(2,900)
Net cash provided (used) by financing activities	**8,500**	(5,060)
Effect of exchange rate changes on cash	**1,400**	(840)

Net increase (decrease) in cash and cash equivalents	**1,500**	(3,300)
Cash and cash equivalents at beginning of year	**6,000**	9,300
Cash and cash equivalents at end of year	**$7,500**	$6,000

See accompanying notes.

ABC, Inc.

Notes to Consolidated Financial Statements

*December 31, 19X5

1. Accounting Policies

Description of Business

The Company manufactures and sells automotive parts primarily to original equipment manufacturers (OEMs) and automotive aftermarket customers. The Company performs periodic credit evaluations of its customers' financial condition and generally does not require collateral. At December 31, 19X5 and 19X4, accounts receivable from OEM customers were approximately $16 million and $12 million, respectively. Receivables generally are due within 60 days. Credit losses relating to OEM customers consistently have been within management's expectations and comparable to losses for the portfolio as a whole.

Principles of Consolidation

The consolidated financial statements include the accounts of the Company and its subsidiaries, all of which are wholly owned. Significant intercompany accounts and transactions have been eliminated in consolidation. The Company's 20%-owned affiliate is accounted for by the equity method.

Inventories

Inventories are carried at the lower of cost or market using the last-in, first-out (LIFO) method for domestic inventories and the first-in, first-out (FIFO) method for all other inventories.

---

*Note: It is also acceptable to indicate the dates of the financial statements for both years presented (e.g., December 31, 19X5 and 19X4).

ABC, Inc.

Notes to Consolidated Financial Statements *(continued)*

1. Accounting Policies *(continued)*

Property, Plant, and Equipment

Property, plant, and equipment is stated at cost. Depreciation is computed principally by the straight-line method for financial reporting purposes.

Cash Equivalents

The Company considers all highly liquid investments with a maturity of three months or less when purchased to be cash equivalents.

Income Taxes

All income tax amounts and balances have been computed in accordance with APB Opinion No. 11, "Accounting for Income Taxes." In December, 1987, the Financial Accounting Standards Board issued Statement of Financial Accounting Standards No. 96, "Accounting for Income Taxes." The Company will be required to comply with the new rules by 1992.

The Company has not completed all of the complex analyses required to estimate the impact of the new Statement, and it has not decided whether it will implement the Statement early or restate any periods. However, the adoption of Statement 96 is not expected to have an adverse impact on the Company's financial position.

ABC, Inc.

Notes to Consolidated Financial Statements *(continued)*

1. Accounting Policies *(continued)*

*Earnings Per Share

Earnings per share is based on the average number of shares of common stock outstanding during each year. Fully diluted earnings per share assumes that the 7% convertible sinking fund debentures were converted into common stock as of the beginning of each year, and that the interest expense thereon, net of income taxes, was added to net income.

2. Mergers and Acquisitions

In December 19X5, the Company purchased certain assets and the business of Future Corp. (a manufacturer of electric motors) for $10 million. The pro forma unaudited results of operations for the years ended December 31, 19X5 and 19X4, assuming the purchase of Future Corp. had been consummated as of January 1, 19X4, are as follows:

	19X5	19X4
	(In Thousands)	
Net sales	**$175,000**	$147,000
Net income	**8,400**	5,250

3. Inventories

Current cost exceeds the LIFO value of inventories by approximately $20.5 million and $14 million at December 31, 19X5 and 19X4, respectively. Year-end inventories valued under the LIFO method were $50 million in 19X5 and $43 million in 19X4.

Note: Earnings per share is not required for nonpublic enterprises (FASB Statement No. 21).

ABC, Inc.

Notes to Consolidated Financial Statements *(continued)*

4. Research and Development Expenses

Research and development expenses of $1.7 million in 19X5 and $1 million in 19X4 were charged to expense as incurred.

5. Credit Arrangements

The Company has line-of-credit arrangements for short-term debt with three banks, under which the Company may borrow up to $10 million on such terms as the Company and the banks may mutually agree upon. These arrangements do not have termination dates but are reviewed annually for renewal. At December 31, 19X5, the unused portion of the credit lines was $7 million, of which the Company has assigned $3 million to support outstanding commercial paper.

In connection with these credit lines, the Company maintains average compensating balances, based upon bank ledger balances adjusted for uncollected funds, equal to 10% of the Company's short-term borrowings. Based on outstanding borrowings and the total credit lines at December 31, 19X5, the Company is required to maintain average compensating balances of $1.3 million, which—stated in terms of the Company's book cash balances—is approximately $870,000. The difference is attributable to uncollected funds and float. During 19X5, the Company maintained average compensating balances of approximately $1,140,000. Compensating balances are not restricted as to withdrawal. Commitment fees, which are 0.5% of the unused line of credit, approximated $33,000 and $5,000 for the years ended December 31, 19X5 and 19X4, respectively.

ABC, Inc.

Notes to Consolidated Financial Statements *(continued)*

6. Long-Term Debt

Long-term debt consisted of the following:

	19X5	19X4
	(In Thousands)	
10% notes due through 19Y6	$15,000	—
7% convertible sinking fund notes due through 19X8	14,000	$15,000
Other, principally at 12% due through 19X9	7,000	7,000
	36,000	22,000
Less current portion	1,000	1,000
	$35,000	$21,000

Maturities of long-term debt for the five years succeeding December 31, 19X5 are $1 million in 19X6, $1 million in 19X7, $15.5 million in 19X8, $5.5 million in 19X9, and $2 million in 19Y0. Through June 30, 19X8, the 7% debentures are convertible into shares of common stock at the rate of one share for each $40 face amount.

The loan agreements for both note issues include, among other things, provisions relative to additional borrowings, maintenance of working capital, and restrictions on the amount of retained earnings available for the payment of dividends. Under the most restrictive of these covenants, retained earnings in the amount of $32 million were free of such limitations at December 31, 19X5.

Interest payments were $6.175 million and $4.8 million in 19X5 and 19X4, respectively, of which $600,000 and $350,000, respectively, was capitalized as part of the cost of the Company's newly constructed manufacturing plant.

ABC, Inc.

Notes to Consolidated Financial Statements *(continued)*

7. Shareholders Equity

At December 31, 19X5, 1 million shares of Series A Preferred Stock with a stated value of $10 per share were authorized, none of which have been issued.

At December 31, 19X5, the Company has reserved 350,000 shares for the conversion of the 7% convertible sinking fund notes.

A subsidiary of the Company is subject to debt agreements that limit cash dividends and loans to the Company. At December 31, 19X5, restricted net assets of the subsidiary were $20 million.

8. Income Taxes

Income before income taxes consisted of the following:

	19X5	19X4
	(In Thousands)	
Domestic	$10,000	$6,000
Foreign	4,000	3,000
	$14,000	$9,000

ABC, Inc.

Notes to Consolidated Financial Statements *(continued)*

8. Income Taxes *(continued)*

Federal, foreign, and state income taxes consisted of the following:

	19X5		19X4	
	Current	Deferred	Current	Deferred
	(In Thousands)			
Federal	$3,150	$1,400	$1,700	$550
Foreign	1,000	250	910	240
State	850	50	540	60
	$5,000	$1,700	$3,150	$850

The deferred tax provision relates to the following:

	19X5	19X4
	(In Thousands)	
Depreciation	$1,600	$800
Other	100	50
	$1,700	$850

Total income tax payments during 19X5 and 19X4 were $2 million and $3.5 million, respectively.

Provision has been made for U.S. federal income taxes to be paid on the portion of undistributed earnings of foreign subsidiaries expected to be remitted to the Company. Undistributed earnings intended to be invested indefinitely in foreign subsidiaries was $10 million and $8 million at the end of 19X5 and 19X4, respectively. Deferred income taxes have not been provided on such earnings; however, if such earnings were remitted, estimated withholding taxes would be $2 million and $1.6 million, respectively.

ABC, Inc.

Notes to Consolidated Financial Statements *(continued)*

8. Income Taxes *(continued)*

The effective income tax rate varied from the statutory federal income tax rate as follows:

	19X5	19X4
Statutory federal income tax rate	**34.0%**	40.0%
Increases (decreases):		
State income taxes, net of federal tax benefit	**5.5**	3.6
Effect of foreign income tax rates	**3.5**	(1.6)
Alternative minimum tax	**3.2**	—
Research and experimentation credit	**(1.1)**	—
Other items	**2.7**	2.4
Effective income tax rate	**47.8%**	44.4%

9. Pension Plans and Postretirement Benefits

The Company and its subsidiaries have two defined benefit pension plans that cover substantially all non-union employees, including certain employees in foreign countries. Benefits are based on years of service and each employee's compensation during the last five years of employment. The Company's funding policy is to make the minimum annual contributions required by applicable regulations.

The following table sets forth the funded status and amount recognized for the Company's defined benefit pension plans in the consolidated balance sheets at December 31:

ABC, Inc.

Notes to Consolidated Financial Statements *(continued)*

9. Pension Plans and Postretirement Benefits *(continued)*

	19X5	19X4
	(In Thousands)	
Actuarial present value of accumulated benefit obligation, including vested benefits of $24,800,000 in 19X5 and $23,700,000 in 19X4	$(32,000)	$(30,600)
Actuarial present value of projected benefit obligation for services rendered to date	$(36,100)	$(33,000)
Plan assets at fair value, primarily listed stocks and U.S. bonds	29,100	27,700
Projected benefit obligation in excess of plan assets	(7,000)	(5,300)
Unrecognized net loss from past experience different from that assumed and effects of changes in assumptions	600	200
Prior service cost not yet recognized in net periodic pension cost	1,400	1,000
Unrecognized net obligation at January 1, 19X5 and 19X4	3,000	2,000
Accrued pension cost	$ (2,000)	$ (2,100)

ABC, Inc.

Notes to Consolidated Financial Statements *(continued)*

9. Pension Plans and Postretirement Benefits *(continued)*

Net pension cost included the following components:

	19X5	19X4
	(In Thousands)	
Service cost—benefits earned during the period	$ 800	$ 600
Interest cost on projected benefit obligation	3,300	3,000
Actual return on plan assets	(3,100)	(2,700)
Net amortization and deferral	500	700
Net pension cost	$1,500	$1,600

The Company also makes contributions to a union-sponsored multi-employer defined benefit pension plan. Such contributions were $1.2 million in 19X5 and $975,000 in 19X4.

Following is a summary of significant actuarial assumptions used:

	19X5	19X4
Discount rates	9%	10%
Rates of increase in compensation levels	6%	6%
Expected long-term rate of return on assets	10%	10%

The Company and its subsidiaries provide certain health care and life insurance benefits for retired employees. Substantially all of the Company's employees, including employees in foreign countries, may become eligible if they reach normal retirement age while still working for the Company. These benefits are provided through an insurance company whose premiums are based on the benefits paid during the year. The cost of retiree health care and life insurance benefits is recognized as expense as premiums are incurred. For 19X5 and 19X4, those costs approximated $225,000 and $200,000, respectively.

ABC, Inc.

Notes to Consolidated Financial Statements *(continued)*

9. Pension Plans and Postretirement Benefits *(continued)*

In December 1990, the Financial Accounting Standards Board issued new rules that require that the projected future cost of providing postretirement benefits, such as health care and life insurance, be recognized as an expense as employees render service instead of when paid. Companies can elect to record the cumulative effect of the accounting change as a charge against income in the year the rules are adopted, or alternatively, on a delayed basis as a part of the future annual benefit cost. The Company will be required to comply with the new rules by 1993. The Company has not yet completed the complex analysis required to estimate the financial statement impact of the new rules, nor has it decided how or when it will initially adopt them. In a related matter, the FASB is considering amending the accounting rules for income taxes, and the outcome of that consideration could have a significant impact on the financial statement effects of adopting the new rules on postretirement benefits.

10. Leases

The Company leases a building and machinery and equipment under capital leases. The lease for the building may be renewed for two five-year periods after 19X3. The lease for the machinery and equipment requires the payment of contingent rentals based on usage in excess of a specified minimum, and future rental payments may be adjusted for increases in maintenance and insurance above specified amounts. The Company also leases certain equipment under noncancelable operating leases that expire in various years through 19X9. These leases may be renewed for periods ranging from one to three years.

ABC, Inc.

Notes to Consolidated Financial Statements *(continued)*

10. Leases *(continued)*

Property, plant, and equipment includes the following amounts for leases that have been capitalized:

	19X5	19X4
	(In Thousands)	
Building	**$17,000**	$17,000
Machinery and equipment	**1,400**	1,400
	18,400	18,400
Less accumulated amortization	**5,900**	4,900
	$12,500	$13,500

Amortization of leased assets is included in depreciation and amortization expense.

ABC, Inc.

Notes to Consolidated Financial Statements *(continued)*

10. Leases *(continued)*

Future minimum payments under capital leases and noncancelable operating leases with initial terms of one year or more consisted of the following at December 31, 19X5:

	Capital Leases	Operating Leases
	(In Thousands)	
19X6	$ 2,060	$1,135
19X7	2,060	1,120
19X8	2,060	1,120
19X9	2,060	1,120
19Y0	2,060	1,120
Thereafter	22,080	3,200
Total minimum lease payments	32,380	$8,815
Executory costs	(80)	
Amounts representing interest	(17,400)	
Present value of net minimum lease payments (including current portion of $400,000)	$14,900	

Rental expense consisted of the following:

	19X5	19X4
	(In Thousands)	
Minimum rentals under operating leases	$ 970	$ 950
Contingent rentals under capital leases	180	150
	$1,150	$1,100

ABC, Inc.
Consolidating Balance Sheet
December 31, 19X5

	Consolidated	Consolidation Adjustments	ABC, Inc.	Beta Co.	XYZ Co.	ABCDEF International
Assets (*In Thousands*)						
Current assets:						
Cash and cash equivalents	$ 7,500		$ 3,250	$ 150	$ 2,500	$ 1,600
Accounts receivable	29,300	$ (2,000)	2,000	6,500	16,000	6,800
Less: Allowance for doubtful accounts	300			50	150	100
Net trade accounts receivable	29,000	(2,000)	2,000	6,450	15,850	6,700
Inventories	59,000		26,900	10,000	13,100	9,000
Prepaid expenses	500		50	300	100	50
Total current assets	96,000	(2,000)	32,200	16,900	31,550	17,350
Investment in subsidiaries	4,200	(16,600)	16,600			
Investment in affiliated company			4,200			
Property, plant, and equipment	104,050		34,550	12,450	42,000	15,050
Accumulated depreciation and amortization	35,550		500	2,750	27,500	4,800
	68,500		34,050	9,700	14,500	10,250
Other assets	800		200	150	300	150
Total assets	$169,500	$(18,600)	$87,250	$26,750	$46,350	$27,750

ABC, Inc.
Consolidating Balance Sheet
December 31, 19X5

	Consolidated	Consolidation Adjustments	ABC, Inc.	Beta Co.	XYZ Co.	ABCDEF International
Liabilities and Shareholders' Equity						
(In Thousands)						
Current liabilities:						
Notes payable to banks	$ 3,000		$ 2,500	$ —	$ 500	$ —
Commercial paper	3,000		1,500		1,500	
Accounts payable and accrued expenses	23,600	$ (2,000)	1,000	4,500	15,000	5,100
Income taxes	5,000		500	2,500	1,000	1,000
Deferred income taxes	700		150	350	100	100
Current portion of long-term debt and capital lease obligations	1,400		200	600	400	200
Total current liabilities	36,700	(2,000)	5,850	7,950	18,500	6,400
Long-term debt, less current portion	35,000			10,000	13,900	11,100
Capital lease obligations, less current portion	14,500		500	7,000	6,500	500
Accrued pension cost	2,000		2,000			
Deferred income taxes	3,000		600	1,400	450	550
Shareholders' equity						
Common stock	3,000	(2,250)	3,000	250	1,500	500
Additional paid-in capital	15,000	(750)	15,000	50	500	200
Retained earnings	59,300	(12,600)	59,300	100	5,000	7,500
Currency translation adjustments	1,000	(1,000)	1,000			1,000
Total shareholders' equity	78,300	(16,600)	78,300	400	7,000	9,200
Total liabilities and shareholders' equity	$169,500	$(18,600)	$87,250	$26,750	$46,350	$27,750

Example Form 10-K

The SEC encourages, but does not require, the incorporation by reference of portions of the annual shareholders report into Form 10-K. Regulation S-K contains the uniform requirements for most of the information other than financial statements required in various SEC forms and annual shareholders reports. Some S-K items, or portions thereof, are required in both the annual shareholders report and Form 10-K. And financial statements for both documents must comply with Regulation S-X.

Annual shareholders reports of companies registered under Sections 12(b) or 12(g) of the Securities Exchange Act of 1934 are required to comply with the SEC proxy rules (Rule 14a-3) and must include the following:[1]

> Consolidated financial statements—Audited balance sheets for the two most recent fiscal years and statements of income and cash flows for each of the three most recent fiscal years prepared in accordance with Regulation S-X. Financial statement schedules, exhibits, and separate financial statements (e.g., significant investees) may be omitted from the annual shareholders report.

> Supplementary financial information—Item 302 of Regulation S-K—two years of quarterly information and information about oil and gas producing activities.

---

[1] Companies reporting under Section 15(d) of the Securities Exchange Act of 1934 are required to file on Form 10-K but need not file an annual shareholders report that complies with the SEC proxy rules.

Changes in and disagreements with accountants on accounting and financial disclosure—Item 304 of Regulation S-K.

Management's discussion and analysis of financial condition and results of operations—Item 303 of Regulation S-K.

A brief description of business for the latest year.

Industry segment information—Item 101 of Regulation S-K, paragraphs (b), (c)(1)(i) and (d). Selected financial data—Item 301 of Regulation S-K.

Director and executive officer information.

Market price of and dividends on the issuer's common equity and related stockholder matters—Item 201 of Regulation S-K.

The requirements in annual shareholders reports for financial statements (except schedules, exhibits, and separate financial statements), supplementary information, selected financial data, management's discussion and analysis, market price and dividends on common equity and related stockholder matters, and disagreements with prior independent auditors are identical to the related Form 10-K requirements. Additionally, Form 10-K requirements for the description of business, including segment data, and the officer and director data include the related annual shareholders report requirements.

This Appendix provides an example of a Form 10-K for a commercial and industrial company in which the industry segment information, common stock market data, selected financial data, management's discussion and analysis, consolidated financial statements, and quarterly results of operations have been incorporated by reference.

A company is not required to incorporate portions of its annual shareholders report into Form 10-K. If the financial statements in the annual shareholders report are not incorporated by reference into Form 10-K, the SEC expects the financial statements in Form 10-K and the annual shareholders report to be *identical*.[2] However, if there is no incorporation by reference, the disclosure of other requirements in those documents (market price and dividends on common equity and related stockholder matters, supplementary financial information, selected financial data, management's discussion and analysis and disagreements with prior independent auditors) must be similar. Accordingly, a Form

---

[2] The financial statements in annual shareholders reports of investment companies and banks are only required to substantially comply with the special Regulation S-X articles applicable to them (Articles 6 and 9).

10-K which does not incorporate the financial statements by reference would be the same as this example, except that the data would be included under the appropriate Item instead of the phrase "is incorporated herein by reference."

A box is used in the following examples to highlight explanatory comments.

EXAMPLE FORM 10-K

Business

Industry Segment Data

The Company operates in three principal industries—construction materials, metal products, and paper products. The Company's construction materials division markets residential heating systems, electrical parts and motors, plumbing supplies and miscellaneous metal goods (including metal products division products) through a chain of wholesale supply warehouses. The Company's metal products, which are sold to its own and to independent wholesale supply warehouses, include vent systems, range hoods, flexible metal hose, and light coverings. Paper product operations include the manufacture and distribution of boxes, cartons, and other packing materials for industrial uses. They are marketed directly to consumers.

	Year Ended December 31		
	19X5	19X4	19X3
	(Thousands of dollars)		
Net Sales			
Construction materials	$110,000	$ 98,000	$ 90,000
Metal products			
Unaffiliated customers	20,000	12,000	10,000
Intersegment	10,000	8,000	8,000
	30,000	20,000	18,000
Paper products	20,000	15,000	14,000
Other industries	10,000	8,000	8,000
Eliminations—intersegment			
sales	(10,000)	(8,000)	(8,000)
Total Revenue	$160,000	$133,000	$122,000

	Year Ended December 31		
	19X5	19X4	19X3
	(Thousands of dollars)		
Operating Profit			
Construction materials	$ 9,000	$ 5,000	$ 9,100
Metal products	5,000	3,500	3,500
Paper products	4,000	3,000	2,000
Other industries	2,000	2,000	1,500
Total Operating Profit	20,000	13,500	16,100
Corporate expenses	(1,450)	(1,100)	(450)
Interest expense	(5,550)	(4,400)	(4,650)
Income Before Income Taxes	$ 13,000	$ 8,000	$ 11,000
Identifiable Assets			
Construction materials	$ 112,500	$ 90,000	$ 85,000
Metal products	20,000	20,000	18,000
Paper products	20,000	19,000	15,000
Other industries	10,000	8,000	6,000
	162,500	137,000	124,000
Corporate assets	7,000	6,500	6,000
Total Assets	$169,500	$143,500	$130,000

Sales of the Construction Materials Division include the following product lines:

Year Ended December 31	Heating Systems	Other Products
(Thousands of dollars)		
19X5	$60,000	$50,000
19X4	55,000	43,000
19X3	48,000	42,000

Note: Although product classes reported in these examples cover all sales of the Construction Materials Division, Regulation S-K does not require that classes of product sales be reconciled to segment totals.

GEOGRAPHIC AREA DATA

| | Year Ended December 31 | | |
	19X5	19X4	19X3
	(Thousands of dollars)		
Net Sales and Other Income			
United States:			
Unaffiliated customers	$125,000	$109,000	$100,000
Interarea transfers	15,000	10,000	10,000
	140,000	119,000	110,000
Canada	15,000	14,000	12,000
Other countries	20,000	10,000	10,000
Eliminations-transfers	(15,000)	(10,000)	(10,000)
	$160,000	$133,000	$122,000
Operating Profit			
United States	$ 16,000	$ 11,000	$ 14,100
Canada	3,000	1,500	1,500
Other countries	1,000	1,000	500
	$ 20,000	$ 13,500	$ 16,100
Indentifiable Assets			
United States	$127,500	$110,000	$ 99,000
Canada	10,000	7,000	7,000
Other countries	25,000	20,000	18,000
	$162,500	$137,000	$124,000
Export Sales			
Primarily to Europe	$ 20,000	$ 16,000	$ 15,000

Notes:

1. This example, along with Note L to the consolidated financial statements, illustrates the minimum industry segment disclosures which should be included in annual shareholders reports. Discussion of the development of business since the beginning of the fiscal year is not presented in this example. When preparing Form 10-K, additional disclosures are necessary to fulfill the requirements of Regulation S-K that are not called for in annual shareholders reports.

2. Regulation S-K does not require that operating profit be reconciled to income before taxes, nor that identifiable assets be reconciled to total assets. These disclosures are required by FASB Statement No. 14 and are included in the above example to facilitate convenient incorporation by reference. The SEC's required information on classes of similar products is required in annual shareholders reports but not within the financial statements. Statement No. 14 requires the fact that a major customer exists to be disclosed in the financial statements. The SEC requires the customer's name in Form 10-K, unless the loss of the customer would not have a material effect on the consolidated entity as a whole. Certain segment information required by Statement No. 14 (depreciation and capital expenditures by industry segment) which is not required by Regulation S-K is included in this example in the notes to the financial statements. However, many registrants elect to consolidate all segment disclosures within the description of business.

3. Industry segment information may be presented in either the description of business or the financial statements, and cross-referenced.

COMMON STOCK MARKET PRICES AND DIVIDENDS

The Company's common stock is traded on the New York Stock Exchange (ticker symbol ABC). The approximate number of record holders of the Company's common stock at December 31, 19X5 was 5,100.

High and low stock prices and dividends for the last two years were:

Quarter Ended	19X5 Sales Price High	19X5 Sales Price Low	19X5 Cash Dividends Declared	19X4 Sales Price High	19X4 Sales Price Low	19X4 Cash Dividends Declared
March 31	$21¼	$17½	$.20	$20¼	$16¾	$.20
June 30	22½	18¾	.20	21½	16½	.20
September 30	23	19¼	.20	21¾	17	.20
December 31	24¾	18¼	.40	22½	17¼	.40

The Company expects to continue its policy of paying regular cash dividends, although there is no assurance as to future dividends because they are dependent on future earnings, capital requirements, and financial condition. In addition, the payment of dividends is subject to the restrictions described in Note F to the financial statements and discussed in management's discussion and analysis.

> *Note:* Dividend policy disclosure is encouraged but not required. The data must be adjusted to give retroactive effect to material changes resulting from stock dividends, stock splits, or reverse stock splits. Restrictions on the transfer of funds to the parent from subsidiaries must be disclosed or reference made to financial statement footnote disclosures and discussion in management's discussion and analysis.

SELECTED FINANCIAL DATA

| | Year Ended December 31 | | | | |
	19X5	19X4	19X3	19X2	19X1
	(In thousands of dollars, except per-share data)				
Net sales and other operating revenues	$160,000	$133,000	$122,000	$116,000	$106,000
Net income	8,000	5,000	6,500	5,500	5,000
Total assets	169,500	143,500	130,000	139,000	133,000
Long-term debt and capital lease obligations, less current portion	49,500	35,900	39,450	41,000	45,000
Per common share:					
Net income- Primary	2.65	1.69	2.21	1.93	1.81
-Fully diluted	2.53	1.67	2.12	1.86	1.75
Cash dividends declared	1.00	1.00	.80	.80	.80

> *Note:* Companies must disclose matters that affect the comparability of the information and material uncertainties that might cause the trend information to be misleading.

MANAGEMENT'S DISCUSSION AND ANALYSIS OF FINANCIAL
CONDITION AND RESULTS OF OPERATIONS

Results of Operations

Record net income was achieved in 19X5 as earnings increased 60%
over 19X4 and 23% over the previous record year of 19X3. This increase
represents continued progress in the Company's efforts to improve earnings by expanding operations, introducing new products, and modernizing productive facilities. The contribution each segment made to this
growth is discussed below.

A $700,000 increase in research and development expense in 19X5
resulted in developing a more efficient electrical motor line. A special
advertising campaign in 19X4 introduced the new flexible metal hose
product line, increasing selling and administrative expenses in 19X4 by
$4,000,000. Other factors, including higher salaries and wages and
increased distribution expenses, also contributed to increased selling and
administrative expenses in 19X5 and 19X4.

Interest expense increased during 19X5 reflecting higher interest rates
on short-term borrowings and interest on the $15,000,000 of debentures
issued during the year.

Construction Materials Segment: This segment had increases in both
sales (12%) and operating profit (80%) over 19X4. Approximately 60%
of the sales increase was due to increased selling prices. Fortunately,
competitive pressures eased during the first quarter of 19X5, allowing
the first major price increase since the second quarter of 19X3. The
remaining increase was due to increased volume and production efficiencies. During the first quarter of 19X5, the Company became the exclu-
sive supplier of heating systems and plumbing supplies for two
nationwide residential construction companies.

It is anticipated that additional production will be required to meet
these two construction companies' supply requirements; therefore, the
Company plans to build a new plant to handle the additional capacity.
Management estimates that approximately $20,000,000 will be required
to finance the new plant. In addition, the Company's expansion will
require increases in inventory of about $10,000,000, which are antici-
pated to be financed principally by trade credit. Funds required to
finance the Company's new plant are expected to come primarily from

new credit facilities and the remainder provided by funds generated from operations. The Company recently entered into a new borrowing agreement with a bank, which provides for additional borrowings of up to $30,000,000 for future expansion.

Sales in 19X4 increased by only 9%, while operating profits decreased 45%. Strong replacement demand and gains in market share more than offset the effect of the unfavorable trend in new construction. The relatively large increase in cost of products sold during 19X4 was principally due to a new labor agreement affecting the employees at the Company's plant in Charlotte. The cost of new contract benefits approximated $3,500,000 in 19X4 ($3,700,000 in 19X5). Increased materials costs and the introduction of the new product line also contributed to the increase in cost of products sold during 19X4.

Non-U.S. sales were up in 19X5 because of stronger markets and expanded distribution in countries other than Canada, as well as the fall in the value of the dollar. 19X4 non-U.S. sales were flat with 19X3.

Metal Products Segment: Sales in this segment increased 50% over 19X4, primarily due to increased volume while operating profits increased 43%. This increase results from the completion of a new plant in Iowa during the first quarter of 19X5 and the introduction of a new product line, flexible metal hose, in the fourth quarter of 19X4. However, because of competitive pressures and start-up costs at the new plant, the gross margin percentage has decreased over the past three years. With the new plant in full production in 19X6 and planned expenditures for modernization of existing facilities, the Company expects to improve its operational efficiency in the coming year and thus to improve its margins. However, these anticipated efficiencies will be partially offset by an average 10% increase in the cost of raw materials, expected to impact the Company in the first half of 19X6.

With the introduction of the new product line, unit volumes have declined approximately 10% in an older product line, which represents approximately 25% of overall revenues. The older product lines continue to approach the end of their life cycles and unit volumes are expected to decline each year in the future. If the Company does not continue to replace these older products with new products, the phase-out of the older products may have an adverse effect on future revenues and operating profits.

Sales and operating profits in 19X4 were flat with 19X3. This was due to intense price competition, which further eroded margins, and expenses for product development.

Paper Products Segment: Sales in this segment increased 33% over 19X4. Operating profits have also increased by 33%. This was due to favorable raw materials costs coupled with increased selling prices for our finished products, which accounted for half the increase in sales. The slump in the housing industry over the past several years has resulted in reductions in demand for wood-based raw materials and a softening of prices. Management does not believe that this environment will continue, as the forest products industry has now adjusted to this environment and prices have firmed. Additionally, the union contract covering most of the employees in this industry expires in 19X6. This, coupled with economic forecasts of an improvement in housing starts during the second quarter of 19X6, may result in increases in wood-related raw material prices. Therefore, operating profits for this segment may decrease if the Company cannot pass price increases on to customers.

19X4 sales increased 7% and operating profits increased 50%. The significant improvement in operating profits results principally from significant charges incurred in 19X3 related to clean up activities at a chemical waste disposal site. These activities were completed in 19X3 and did not have a significant impact on operating costs in 19X4 or 19X5.

Liquidity and Sources of Capital

Cash flow from operations, along with the proceeds of the $15,000,000 debt offering, were sufficient to fund the acquisition of Future Corporation ($10,000,000) and to complete construction of the Company's new plant ($11,500,000).

The ratio of current assets to current liabilities was 2.7 at the end of 19X5, compared to 2.6 at the end of 19X4 and 2.4 at the end of 19X3. Working capital continues to increase, reflected principally in higher inventory levels attributable to a planned build-up in anticipation of increased sales. The increase in inventories has been financed principally from the Company's cash flow from operations. Even though inventories have increased, inventory turnover improved to 2.2 in 19X5 from slightly under 2 in 19X4 and 19X3 because of more efficient production scheduling methods and increased sales.

To maintain flexibility in financing interim needs, the Company plans to change the mix of working capital in the coming year by reducing inventories, through further improvements in production scheduling and timing of materials purchases, and by increasing short-term investments. Current financial resources (working capital and short-term borrowing arrangements) and anticipated funds from operations are expected to be adequate to meet cash requirements in the year ahead.

The Company had $7,000,000 in available credit at the end of 19X5 under short-term borrowing arrangements with banks, of which $3,000,000 is assigned to support outstanding commercial paper. Due to the levels of cash flow from operations generated in the past three years, average borrowings have been steadily reduced from $9,750,000 in 19X3, to $8,975,000 in 19X4 and to $3,400,000 in 19X5. The Company plans to continue using commercial paper and short-term bank borrowings to finance interim needs in the coming year. However, the Company does not plan to increase average borrowings over 19X5 levels.

In 19X5, the Company sold $15,000,000 in 10% debentures to finance the purchase of Future Corp. and construction of the Company's new plant. Accordingly, at the end of 19X5, the ratio of long-term debt and capital lease obligations to equity was .63:1 as compared to .51:1 at the end of 19X4 and .56:1 at the end of 19X3. The debentures mature in annual installments of $2,000,000 beginning in 19X9.

Certain of the Company's subsidiaries are parties to debt agreements that limit the amount of cash dividends and loans that can be advanced to the Company. At December 31, 19X5, subsidiaries' net assets of $20,000,000 were restricted due to these agreements. However, these restrictions have no significant impact on the Company's liquidity. As these subsidiaries are in growth markets, management intends to continue reinvesting the subsidiaries' earnings to expand their productive capacity and develop new markets.

Capital expenditures during the year totaled $23,800,000, including $10,000,000 in additions to property, plant, and equipment arising from the acquisition of Future Corp. and $11,500,000 to complete construction and equip the Company's new plant in Iowa. In October, the Company announced a three-year $30,000,000 capital expenditures program. It is anticipated that funds for the program will come from future cash flow from operations, generally maintaining the Company's present

debt-to-equity ratio. A third of the funds will be used to expand manufacturing capacity, particularly for the Company's new flexible metal
hose product line. The remainder will be used for cost-saving machinery
and equipment and general modernization of existing facilities.

Environmental Matters

In the course of its construction materials, metal, and paper products
operations, the Company is subject to occasional governmental proceedings and orders pertaining to noise, air emissions, and water discharges
into the environment. As part of its continuing environmental program,
the Company has been able to comply with such proceedings and orders
without any materially adverse effect on its business.

In May 19X3, the Company received a letter from the United States
Environmental Protection Agency ("EPA") regarding remedial actions
at a chemical waste disposal site in Anytown, USA. Records indicate
that the company may have generated a portion of the waste placed at the
site and the Company has therefore been deemed by the EPA to be a
potentially responsible party ("PRP") with respect to the site under the
Comprehensive Environmental Response, Compensation and Liability
Act. The Company, together with other companies which also generated
waste placed at the site, has participated with the EPA in a clean-up
study at the site. The Company has also engaged in settlement negotiations with the EPA and with other companies regarding its responsibilities, if any, for clean-up of the site. No settlements have been achieved,
but negotiations are continuing.

The Company provides for costs related to contingencies when a loss
is probable and the amount is reasonably determinable. It is the opinion
of management, based on past experience and advice of counsel, that the
ultimate resolution of this contingency, to the extent not previously provided for, will not have a material adverse effect on the financial condition of the Company.

Impact of Recently Issued Accounting Standards[3]

Income Taxes

---

[3] In the following example, the discussion of pending accounting standards uses
actual dates.

In December 1987, the Financial Accounting Standards Board issued Statement of Financial Accounting Standards No. 96, "Accounting for Income Taxes." Companies are required to adopt the new method of accounting for income taxes no later than 1993. In June 1991, the FASB issued an Exposure Draft of a proposed Statement to supersede Statement 96, which if adopted would be effective for fiscal years beginning after December 15, 1992.

The Company has not completed all of the complex analyses required to estimate the impact of adopting the liability method, and it has not decided whether it will implement the liability method by restating any prior years. However, the adoption of the liability method is not expected to have a significant adverse impact on the company's financial position.

Other Postretirement Benefits

In December 1990, the Financial Accounting Standards Board issued new rules that require that the projected future cost of providing postretirement benefits, such as health care and life insurance, (referred to as OPEBs) be recognized as an expense as employees render service instead of when the benefits are paid. Companies can elect to record the cumulative effect of the accounting change as a charge against income in the year the rules are adopted, or alternatively, on a prospective basis as a part of the future annual benefit cost.

The Company currently is accumulating the necessary data and expects to apply the new rules starting in the first quarter of 19X6 on a prospective basis. Based on preliminary estimates, the new rules are expected to result in an increase in 19X6 net periodic postretirement benefit cost of approximately $800,000–$1,000,000. As discussed above, the FASB is considering amending the accounting rules for income taxes, which could have a significant impact on the financial statement effects of adopting the new rules on postretirement benefits.

Impact of Inflation[4]

Although inflation has slowed in recent years, it is still a factor in our economy and the Company continues to seek ways to cope with its

---

[4] Inflation information that has a material effect on a company's business must be discussed in MD&A (FRR 30—Release No. 33-6728).

impact. To the extent permitted by competition, in general the Company passes increased costs on by increasing sales prices over time. Sales reported in the company's financial statements have increased in the last two years due to increases in selling prices and increased sales volume. Approximately 75% of the increase in 19X4 reported sales and 40% of the 19X5 increase were due to increased selling prices. The introduction of a new product line, flexible metal hose, in the last half of 19X4 is primarily responsible for increased sales volume. Although the Company has been able to pass most cost increases through to its customers, the costs of a new labor contract in 19X4 have been primarily responsible for the reductions in operating margins.

The Company uses the LIFO method of accounting for its inventories. Under this method, the cost of products sold reported in the financial statements approximates current costs and thus reduces the distortion in reported income due to increasing costs. The charges to operations for depreciation represent the allocation of historical costs incurred over past years and are significantly less than if they were based on the current cost of productive capacity being consumed.

Approximately 67% of the company's properties have been acquired over the past five years and have a remaining useful life ranging from five years for equipment to thirty-five years for buildings. Assets acquired in prior years will, of course, be replaced at higher costs but this will take place over many years. Again, these new assets will result in higher depreciation charges; but in many cases, due to technological improvements, there will be operating cost savings as well. The Company considers these matters in setting its pricing policies.

Present tax laws do not allow deductions for adjustments for the impact of inflation. Thus, taxes are levied on the Company at rates which, in real terms, exceed established statutory rates. In general, during periods of inflation, this tax policy results in a tax on shareholders' investment in the Company.

Notes:

1. This example illustrates the discussion that might be presented in the Form 10-K and annual shareholders report of ABC, Inc. Of course, the content and length of management's discussion will vary among companies, and it is impossible to illustrate the disclosures that might

be required under all circumstances. This example does not reflect the following discussion areas that could be necessary in more complex situations: (1) proposed actions to remedy a deficiency in liquidity, (2) infrequent events or transactions, (3) known trends as may be reflected in the table of selected financial data, and (4) the effect of foreign operations and translation adjustments on operations and liquidity.

2. Regulation S-K requires a discussion of any material effects of inflation on the company's results of operations.

3. FRR 36 indicates that registrants are expected to use the statement of cash flows and other appropriate indicators in analyzing their liquidity and to present a balanced discussion dealing with cash flows from investing and financing activities as well as from operations.

4. Management's discussion must address the liquidity of the parent company when the flow of funds from a subsidiary to the parent is restricted. This discussion is required when footnote disclosures about the restrictions are in the notes to the financial statements.

5. The information required by Schedule IX (Short-term borrowings—Rule 12-10 of Regulation S-X) may be presented in management's discussion if it results in a more meaningful presentation. Schedule IX would then incorporate that information by reference.

6. SAB 74 addresses disclosure requirements with respect to accounting standards which have been issued but not yet adopted by the registrant. The staff believes that disclosure of impending accounting changes is necessary to inform the reader about expected impacts on financial information to be reported in the future, and therefore, should be disclosed in accordance with existing MD&A requirements.

With regard to income taxes, the example above illustrates the discussion that might be presented for a company that had not yet adopted Statement 96. Although the requirements of SAB 74 do not extend to Exposure Drafts of pending accounting standards, the following example may be appropriate for a company that had previously adopted Statement 96:

In June 1991, the FASB issued an Exposure Draft of a proposed Statement to supersede Statement 96, which if adopted would be effective for fiscal years beginning after December 15, 1992. The proposed Statement addresses two principal criticisms leveled against Statement 96—the overly restrictive criteria for recognition of deferred tax assets and the complexities involved in its implementation. The proposed change in accounting for deferred tax assets could result in the recognition of a significant addition to deferred tax assets in the company's balance sheet.

SAB 74 does not require a company to make a calculation of the effects of a new accounting standard. However, the SEC staff does expect companies to disclose the expected effects on the financial statements of adopting a pending Statement to the extent those effects are known. The following example may be appropriate for a company that has reasonably quantified the impact of adoption under the cumulative effect method:

> In December 1990, the Financial Accounting Standards Board issued new rules that require that the projected future cost of providing postretirement benefits, such as health care and life insurance, be recognized as an expense as employees render service instead of when the benefits are paid. Companies can elect to record the cumulative effect of the accounting change as a charge against income in the year the rules are adopted, or alternatively, on a prospective basis as a part of the future annual benefit cost.

> The Company currently is accumulating the necessary data and expects to apply the new rules starting in the first quarter of 1993 using the cumulative effect method. Based on preliminary estimates, the cumulative effect accounting change at January 1, 1993 is expected to approximate $15 million. The new rules are expected to result in an increase in 1993 net periodic postretirement benefit cost of approximately $350,000.

If the effects are not known (for example, the company is considering substantial changes to its OPEB plan before the effective date of Statement 106, and the effects of those changes are not presently known), companies should disclose that fact. It may be appropriate to disclose a range of possible effect if an approximate amount is not known. The SEC staff has indicated that qualitative disclosures should be included where quantitative information is not available. For companies that have not yet determined the effect of Statement 106, the following represents a possible disclosure alternative:

> In December 1990, the Financial Accounting Standards Board issued new rules that require that the projected future cost of providing postretirement benefits, such as health care and life insurance be recognized as expense as employees render service instead of when the benefits are paid. Companies can elect to record the cumulative effect of the accounting change as a charge against

income in the year the rules are adopted, or alternatively, on a prospective basis as a part of the future annual benefit cost.

The Company will be required to comply with the new rules beginning in 1993. The Company has not yet completed the complex analysis required to estimate the financial statement impact of the new rules, nor has it decided how or when it will initially adopt them. It is expected that adoption of the new rules will significantly decrease shareholders equity if adopted on a cumulative basis or increase operating expense if adopted on a prospective basis. In a related matter, the FASB is considering amending the accounting rules for income taxes and the outcome of that consideration could have a significant impact on the financial statement effects of adopting the new rules on postretirement benefits by increasing the tax benefit recognized as a deferred tax asset.

QUARTERLY RESULTS OF OPERATIONS

The following is a summary of the quarterly results of operations for the years ended December 31, 19X5 and 19X4.

| | Three Months Ended | | | |
	Mar. 31	Jun. 30	Sep. 30	Dec. 31
	(Thousands of dollars, except per-share data)			
19X5				
Net sales	$45,000	$30,000	$40,000	$35,000
Cost of products sold	36,000	24,500	32,000	28,000
Net income	2,400	1,600	2,150	1,850
Net income per common share:				
Primary	.80	.53	.71	.61
Fully diluted	.73	.49	.65	.59

| | Three Months Ended | | | |
	Mar. 31	Jun. 30	Sep. 30	Dec. 31
	(Thousands of dollars, except per-share data)			
19X4				
Net sales	$25,000	$37,500	$33,500	$29,000
Cost of products sold	19,500	29,500	26,000	22,500
Net income	1,000	1,500	1,300	1,200
Net income per common share:				
Primary	.34	.51	.46	.38
Fully diluted	.34	.49	.45	.37

Note: Selected quarterly financial data is required to be presented only by companies that meet certain tests. These tests (and the required disclosures) are in Item 302 of Regulation S-K.

Item 302 requires the disclosure of gross profit. If a company wishes to make its annual and quarterly disclosures on the same basis, SAB Topic 6G allows disclosure of the cost of sales instead of gross profit. However, users must be able to compute gross profit from the information provided. The example above illustrates this optional disclosure.

If the information is included in the footnotes to financial statements (it need not be presented there) it should be labeled unaudited.

REPORT OF INDEPENDENT AUDITORS

Shareholders and Board of Directors
ABC, Inc.

We have audited the accompanying consolidated balance sheets of ABC, Inc. and subsidiaries as of December 31, 19X5 and 19X4, and the related consolidated statements of income, shareholders' equity, and cash flows for each of the three years in the period ended December 31, 19X5. These financial statements are the responsibility of the company's management. Our responsibility is to express an opinion on these financial statements based on our audits.

We conducted our audits in accordance with generally accepted auditing standards. Those standards require that we plan and perform the audit to obtain reasonable assurance about whether the financial statements are free of material misstatement. An audit includes examining, on a test basis, evidence supporting the amounts and disclosures in the financial statements. An audit also includes assessing the accounting principles used and significant estimates made by management, as well as evaluating the overall financial statement presentation. We believe that our audits provide a reasonable basis for our opinion.

In our opinion, the financial statements referred to above present fairly, in all material respects, the consolidated financial position of ABC, Inc. and subsidiaries at December 31, 19X5 and 19X4, and the consolidated results of their operations and their cash flows for each of the three years in the period ended December 31, 19X5, in conformity with generally accepted accounting principles.

Ernst & Young

City, State

Date

CONSOLIDATED BALANCE SHEETS

ABC, Inc. and Subsidiaries

	December 31	
	19X5	19X4
	(Thousands of dollars)	
Assets		
Current Assets		
Cash and cash equivalents—Notes A and E	$ 7,500	$ 6,000
Accounts receivable, less allowance of		
$300,000 in 19X5 and 19X4	29,000	28,000
Inventories—Note C:		
Finished products	17,000	16,000
Products in process	35,000	29,000
Raw materials and supplies	7,000	6,000
	59,000	51,000
Prepaid expenses	500	500
Total Current Assets	96,000	85,500

	December 31	
	19X5	19X4
	(Thousands of dollars)	
Property, Plant and Equipment—Note J		
Land	6,000	5,000
Buildings	38,350	30,850
Machinery and equipment	59,700	47,200
	104,050	83,050
Less allowances for depreciation and amortization	35,550	30,550
	68,500	52,500
Other Assets		
Equity investee	4,200	4,100
Other	800	1,400
	5,000	5,500
	$169,500	$143,500

Notes: The cash caption should include only cash and investments that can be immediately converted into cash and are not usually subject to any market fluctuations. Time deposits, short-term certificates of deposit, and money market funds could normally be classified as cash. Marketable securities is a separate caption in Regulation S-X and should not be combined with cash.

Note references on the face of the financial statements, although preferred by the SEC, are not required.

Current assets which exceed 5% of total current assets and other assets which exceed 5% of total assets must be separately stated on the balance sheet or in notes thereto.

	December 31	
	19X5	19X4
	(Thousands of dollars)	
Liabilities and Shareholders' Equity		
Current Liabilities		
Notes payable to banks—Note E	$ 3,000	$ 7,000
Commercial paper—Note E	3,000	2,000
Accounts payable	14,800	13,500
Employee compensation	6,300	4,900
Taxes, other than income taxes	2,500	1,000
Income taxes	4,000	2,000
Current portion of long-term debt and capital lease obligations	1,400	1,350
Other liabilities	1,000	800
Total Current Liabilities	36,000	32,550
Long-Term Debt, less current portion—Note F	35,000	21,000
Capital Lease Obligations, less current portion—Note J	14,500	14,900
Accrued Pension Cost—Note I	2,000	2,100
Deferred Income Taxes—Note H	3,000	2,000
Shareholders' Equity—Notes F and G		
Common stock, $1 par value: Authorized shares—5,000,000 Issued and outstanding shares— 3,000,000 in 19X5 and 2,900,000 in 19X4	3,000	2,900
Additional paid-in capital	15,000	14,100
Retained earnings	60,000	54,950
Currency translation adjustments	1,000	(1,000)
	79,000	70,950
Contingencies and Commitments—Note J		
	$169,500	$143,500

See notes to consolidated financial statements.

Note: Current liabilities which exceed 5% of total current liabilities and other liabilities which exceed 5% of total liabilities must be separately stated on the balance sheet or in notes thereto.

CONSOLIDATED STATEMENTS OF INCOME

ABC, Inc. and Subsidiaries

Year Ended December 31

	19X5	19X4	19X3
	(Thousands of dollars)		
Net Sales*	$150,000	$125,000	$115,000
Other income	10,000	8,000	7,000
	160,000	133,000	122,000
Costs and expenses:			
Costs of products sold—Note C	120,500	97,500	88,500
Selling and administrative **	20,950	23,100	17,850
Interest—Notes E and F	5,550	4,400	4,650
	147,000	125,000	111,000
Income Before Income Taxes	13,000	8,000	11,000
Federal, foreign and state income taxes—Note H	5,000	3,000	4,500
Net Income	$ 8,000	$ 5,000	$ 6,500
Per share amounts			
Primary	$2.65	$1.69	$2.21
Fully diluted	$2.53	$1.67	$2.12

See notes to consolidated financial statements.

Notes:

    * If any of the following is 10% or more of the sum of all these items, it must be stated separately:

    Net sales of tangible products
    Operating revenues of public utilities.
    Income from rentals.

Revenues from services.
Other revenues.

The related costs and expenses must be similarly grouped. If excise taxes are 1% or more of total sales and revenues, the amount must be shown on the face of the statement.

** The provision for doubtful accounts is required as a separate caption on the face of the income statement if the amount is material.

CONSOLIDATED STATEMENTS OF SHAREHOLDERS' EQUITY

ABC, Inc. and Subsidiaries

	Common Stock	Additional Paid-In Capital	Retained Earnings	Currency Translation Adjustments	Total
	(Thousands of dollars)				
Balance at January 1, 19X3	$2,900	$14,100	$48,670	$2,000	$67,670
Net income for 19X3			6,500		6,500
Currency translation adjustments				(1,500)	(1,500)
Cash dividends paid—$.80 a share			(2,320)	(2,320)	
Balance at December 31, 19X3	2,900	14,100	52,850	500	70,350
Net income for 19X4			5,000		5,000
Currency translation adjustments				(1,500)	(1,500)
Cash dividends paid—$1 a share			(2,900)		(2,900)
Balance at December 31, 19X4	2,900	14,100	54,950	(1,000)	70,950
Proceeds from issuance of 100,000 shares of common stock upon exercise of stock options	100	900			1,000
Net income for 19X5			8,000		8,000
Currency translation adjustments				2,000	2,000
Cash dividends paid—$1 a share			(2,950)		(2,950)

	Common Stock	Additional Paid-In Capital	Retained Earnings	Currency Translation Adjustments	Total
		(Thousands of dollars)			
Balance at December 31, 19X5	$3,000	$15,000	$60,000	$1,000	$79,000

See notes to consolidated financial statements.

Note: Regulation S-X Rules 5-02.28-31 require the changes in shareholders' equity accounts to be presented either in a statement or in the notes for the same periods for which income statements are required (three years).

CONSOLIDATED STATEMENTS OF CASH FLOWS

ABC, Inc. and Subsidiaries

	Year Ended December 31		
	19X5	19X4	19X3
	(Thousands of dollars)		
Operating Activities			
Net income	$8,000	$5,000	$6,500
Adjustments to reconcile net income to net cash provided by operating activities:			
Depreciation and amortization	8,000	7,500	7,300
Deferred income taxes	1,000	850	800
Provision for doubtful accounts	35	35	25
Equity in earnings of investee	(550)	(500)	(600)
Dividends received from investee	450	330	270
Increase in accounts receivable	(1,135)	(1,365)	(795)
Increase in inventories	(7,800)	(4,500)	(400)
Increase in liabilities	6,400	950	1,920
Cash provided by operating activities	14,400	8,300	15,020

	Year Ended December 31		
	19X5	19X4	19X3
	(Thousands of dollars)		

Investing Activities
Purchases of property, plant and

	19X5	19X4	19X3
equipment	(13,800)	(5,900)	(7,950)
Acquisition of Future Corp.	(10,000)		
Proceeds from disposal of property, plant and equipment	1,000	200	400
Cash used in investing activities	(22,800)	(5,700)	(7,550)

Financing Activities

Proceeds from issuing 10% debentures	15,000		
Proceeds from sale of common stock under option plan	1,000		
Payments on long-term debt	(1,200)	(860)	(890)
Payments on capitalized lease obligations	(350)	(300)	(350)
Net (decrease) in short-term borrowings	(3,000)	(1,000)	(2,500)
Dividends paid	(2,950)	(2,900)	(2,320)
Cash provided (used) by financing activities	8,500	(5,060)	(6,060)
Effect of exchange rate changes on cash	1,400	(840)	(410)
Increase (Decrease) in Cash and Cash Equivalents	1,500	(3,300)	1,000
Cash and cash equivalents at beginning of year	6,000	9,300	8,300
Cash and Cash Equivalents at End of Year	$7,500	$6,000	$9,300

See notes to consolidated financial statements.

Notes:

1. The example statement of cash flows complies with the guidance in FASB Statement No. 95, ''Statement of Cash Flows.'' The example

> follows the indirect method of reporting cash flows from operating activities. When the indirect method is used, separate disclosure of interest paid and of income taxes paid are required. In the example financial statements, those disclosures are included in Notes F and H (respectively) to the financial statements.

NOTES TO CONSOLIDATED FINANCIAL STATEMENTS

ABC, Inc. and Subsidiaries

December 31, 19X5

NOTE A—ACCOUNTING POLICIES

Principles of Consolidation: The consolidated financial statements include the accounts of the Company and its subsidiaries, all of which are wholly owned. Significant intercompany accounts and transactions have been eliminated in consolidation. The company's 20% owned investee, XYZ Corp., is accounted for by the equity method. The market value of the company's investment in XYZ Corp. at December 31, 19X5 was approximately $6,000,000.

Inventories: Inventories are priced at the lower of cost or market using the last-in, first-out (LIFO) method for domestic inventories and the first-in, first-out (FIFO) method for all other inventories.

The Company hedges the excess of its raw materials inventory of copper over sales commitments against price fluctuations through the sale of futures contracts. In accordance with FASB Statement No. 80, gains and losses on the hedging transactions are deferred as an adjustment to the carrying amount of the inventory and are recognized in income when the inventory is sold.

Property, Plant and Equipment: Property, plant and equipment is stated on the basis of cost. Depreciation is computed principally by the straight-line method for financial reporting purposes and by accelerated methods for income tax purposes.

Cash Equivalents: The Company considers all highly liquid investments with a maturity of three months or less when purchased to be cash equivalents.

Net Income Per Common Share: Primary net income per common share is based on the average number of shares of common stock outstanding during each year and common stock equivalents of dilutive stock options. Fully diluted net income per common share assumes that the 7% convertible sinking fund debentures were converted into common stock as of the beginning of each year, and that the interest expense thereon, net of income taxes, was added to net income.

Foreign Currency Translation: The financial statements of foreign subsidiaries have been translated into U.S. dollars in accordance with FASB Statement No. 52. All balance sheet accounts have been translated using the current exchange rates at the balance sheet date. Income statement amounts have been translated using the average exchange rate for the year. The gains and losses resulting from the change in exchange rates from year to year have been reported separately as a component of shareholders' equity. The effect on the statements of income of transaction gains and losses is insignificant for all years presented.

NOTE B—MERGERS AND ACQUISITIONS

In December 19X5, the Company purchased certain assets and the business of Future Corp. (a manufacturer of electric motors) for $10,000,000 cash raised through the issuance of 10% debentures. The pro forma unaudited results of operations for the years ended December 31, 19X5 and 19X4, assuming the purchase of Future Corp. had been consummated as of January 1, 19X4, are as follows:

	19X5	19X4
Net sales	$175,000,000	$147,000,000
Net income	8,400,000	5,250,000
Net income per common share:		
Primary	2.78	1.78
Fully diluted	2.65	1.75

Note: Generally accepted accounting principles (APB Opinion No. 16) only require the pro forma information be shown for the year of acquisition and the preceding year. However, one of the effects of the SEC rule requiring three years' income statements is to prolong disclosures of prior years' events. For example, had the company made a purchase acquisition in 19X3 (the earliest year for which an income statement is presented), disclosure of that acquisition also would be required.

NOTE C—INVENTORIES

Current cost exceeds the LIFO value of inventories by approximately $20,500,000 and $14,000,000 at December 31, 19X5 and 19X4, respectively. Year-end inventories valued under the LIFO method were $50,000,000 in 19X5 and $43,000,000 in 19X4.

Note: The disclosure of the difference between current cost and LIFO is intended to be responsive to Regulation S-X Rule 5-02.6. The disclosure of the amount of inventory valued under the LIFO method is responsive to a recommendation included in the AICPA's LIFO Issues Paper endorsed by the SEC in Staff Accounting Bulletin No. 58 (Topic 5.L).

If a material amount of income is recognized as a result of a liquidation of LIFO inventory quantities, SAB No. 40 (Topic 11.F—LIFO Liquidation) calls for disclosure of the amount either on the face of the income statement or in a footnote to the financial statements. The following disclosure would be appropriate:

"During 19X5, inventory quantities were reduced. This reduction resulted in a liquidation of LIFO inventory quantities carried at lower costs prevailing in prior years as compared with the cost of 19X5 purchases, the effect of which increased net income by approximately $XXX, or $X per share."

The IRS permits *supplemental* disclosures of the effect of using LIFO. Thus, the IRS LIFO conformity requirements only extend to the face of the financial statements. However, the SEC has concerns that supplemental disclosures of FIFO earnings may be misleading. To guard against this, the SEC states in Section 205.02.c of the Codification of Financial Reporting Policies (ASR 293) that such supplemental disclosures should:

1. Indicate that LIFO better matches costs and revenues during periods of inflation.

2. Indicate why supplemental income disclosures are being provided (e.g., comparability with non-LIFO companies).

3. Explain important assumptions used in calculating the information such as assumed tax rates, effect on bonus or profit sharing plans, etc.

LIFO disclosures should not appear in financial highlights, press releases or president's letters. They would be appropriate in management's discussion and analysis or footnotes to the financial statements.

Accordingly, companies may want to provide the following footnote disclosure:

The Company uses the LIFO method of inventory valuation because it results in a better matching of current costs and revenues. A number of the company's competitors use the FIFO method of inventory valuation. Had the company reported its LIFO inventories at values approximating current cost, as would have resulted from using the FIFO method; had a 34% tax rate been applied to changes in income resulting therefrom; and had no other assumptions been made as to changes in income, net income would have been $X,XXX,XXX ($X.XX per share) for 19X5, $X,XXX,XXX ($X.XX per share) for 19X4, and $XXX,XXX ($X.XX per share) for 19X3.

NOTE D—RESEARCH AND DEVELOPMENT EXPENSE

The Company incurred research and development expense of $1,700,000 in 19X5, $1,000,000 in 19X4, and $950,000 in 19X3, which amounts were charged to cost of products sold as incurred.

NOTE E—CREDIT ARRANGEMENTS

Under line of credit arrangements for short-term debt with three banks, the Company may borrow up to $10,000,000 on such terms as the Company and the banks may mutually agree upon. These arrangements do not have termination dates but are reviewed annually for renewal. At December 31, 19X5, the unused portion of the credit lines was $7,000,000, of which the Company has assigned $3,000,000 to support outstanding commercial paper.

In connection with these credit lines, the Company maintains average compensating balances, based upon bank ledger balances adjusted for uncollected funds, equal to 10% of the company's short-term borrowings plus 10% of its total credit lines. Based on outstanding borrowings and the total credit lines at December 31, 19X5, the Company should maintain average compensating balances of $1,300,000 which, stated in terms of the company's book cash balances, is approximately $870,000. The difference is attributable to uncollected funds and float. During 19X5, the Company maintained average compensating balances of approximately $1,140,000. Compensating balances are not restricted as to withdrawal. Commitment fees, which are 1/2% of the unused line of credit, approximated $3,300, $5,200 and $3,200 for the years ended December 31, 19X5, 19X4 and 19X3, respectively.

Note: Disclosure of average interest rates, maximum amounts outstanding at month-end, average amounts outstanding and weighted average interest rates of short-term debt are required in **SEC** filings in Schedule IX, Short-Term Borrowings.

NOTE F—LONG-TERM DEBT

Long-term debt consisted of the following:

	19X5	19X4
	(Thousands of dollars)	
7% convertible sinking fund debentures due through 19X8	$14,000	$15,000
10% debentures due through 19Y6	15,000	
Other, principally at 12% due through 19X9	7,000	7,000
	36,000	22,000
Less current portion	1,000	1,000
	$35,000	$21,000

Maturities of long-term debt for the five years succeeding December 31, 19X5 are $1,000,000 in 19X6, $1,000,000 in 19X7, $15,500,000 in 19X8, $5,500,000 in 19X9, and $2,000,000 in 19Y0.

Through June 30, 19X8, the 7% debentures are convertible at the option of the holder into shares of common stock at the rate of one share for each $40 face amount. The 7% convertible sinking fund debentures are secured by accounts receivable, inventory and other general assets of the company.

In 19X5, the Company sold $15,000,000 in 10% debentures to finance the purchase of Future Corp. and construction of the company's new plant. The debt is secured by the new plant.

The indentures for both issues of debentures include, among other things, provisions relative to additional borrowings, maintenance of working capital, and restrictions on the amount of retained earnings available for the payment of dividends. Under the most restrictive of these covenants, retained earnings in the amount of $32,000,000 were free of such limitations at December 31, 19X5.

During 19X5, 19X4, and 19X3 interest paid totaled $6,150,000, $4,750,000, and $4,650,000 respectively, of which $600,000, $350,000, and $0 respectively, was capitalized as part of the cost of the company's newly constructed manufacturing plant.

NOTE G—SHAREHOLDERS' EQUITY

At December 31, 19X5 there were authorized 1,000,000 shares of Series A Preferred Stock, stated value $10 per share, none of which have been issued.

> *Note:* This disclosure may be made on the face of the balance sheet.

Options granted under the 19X1 qualified stock option plan are at the fair market value at date of grant and, subject to termination of employment, expire five years from date of grant, are not transferable other than on death, and are exercisable in four equal annual installments commencing one year from date of grant.

At December 31, 19X5, the Company has reserved 270,000 shares of common stock for issuance in connection with the stock option plan and 350,000 shares for conversion of 7% convertible sinking fund debentures.

At December 31, 19X5 and 19X4 there were outstanding options for the purchase of 250,000 and 200,000 shares, respectively, at prices ranging from $10 to $23 per share in 19X5 and $10 to $19 per share in 19X4. During 19X5 options for 100,000 shares were exercised at $10.00 per share. No options were exercised during 19X4 and 19X3. At December 31, 19X5 and 19X4, options for 60,000 and 170,000 shares, respectively, were exercisable.

At December 31, 19X5, consolidated retained earnings included $1,200,000 of undistributed earnings of the company's 20% owned investee accounted for by the equity method.

A subsidiary of the Company is subject to debt agreements that limit cash dividends and loans to the Company. At December 31, 19X5 restricted net assets of the subsidiary were $20,000,000.

Note: In this example, restricted assets of $20,000,000 exceed 25% of consolidated net assets as of the end of the most recently completed fiscal year, therefore Schedule III would be required.

Note: Companies listed on the New York or American stock exchanges must provide certain option data which exceeds the disclosures required by GAAP. This additional information is required for the current year only. The exchanges' requirements are:

> "The Corporation will disclose in its annual report to shareholders, for the year covered by the report, (1) the number of shares of its stock issuable under outstanding options at the beginning of the year; separate totals of changes in the number of shares of its stock under options resulting from issuance, exercise, expiration or cancellation of options; and the number of shares issuable under outstanding options at the close of the year, (2) the number of unoptioned shares available at the beginning and at the close of the year for the granting of options under an option plan, and (3) any changes in the exercise price of outstanding options, through cancellation and reissuance or otherwise, except price changes resulting from the normal operation of anti-dilution provisions of the options."

To avoid future post-effective amendments, Item 3 of Form S-8 permits certain option data to be incorporated by reference from the annual shareholders report or proxy statement. The **SEC** has stated that it believes: "The choice as to where the information should be set forth should be left to the issuer. The issuer should be in the best position to determine which form of presentation will involve the least duplication or expense."

Specifically, Form S-8 requires disclosure of options outstanding, exercise prices and expiration dates, grouped by prices and expiration dates. (However, if this produces more than five separate groups, only the *range* of expiration dates and *average* purchase prices need be shown.) The following are examples of the information that normally would be added to stock option disclosures already included in proxy statements or annual shareholders reports if the issuer chose to omit it from the Form S-8 prospectus.

Example 1—Grouping by prices and expiration dates produces five or fewer separate groups.

The following options to purchase the company's common shares were outstanding under the Plan on December 31, 19X5:

Year of Grant	Number of Shares	Exercise Price	Expiration Date
19X1	41,850	$10.00	9/25/X6
19X2	48,100	12.00	7/16/X7
19X3	53,750	19.00	8/23/X8
19X4	49,800	17.50	9/27/X9
19X5	56,500	23.00	9/02/Y0
	250,000		

Example 2—Grouping by prices and expiration dates produces more than five separate groups.

At December 31, 19X5, employees of the company held options to purchase 212,200 common shares at an average option price of $13.72 per share. These options expire on various dates beginning May 15, 19X6 and ending on May 31, 19Y1.

NOTE H—INCOME TAXES[5]Income before income taxes consisted of the following:

	19X5	19X4	19X3
	(Thousands of dollars)		
Domestic	$ 9,000	$5,500	$ 9,000
Foreign	4,000	2,500	2,000
	$13,000	$8,000	$11,000

[5] In this example, the discussion of pending accounting standards uses actual dates.

Note: Disclosure of foreign and domestic pre-tax income is required. The SEC definition of foreign income is that generated from foreign operations, similar to the industry segment disclosure. The SEC's intent is to require disclosure of the amount that relates to the foreign income taxes.

Federal, foreign and state income taxes consisted of the following:

	19X5		19X4		19X3	
Current	Current	Deferred	Current	Deferred	Current	Deferred
		(Thousands of dollars)				
Federal	$2,400	$ 700	$1,100	$550	$2,400	$650
Foreign	1,050	250	710	240	750	—
State	550	50	340	60	550	150
	$4,000	$1,000	$2,150	$850	$3,700	$800

The components of deferred income tax expense follow:

	19X5	19X4	19X3
	(Thousands of dollars)		
Accelerated depreciation for tax purposes	$ 900	$800	$760
Other	100	50	40
	$1,000	$850	$800

Note: Rule 4-08(h)(1)(ii) requires disclosure of the components of income tax expense, including (A) taxes currently payable and (B) the tax effects of timing differences. Separate disclosure of the estimated tax effect of each of the various types of timing differences is required where the amount of each such tax effect exceeds five percent of the amount computed by multiplying the income before tax by the applicable Federal income tax rate. Statement 96 requires disclosure of the nature or type of temporary differences that give rise to significant portions of a deferred tax asset or liability. The SEC is reconsidering this disclosure requirement in light of Statement 96 and expects to issue final rules in this area upon issuance of the proposed statement that would supersede Statement 96. Pending issuance of such final rules, the staff has indicated that it will not insist on literal compliance with Rule 4-08(h)(1)(ii)(B) for those registrants that have adopted the liability method of accounting for income taxes pursuant to Statement 96.

Total income tax payments during 19X5, 19X4, and 19X3 were $2,000,000, $3,500,000, and $5,500,000, respectively.

Provision has been made for U.S. federal income taxes to be paid on the portion of undistributed earnings of foreign subsidiaries expected to be remitted to the Company. Undistributed earnings intended to be invested indefinitely in foreign subsidiaries were $10,000,000, $8,000,000, and $6,500,000 at the end of 19X5, 19X4, and 19X3, respectively.

The effective income tax rate varied from the statutory federal income tax rate as follows:

	19X5	19X4	19X3
Statutory federal income tax rate	34.0%	34.0%	34.0%
Increases (decreases):			
State income taxes, net of federal tax benefit	3.3	3.6	3.7
Effect of foreign income tax rates	2.2	1.3	2.1
Other items	(1.0)	(1.4)	1.1
	38.5%	37.5%	40.9%

In December 1987, the Financial Accounting Standards Board issued Statement of Financial Accounting Standards No. 96, "Accounting for Income Taxes." Companies are required to adopt the new method of accounting for income taxes no later than 1993. In June 1991, the FASB issued an Exposure Draft of a proposed Statement to supersede Statement 96, which if adopted would be effective for fiscal years beginning after December 15, 1992.

The Company has not completed all of the complex analyses required to estimate the impact of adopting the liability method, and it has not decided whether it will implement the liability method by restating any prior years. However, the adoption of the liability method is not expected to have a significant adverse impact on the company's financial position.

NOTE I—PENSION PLANS AND POSTRETIREMENT BENEFITS[6]

The Company and its subsidiaries have two defined benefit pension plans which cover substantially all of their non-union employees, including certain employees in foreign countries. Benefits are based on years of service and the employee's compensation during the last five years of employment. The company's funding policy is to make the minimum annual contributions required by applicable regulations.

The following table sets forth the funded status and amount recognized for the Company's defined benefit pension plans in the consolidated balance sheets at December 31:

	19X5	19X4
	(Thousands of dollars)	
Actuarial present value of accumulated benefit obligation, including vested benefits of $24,800 in 19X5 and $23,700 in 19X4	$ 32,100	$ 29,800
Actuarial present value of projected benefit obligation for services rendered to date	$(36,500)	$(33,000)
Plan assets at fair value, primarily listed stocks and U.S. bonds	31,100	27,700
Projected benefit obligation in excess of plan assets	(5,400)	(5,300)
Unrecognized net loss from past experience different from that assumed and effects of changes in assumptions	600	200
Prior service cost not yet recognized in net periodic pension cost	1,400	1,800
Unrecognized net obligation at January 1, 19X5 and 19X4	1,400	1,600
Adjustment required to recognize minimum liability	–	(400)
Accrued pension cost	$(2,000)	$(2,100)

Net pension cost included the following components (in thousands):

---

[6] In this example, the discussion of pending accounting standards uses actual dates.

	19X5	19X4	19X3
Service cost—benefits earned during the period	$ 800	$ 600	$1,000
Interest cost on projected benefit obligation	3,300	3,000	2,800
Actual return on plan assets	(3,100)	(2,700)	(3,200)
Net amortization and deferral	500	700	800
Net pension cost	$1,500	$1,600	$1,400

The company also makes contributions to a union-sponsored multi-employer defined benefit pension plan. Such contributions amounted to $1,200,000 in 19X5, $975,000 in 19X4 and $900,000 in 19X3.

Following is a summary of significant actuarial assumptions used:

	As of December 31,		
	10X5	19X4	19X3
Weighted-average discount rates	9.0%	10.0%	8.0%
Rates of increase in compensation levels	6.0%	6.0%	8.0%
Expected long-term rate of return on assets	10.0%	10.0%	10.0%

Notes:

1. The above example assumes that the plan is underfunded (i.e., the actuarial present value of accumulated plan benefits exceed the fair value of the plan's assets). The adjustment made to recognize this minimum liability appears as a line item in the reconciliation of the funded status of the plan with amounts reported in the sponsor's balance sheet. The offset in the balance sheet would be an intangible asset and/or a reduction of stockholders' equity.

2. The above example also reflects the disclosure of an immaterial foreign pension plan. To the extent that those arrangements are in substance similar to pension plans in the U.S., they are subject to the provisions of Statement 87. In addition, it is customary or required in some countries to provide benefits in the event of a voluntary or involuntary severance of employment (termination indemnities). If such an arrangement is in substance a pension plan, disclosure is required.

3. As a general rule, the disclosures required by Statement 87 may be aggregated for all of an employer's domestic single employer defined

benefit plans, or plans may be disaggregated into groups so as to provide "the most useful information" (not defined). However for purposes of the disclosures regarding the reconciliation of the funded status of the plan with amounts reported in the sponsor's balance sheet, the disclosures are required to be presented in two groups:

Aggregate amounts for plans with assets in excess of the accumulated benefit obligation.

Aggregate amounts for plans with an accumulated benefit obligation in excess of plan assets.

Companies with more than one plan may find that each plan has unique weighted average assumed discount rates, salary scales (if applicable), and expected long-term rates of return. We believe either of the following two approaches are acceptable in this situation:

Disclose the range of rates pertaining to each assumption.

Compute "overall" weighted-average assumed rates for disclosure purposes, based on each individual plan's projected benefit obligation in relation to the total projected benefit obligations of all plans (or in proportion to market related values, as applicable).

In addition to the general rules applicable to domestic plans, Statement 87 stipulates that disclosures for plans outside the U.S. may not be combined with those for U.S. plans unless those plans use similar economic assumptions.

The Company and its subsidiaries provide certain health care and life insurance benefits for retired employees. Substantially all of the Company's employees, including employees in foreign countries, may become eligible if they reach normal retirement age while still working for the Company. These benefits are provided through an insurance company whose premiums are based on the benefits paid during the year. The cost of retiree health care and life insurance benefits is recognized as expense as premiums are incurred. For 19X5, 19X4, and 19X3, those costs approximated $225,000, $200,000, and $180,000, respectively.

In December 1990, the Financial Accounting Standards Board issued new rules that require that the projected future cost of providing postretirement benefits, such as health care and life insurance, (referred to as OPEBs) be recognized as an expense as employees render service instead of when the benefits are paid. Companies can elect to record the cumulative effect of the accounting change as a charge against income in the year the rules are adopted, or alternatively, on a prospective basis as a part of the future annual benefit cost.

The Company currently is accumulating the necessary data and expects to apply the new rules starting in the first quarter of 19X6 on a prospective basis. Based on preliminary estimates, the new rules are expected to result in an increase in 19X6 net periodic postretirement benefit cost of approximately $800,000-$1,000,000. As discussed in Note H, the FASB is considering amending the accounting rules for income taxes which could have a significant impact on the financial statement effects of adopting the new rules on postretirement benefits.

NOTE J—CONTINGENCIES AND COMMITMENTS

In May 19X3, the Company received a letter from the United States Environmental Protection Agency ("EPA") regarding remedial actions at a chemical waste disposal site in Anytown, USA. Records indicate that the company may have generated a portion of the waste placed at the site and the Company has therefore been deemed by the EPA to be a potentially responsible party ("PRP") with respect to the site under the Comprehensive Environmental Response, Compensation and Liability Act. The Company, together with other companies which also generated waste placed at the site, has participated with the EPA in a cleanup study at the site. The Company has also engaged in settlement negotiations with the EPA and with other companies regarding its responsibilities, if any, for cleanup of the site. No settlements have been achieved, but negotiations are continuing.

The Company provides for costs related to contingencies when a loss is probable and the amount is reasonably determinable. It is the opinion of management, based on past experience and advice of counsel, that the ultimate resolution of this contingency, to the extent not previously provided for, will not have a material adverse effect on the financial condition of the Company.

The Company leases a building and machinery and equipment under capital leases. The lease for the building may be renewed for two five-year periods after 19Y3. The lease for the machinery and equipment requires the payment of contingent rentals based on usage in excess of a specified minimum and future rental payments may be adjusted for increases in maintenance and insurance above specified amounts. The Company also leases certain equipment under noncancellable operating leases that expire in various years through 19X9. These leases may be renewed for periods ranging from one to three years.

Property, plant and equipment includes the following amounts for leases that have been capitalized:

	19X5	19X4
	(Thousands of dollars)	
Building	$17,000	$17,000
Machinery and equipment	1,400	1,400
	18,400	18,400
Less allowances for amortization	5,900	4,900
	$12,500	$13,500

Amortization of leased assets is included in depreciation and amortization expense.

Future minimum payments under capital leases and noncancellable operating leases with initial terms of one year or more consisted of the following at December 31, 19X5:

	Capital Leases	Operating Leases
	(Thousands of dollars)	
19X6	$ 2,060	$1,135
19X7	2,060	1,120
19X8	2,060	1,120
19X9	2,060	1,120
19X0	2,060	1,120
Thereafter	22,080	3,200
Total minimum lease payments	32,380	$8,815
Executory costs	(80)	
Amounts representing interest	(17,400)	
Present value of net minimum lease payments (including current portion of $400,000)	$14,900	

Rental expense consisted of the following:

	19X5	19X4	19X3
	(Thousands of dollars)		
Minimum rentals under operating leases	$ 970	$ 950	$ 920
Contingent rentals under capital leases	180	150	130
	$1,150	$1,100	$1,050

NOTE K—FINANCIAL INSTRUMENTS

Off Balance Sheet Risk

The company enters into foreign exchange contracts to hedge certain of its operational commitments and balance sheet exposure against changes in foreign currency exchange rates. Such exposure is a result of the portion of the company's operations, assets and liabilities which are denominated in currencies other than the U.S. dollar. When the company's foreign exchange contracts hedge operational commitments, the effects of movements in currency exchange rates on these instruments are recognized when the related operating revenues and expenses are recognized. When foreign exchange contracts hedge balance sheet exposure such effects are recognized when the exchange rate changes. Because the impact of movements in currency exchange rates on foreign exchange contracts offsets the related impact on the underlying items being hedged, these instruments do not subject the company to risk that would otherwise result from changes in currency exchange rates.

The company had foreign exchange contracts of $2,100,000 outstanding at December 31, 19X5. The foreign exchange contracts require the company to exchange foreign currencies for U.S. dollars and generally mature within six months.

Concentrations of credit risk

Financial instruments which potentially subject the company to significant concentrations of credit risk consist principally of cash investments and trade accounts receivable.

The company maintains cash and equivalents, short and long-term investments and certain other financial instruments with various financial institutions. These financial institutions are located throughout the country and company policy is designed to limit exposure to any one institution. The company performs periodic evaluations of the relative credit standing of these financial institutions which are considered in the company's investment strategy.

Concentrations of credit risk with respect to trade accounts receivable are limited due to the large number of entities comprising the company's customer base and their dispersion across many different industries.

As of December 31, 19X5, the company had no significant concentrations of credit risk.

NOTE L—OPERATIONS BY INDUSTRY SEGMENT AND GEOGRAPHIC AREA

Industry segment data and geographic area data for the years ended December 31, 19X5, 19X4 and 19X3 included on pages xx and xx of this report are an integral part of these financial statements. The following summarizes additional information about the reported industry segments:

	19X5	19X4	19X3
	(Thousands of dollars)		
Depreciation and Amortization Expense			
Construction materials	$ 3,600	$3,250	$3,200
Metal products	1,500	1,450	1,375
Paper products	1,100	1,050	1,000
Other industries	1,000	1,000	975
Corporate	800	750	750
Capital Expenditures			
Construction materials	10,500[7]	1,900	4,750
Metal products	12,000	3,000	2,300
Paper products	1,000	1,000	900
Other industries	300		

Intersegment sales are accounted for at prices comparable to unaffiliated customer sales. Operating profit is total revenue less operating expenses, excluding interest and corporate expenses. Identifiable assets by industry segment include both assets directly identified with those

---

[7] Includes $10 million acquired in the purchase of Future Corp.

operations and an allocable share of jointly-used assets. Corporate assets consist primarily of cash and other investments.

Sales of the construction materials division include sales to a major supply wholesaler of $20,000,000 in 19X5, $18,000,000 in 19X4 and $16,000,000 in 19X3.

Additional information as to the Company's operations by geographic area is summarized below:

	19X5	19X4
	(Thousands of dollars)	
Total Assets		
United States	$134,000	$116,000
Canada	10,500	7,500
Other countries	25,000	20,000
	$169,500	$143,500
Total Liabilities		
United States	$ 70,500	$ 56,550
Canada	5,000	4,000
Other countries	15,000	12,000
	$ 90,500	$ 72,550

Transfers between geographic areas are accounted for at prices comparable to normal, unaffiliated customer sales.

Note: In the above example, disclosure of total foreign assets and liabilities was presented to illustrate compliance with ARB No. 43. As illustrated here, this disclosure usually is made along with FASB Statement No. 14, Geographic Disclosures.

Note: Quarterly results of operations are presented outside the financial statements in this example.

Note: The names and their relationship to the company, if any, of customers to whom 10% or more of sales were made must be disclosed in Form 10-K unless the loss of the customer would not have a material effect on the consolidated entity as a whole. These disclosures are not required in the annual shareholders report.

SECURITIES AND EXCHANGE COMMISSION
Washington, D.C. 20549

FORM 10-K

[ ] Annual Report Pursuant to Section 13 or 15(d) of the Securities Exchange Act of 1934 [Fee Required]

For the fiscal year ended December 31, 19X5.

[ ] Transition Report Pursuant to Section 13 or 15(d) of the Securities Exchange Act of 1934 [No Fee Required].

For the transition period from ___ to ___.

Commission file number 0-000.

ABC, INC.
(Exact name of registrant as specified in its charter)

State	00-0000000
(State or other jurisdiction of incorporation or organization)	(I.R.S. Employer Identification No.)
ABC Building	00000
(Address of principal executive offices)	(Zip Code)

Registrant's telephone number, including area code 000-000-0000

Securities registered pursuant to Section 12(b) of the Act:

Title of each class   Name of each exchange on which registered:

Common Stock, $1 Par Value   New York Stock Exchange

Securities pursuant to section 12(g) of the Act:

7% Convertible Sinking Fund Debentures due 19X8
(Title of class)

Indicate by check mark whether the registrant (1) has filed all reports required to be filed by Section 13 or 15(d) of the Securities Exchange Act of 1934 during the preceding 12 months (or for such shorter period that the registrant was required to file such reports), and (2) has been subject to such filing requirements for the past 90 days. Yes X No __.

Indicate by check mark if disclosure of delinquent filers pursuant to Item 405 of Regulation S-K (§229.405 of this chapter) is not contained herein, and will not be contained, to the best of registrant's knowledge, in definitive proxy or information statements incorporated by reference in Part III of this Form 10-K or any amendment to this Form 10-K.[ ].

The aggregate market value of the voting stock held by non-affiliates of the registrant as of February 28, 19X6:

Common Stock, $1 par value—$71,200,000

> *Note:* The aggregate market value of voting stock held by nonaffiliates and the number of shares outstanding are to be provided as of the latest practical date. If it takes inordinate time and expense to determine affiliate status, the registrant may make reasonable assumptions about common stock held by affiliates if it discloses those assumptions.

The number of shares outstanding of the issuer's classes of common stock as of February 28, 19X6:

Common Stock, $1 Par Value—3,000,000 shares

> *Note:* This information is required as of the latest practical date.

DOCUMENTS INCORPORATED BY REFERENCE

Portions of the annual shareholders report for the year ended December 31, 19X5 are incorporated by reference into Parts I and II.

Portions of the proxy statement for the annual shareholders meeting to be held April 15, 19X6 are incorporated by reference into Part III.

Part I

Item 1. Business

"Business—Industry Segment Data" on pages XX and XX of the annual shareholders report for the year ended December 31, 19X5 is incorporated herein by reference.

Note: Examples of the other disclosures required by Regulation S-K Item 101 are not presented.

Item 2. Properties[8]

Item 3. Legal Proceedings[8]

Item 4. Submission of Matters to a Vote of Security Holders[8]

Part II

Item 5. Market for Registrant's Common Stock and Related Stockholder Matters

Common Stock Market Prices and Dividends on page XX of the annual shareholders report for the year ended December 31, 19X5 is incorporated herein by reference.

Item 6. Selected Financial Data

Selected Financial Data on page XX of the annual shareholders report for the year ended December 31, 19X5 is incorporated herein by reference.

Item 7. Management's Discussion and Analysis of Financial Condition and Results of Operations

Management's Discussion and Analysis of Financial Condition and Results of Operations on pages XX through XX and the related comments in the third paragraph of the President's Letter on page X of the annual shareholders report for the year ended December 31, 19X5 are incorporated herein by reference.

Item 8. Financial Statements and Supplementary Data

---

[8] Examples of disclosures not presented.

The consolidated financial statements included on pages XX through XX of the annual shareholders report for the year ended December 31, 19X5 are incorporated herein by reference.

Quarterly Results of Operations on page XX of the annual shareholders report for the year ended December 31, 19X5 is incorporated herein by reference.

Item 9. Changes in and Disagreements with Accountants on Accounting and Financial Disclosure

None.

Part III

Item 10. Directors and Officers of the Registrant

The information contained on pages XX and XX of ABC, Inc.'s Proxy Statement dated March XX, 19X6, with respect to directors and executive officers of the Company, is incorporated herein by reference in response to this item.

Item 11. Executive Compensation

The information contained on pages XX and XX of ABC, Inc.'s Proxy Statement dated March XX, 19X6, with respect to executive compensation and transactions, is incorporated herein by reference in response to this item.

Item 12. Security Ownership of Certain Beneficial Owners and Management

The information contained on pages XX and XX of ABC, Inc.'s Proxy Statement dated March XX, 19X6, with respect to security ownership of certain beneficial owners and management, is incorporated herein by reference in response to this item.

Item 13. Certain Relationships and Related Transactions

The information contained on pages XX and XX of ABC, Inc.'s Proxy Statement dated March XX, 19X6, with respect to certain relationships and related transactions, is incorporated herein by reference in response to this item.

> *Note:* Part III information must be incorporated by reference from the annual proxy statement if it is filed within 120 days after year end. If they cannot be incorporated by reference from the proxy statement, these items must be either in the Form 10-K when filed or included in an amendment filed up to 120 days after year end.

Part IV

Item 14. Exhibits, Financial Statement Schedules and Reports on Form 8-K.[9]

(a)   (1) and (2)—The response to this portion of Item 14 is submitted as a separate section of this report.

> *Note:* Item 14(a)(1) and (2) requires a list of financial statements and schedules required to be included in Form 10-K Items 8 and 14(d). This list could be provided here rather than by reference to a separate section.

           (3)   Listing of Exhibits
                 Exhibit 11—Statement Re: Per Share Earnings
                 Exhibit 24—Consent of Independent Auditors

> *Note:* Item 14(a)(3) requires a list of all exhibits included in Item 14(c). The above two are shown for illustrative purposes. Additional exhibits may be required in Form 10-K. An auditors' consent is required in a Form 10-K that is incorporated by reference into a previously filed registration statement (such as Form S-3, S-4, or S-8).

(b)   Reports on Form 8-K filed in the fourth quarter of 19X5:

           Form 8-K dated December 27, 19X5
           Item 2. Acquisition or Disposition of Assets—Acquisition of Future
                 Corp.[10]

---

[9] Examples of disclosures not presented.

[10] Examples of disclosures not presented.

Item 7. Financial Statements and Exhibits—Financial Statements of Future Corp.[10]

(c) Exhibits—The response to this portion of Item 14 is submitted as a separate section of this report.

> *Note:* Item 14(c) should include the exhibits required by Item 601 of Regulation S-K. Only exhibits listed under Item 14(a)(3) are presented in this example. Exhibit 22 (not illustrated in this example) requires a list of subsidiaries. Subsidiaries which in the aggregate do not constitute a significant subsidiary may be omitted.

(d) Financial Statement Schedules—The response to this portion of Item 14 is submitted as a separate section of this report.

> *Note:* Financial statements and schedules required by Regulation S-X, but excluded from the annual shareholders report, are required to be filed in this portion of Item 14 (d). They could be presented here rather than by reference to a separate section.

Signatures

Pursuant to the requirements of Section 13 or 15(d) of the Securities Exchange Act of 1934, the registrant has duly caused this report to be signed on its behalf by the undersigned, thereunto duly authorized.

ABC, INC.
_____
(Registrant)

_____
(Signature and date)
(Name and Title)

Pursuant to the requirements of the Securities Exchange Act of 1934, this report has been signed below by the following persons on behalf of the registrant and in the capacities and on the dates indicated.

(Signature and date)	(Signature and date)
(Name and Title)	(Name and Title)
(Signature and date)	(Signature and date)
(Name and Title)	(Name and Title)
(Signature and date)	(Signature and date)
(Name and Title)	(Name and Title)
(Signature and date)	(Signature and date)
(Name and Title)	(Name and Title)

Note: Form 10-K is required to be signed by the registrant, and on behalf of the registrant by its principal executive officer or officers, its principal financial officer, its controller or principal accounting officer, and by at least a majority of the board of directors or persons performing similar functions. Any person who signs in more than one capacity (e.g., specified officer and director) shall indicate each capacity in which he or she signs the report.

ANNUAL REPORT ON FORM 10-K

ITEM 14(a)(1) and (2), (c) and (d)

LIST OF FINANCIAL STATEMENTS AND FINANCIAL

STATEMENT SCHEDULES

CERTAIN EXHIBITS

FINANCIAL STATEMENT SCHEDULES

YEAR ENDED DECEMBER 31, 19X5

ABC, INC.

CITY, STATE

Note: This page would only be presented if the financial information that follows is presented as a separate section of the Form 10-K.

If the consolidated financial statements and supplementary data are not incorporated by reference from the annual shareholders report into Item 8 of Form 10-K and they are presented in this separate section, the second line above would read, "Item 8, Item 14(a)(1) and (2), (c) and (d)" and a line should be added titled "Financial Statements and Supplementary Data." The response to Item 8 in Form 10-K should read, "The response to this Item is submitted in a separate section of this report."

FORM 10-K—ITEM 14(A)(1) AND (2)

ABC, Inc. and Subsidiaries

LIST OF FINANCIAL STATEMENTS AND FINANCIAL STATEMENT SCHEDULES

The following consolidated financial statements of ABC, Inc. and subsidiaries, included in the annual report of the registrant to its shareholders for the year ended December 31, 19X5, are incorporated by reference in Item 8:

Note: When the consolidated financial statements are included in Form 10-K instead of being incorporated by reference from the annual shareholders reports the above paragraph would read: "The following consolidated financial statements of ABC, Inc. and subsidiaries are included in Item 8:"

Consolidated balance sheets—December 31, 19X5 and 19X4

Consolidated statements of income—Years ended December 31, 19X5, 19X4, and 19X3

Consolidated statements of shareholders' equity—Years ended December 31, 19X5, 19X4, and 19X3

Consolidated statements of cash flows—Years ended December 31, 19X5, 19X4, and 19X3

Notes to consolidated financial statements—December 31, 19X5

The following consolidated financial statement schedules of ABC, Inc. and subsidiaries are included in Item 14(d):

Schedule II—Amounts receivable from related parties and underwriters, promoters, and employees other than related parties

Schedule III—Condensed financial information of registrant

Schedule V—Property, plant, and equipment

Schedule VI—Accumulated depreciation, depletion, and amortization of property, plant, and equipment

Schedule VIII—Valuation and qualifying accounts

Schedule IX—Short-term borrowings

Schedule X—Supplementary income statement information

All other schedules for which provision is made in the applicable accounting regulation of the Securities and Exchange Commission are not required under the related instructions or are inapplicable, and therefore have been omitted.

Note: Some registrants may want to indicate on this index the appropriate page number where this information appears.

EXHIBIT 24—CONSENT OF INDEPENDENT AUDITORS

We consent to the incorporation by reference in this Annual Report (Form 10-K) of ABC Inc. of our report dated (date of report), included in the 19X5 Annual Report to Shareholders of ABC Inc.

We also consent to the addition of the financial statement schedules, listed in the accompanying index to financial statements, to the financial statements covered by our report dated (date of report), incorporated herein by reference.

We also consent to the incorporation by reference in the Registration Statement (Form S-8 No. 33-00000) pertaining to the ABC Inc. Non-Incentive Stock Option Plan and in the Registration Statement (Form S-8 No. 33-00000) pertaining to the ABC Inc. 19X5 Stock Option Plan of our report dated (date of report), with respect to the consolidated financial statements incorporated herein by reference and schedules of ABC Inc. included in the Annual Report (Form 10-K) for the year ended December 31, 19X5.

Ernst & Young

City, State

Date

Notes:

1. The auditors' consent for Form 10-K should be filed as Exhibit 24 if the financial statements are incorporated by reference.

2. Rule 12bhr-11 of the General Rules and Regulations under the Securities Exchange Act of 1934 requires that at least one copy filed with the SEC and each stock exchange shall be manually signed.

3. Forms S-3, S-4 and S-8 automatically incorporate by reference future Form 10-K filings. Therefore, a manually signed and dated accountants' consent is required in a subsequently filed Form 10-K if the company has an effective Form S-3, S-4, or S-8.

4. An alternative to the above is to include the auditors' report (including financial statement schedules) in Item 8 of Form 10-K as follows:

Report of Independent Auditors
Shareholders and Board of Directors
ABC, Inc.

We have audited the consolidated financial statements of ABC, Inc. and subsidiaries listed in the accompanying index to financial statements (Item 14 (a)). These financial statements are the responsibility of the company's management. Our responsibility is to express an opinion on these financial statements based on our audits.

We conducted our audits in accordance with generally accepted auditing standards. Those standards require that we plan and perform the audit to obtain reasonable assurance about whether the financial statements are free of material misstatement. An audit includes examining, on a test basis, evidence supporting the amounts and disclosures in the financial statements. An audit also includes assessing the accounting principles used and significant estimates made by management, as well as evaluating the overall financial statement presentation. We believe that our audits provide a reasonable basis for our opinion.

In our opinion, the financial statements listed in the accompanying index to financial statements (Item 14 (a)) present fairly, in all material respects, the consolidated financial position of ABC, Inc. and subsidiaries at December 31, 19X5 and 19X4, and the consolidated results of their operations and their cash flows for each of the three years in the period ended December 31, 19X5, in conformity with generally accepted accounting principles.

Ernst & Young

City, State
Date

SCHEDULE II—AMOUNTS RECEIVABLE FROM RELATED PARTIES AND UNDERWRITERS, PROMOTERS, AND OTHER EMPLOYEES OTHER THAN RELATED PARTIES

ABC, INC. AND SUBSIDIARIES

COL. A	COL. B	COL. C	COL. D		COL. E	
			DEDUCTIONS		BALANCE AT END OF PERIOD	
NAME OF DEBTOR	Balance at Beginning of Period	Additions	(1) Amounts Collected	(2) Amounts Written Off	(1) Current	(2) Not Current
YEAR ENDED DECEMBER 31, 19X5						
Notes receivable:						
Victor I. President	$128,000		$ 16,000		$16,000	$ 96,000
Tom A. Vice President	144,000		18,000		18,000	108,000
Joe Employee		$100,000	100,000			
TOTAL	$272,000	$100,000	$134,000		$34,000	$204,000
YEAR ENDED DECEMBER 31, 19X4						
Notes receivable:						
Victor I. President	$144,000		$ 16,000		$16,000	$112,000
Tom A. Vice President	162,000		18,000		18,000	126,000
Sam (10%) Shareholder		$ 25,000	25,000			
TOTAL	$306,000	$ 25,000	$ 59,000		$34,000	$238,000

YEAR ENDED DECEMBER 31, 19X3

Notes receivable:

Victor I. President	$160,000	$ 16,000	$16,000	$128,000
Tom A. Vice President	180,000	18,000	18,000	144,000
TOTAL	$340,000	$ 34,000	$34,000	$272,000

Note—The notes receivable, which bear interest at the rate of 12% per annum, are unsecured and are payable in ten equal annual installments commencing in 19X3.

Note: SAB (Topic 6.F.1) specifies that this schedule should include amounts due from related parties and underwriters, promoters, and employees other than related parties of all the registrant's subsidiaries whether consolidated or accounted for by the equity method. Receivables arising from loans to officers and employees for the purchase of the company's capital stock should be shown as deductions from shareholders' equity.

SCHEDULE III—CONDENSED FINANCIAL INFORMATION OF REGISTRANT

ABC, Inc.
(Parent Company)

Condensed Balance Sheets

	December 31	
	19X5	19X4
	(Thousands of Dollars)	
Assets		
Current assets		
Cash	$ 5,000	$ 2,500
Accounts receivable (including $125,000 and $167,000 due from subsidiaries in 19X5 and 19X4, respectively), less allowances—$150,000 in 19X5 and 19X4	7,500	8,000
Inventories	3,500	2,500
Prepaid expenses	250	300
Total current assets	16,250	13,300
Property, plant and equipment	25,000	17,500
Less allowances for depreciation	(10,000)	(8,500)
	15,000	9,000
Other assets (Principally investment in and amounts due from wholly-owned subsidiaries)	94,250	79,700
	$125,500	$102,000
Liabilities and shareholders' equity		
Current liabilities	$ 11,500	$ 10,050
Long-term debt	28,000	14,000
Other non-current liabilities	7,000	7,000
Shareholders' equity		
Common stock	3,000	2,900
Other shareholders' equity	76,000	68,050
	79,000	70,950
	$125,500	$102,000

ABC, Inc.
(Parent Company)

CONDENSED STATEMENTS OF INCOME

	Year Ended December 31		
	19X5	19X4	19X3
	(Dollars in thousands)		
Net sales	$17,500	$15,000	$16,000
Management fees from wholly-owned subsidiaries	1,500	2,000	2,500
	19,000	17,000	8,500
Costs and expenses:			
Cost of products sold	7,490	6,060	6,450
Selling and administrative expenses	3,400	4,400	2,100
Interest expense	3,610	2,040	2,550
	14,500	12,500	11,100
Income before income taxes and equity in net income of subsidiaries	4,500	4,500	7,400
Federal and state income tax	(2,250)	(2,250)	(3,200)
Equity in net income of subsidiaries	5,750	2,750	2,300
Net income	$ 8,000	$ 5,000	$ 6,500

ABC, Inc.
(Parent Company)

CONDENSED STATEMENTS OF CASH FLOWS

| | Year Ended December 31 | | |
	19X5	19X4	19X3
	(Thousands of Dollars)		
Cash from Operating Activities	$11,200	$7,500	$8,350
Investing activities			
Acquisition of Future Corporation	(10,000)		
Purchases of property, plant, and equipment	(7,900)	(1,950)	(1,550)
Other	500		200
	(17,400)	(1,950)	(1,350)
Financing activities			
Proceeds from issuing debentures	15,000		
Proceeds from sale of common stock	1,000		
Dividends paid	(2,950)	(2,900)	(2,320)
Payments on long-term obligations	(1,350)	(1,150)	(1,180)
Net decrease in short-term borrowings	(3,000)	(1,000)	(2,500)
	8,700	(5,050)	(6,000)
Increase in Cash	$ 2,500	$ 500	$1,000

ABC, Inc.
(Parent Company)

NOTES TO CONDENSED FINANCIAL STATEMENTS

NOTE A—BASIS OF PRESENTATION

In the parent-company-only financial statements, the Company's investment in subsidiaries is stated at cost plus equity in undistributed earnings of subsidiaries since date of acquisition. The Company's share of net income of its unconsolidated subsidiaries is included in consolidated income using the equity method. Parent-company-only financial statements should be read in conjunction with the company's consolidated financial statements.

NOTE B — LONG-TERM DEBT[11]

Long-term debt consisted of the following:

	19X5	19X4
	(Thousands of Dollars)	
7% convertible sinking fund debentures due through 19X8	$14,000	$15,000
10% debentures due through 19Y6	15,000	
	29,000	15,000
Less current portion	1,000	1,000
	$28,000	$14,000

Maturities of long-term debt for the five years succeeding December 31, 19X5 are $1,000,000 in 19X6, $1,000,000 in 19X7, $12,000,000 in 19X8, $2,000,000 in 19X9 and $2,000,000 in 19Y0.

Through June 30, 19X8, the 7% debentures are convertible at the option of the holder into shares of common stock at the rate of one share for each $40 face amount. The 7% convertible sinking fund debentures are secured by accounts receivable, inventory, and other general assets of the company.

In 19X5, the Company sold $15,000,000 in 10% debentures to finance the purchase of Future Corporation and construction of the company's new plant. The debt is secured by the new plant.

The indentures for both issues of debentures include, among other things, provisions relative to additional borrowings, maintenance of working capital, and restrictions on the amount of retained earnings available for the payment of dividends. Under the most restrictive of these covenants, retained earnings in the amount of $32,000,000 were free of such limitations at December 31, 19X5.

---

[11] If in the consolidated financial statements these were identified as relating to the parent, these notes could be omitted from the schedule.

NOTE C—GUARANTEE[12]

UVW Corp., a subsidiary of the Company, has $7,000,000 of long-term debt outstanding. Under the terms of the debt agreement, the Company has guaranteed the payment of all principal and interest.

NOTE D—DIVIDENDS FROM SUBSIDIARIES AND INVESTEES

Cash dividends paid to ABC, Inc. from the Company's consolidated subsidiaries and investees accounted for by the equity method are summarized as follows:

	19X5	19X4	19X3
	(Dollars in thousands)		
Consolidated subsidiaries	$ 750	$ 800	$700
Investees	450	330	270
	$1,200	$1,130	$970

[12] If in the consolidated financial statements these were identified as relating to the parent, these notes could be omitted from the schedule.

SCHEDULE V—PROPERTY, PLANT AND EQUIPMENT

ABC, INC. AND SUBSIDIARIES

YEAR ENDED DECEMBER 31, 19X5

COL. A	COL. B	COL. C	COL. D	COL. E	COL. F
CLASSIFICATION	Balance at Beginning of Period	Additions at Cost	Retirements	Other Changes-Add (Deduct)-Describe	Balance at End of Period
Land	$ 5,000,000			$ 1,000,000	$ 6,000,000
Buildings	27,850,000	$ 3,000,000	$ 500,000	4,000,000	34,350,000
Building equipment	3,000,000	500,000	500,000	1,000,000	4,000,000
	30,850,000	3,500,000	1,000,000	5,000,000	38,850,000
Machinery and equipment	42,700,000	8,800,000	3,000,000	5,200,000	53,700,000
Automobiles and trucks	4,500,000	1,500,000	1,000,000	1,000,000	6,000,000
	47,200,000	10,300,000	4,000,000	6,200,000	59,700,000
Total	$83,050,000	$13,800,000[1]	$5,000,000	$12,200,000[2]	$104,050,000

(1) Additions principally relate to building and equipment a new plant in Newtown, Iowa and replacements for existing equipment.

(2) $10,000,000 acquired in the purchase of Future Corporation. (See Note B to Consolidated Financial Statements.) Remaining addition of $2,200,000 is due to the effect of exchange rate changes on translating property, plant and equipment of foreign subsidiaries in accordance with FASB Statement No. 52, "Foreign Currency Translation."

(3) The annual provisions for depreciation have been computed principally in accordance with the following ranges of rates:

Buildings and building equipment	4% to 10%
Machinery and equipment	7% to 20%
Automobiles and trucks	20% to 33%

Notes:

1. The rules of this schedule also require disclosure of the depreciation method. This disclosure is generally included in the notes to the financial statements and need not be repeated on the schedule.

2. Companies can omit this schedule when property, plant and equipment net of accumulated depreciation, depletion and amorization at both the beginning and end of the latest fiscal year is less than 25% of the total assets as shown on the related balance sheet. The schedule is required for each year an income statement is required. Thus, the schedule is required for three years even though it may only meet the 25% test in the current year. However, the schedules for prior years are not necessary unless the test is met for the current year.

SCHEDULE V—PROPERTY, PLANT AND EQUIPMENT

ABC, INC. AND SUBSIDIARIES

YEAR ENDED DECEMBER 31, 19X4

COL. A CLASSIFICATION	COL. B Balance at Beginning of Period	COL. C Additions at Cost	COL. D Retirements	COL. E Other Changes-Add (Deduct)-Describe	COL. F Balance at End of Period
Land	$ 5,000,000				$ 5,000,000
Buildings	28,600,000			$ (750,000)	27,850,000
Building equipment	3,000,000				3,000,000
	31,600,000	—	—	(750,000)	30,850,000
Machinery and equipment	39,950,000	$4,800,000	$1,000,000	(1,050,000)	42,700,000
Automobiles and trucks	4,400,000	1,100,000	1,000,000		4,500,000
	44,350,000	5,900,000	2,000,000	(1,050,000)	47,200,000
Total	$80,950,000	$5,900,000⁽¹⁾	$2,000,000	$(1,800,000)⁽³⁾	$83,050,000

(1) Additions principally relate to expansion of existing production facilities and replacements for existing equipment.

(2) The annual provisions for depreciaiton have been computed principally in accordance with the following ranges of rates:

Buildings and building equipment   3% to 10%

Machinery and equipment   7% to 20%

Automobiles and trucks   20% to 33%

(3) Deduction is due to the effect of exchange rate changes on translating property, plant and equipment of foreign subsidiaries in accordance with FASB Statement No. 52, "Foreign Currency Translation."

SCHEDULE V—PROPERTY, PLANT AND EQUIPMENT

ABC, INC. AND SUBSIDIARIES

YEAR ENDED DECEMBER 31, 19X3

COL. A CLASSIFICATION	COL. B Balance at Beginning of Period	COL. C Additions at Cost	COL. D Retirements	COL. E Other Changes-Add (Deduct)-Describe	COL. F Balance at End of Period
Land	$ 5,000,000				$ 5,000,000
Buildings	27,000,000	$2,400,000		$ (800,000)	28,600,000
Building equipment	2,000,000	1,000,000			3,000,000
	29,000,000	3,400,000		(800,000)	31,600,000
Machinery and equipment	38,000,000	$4,050,000	$1,000,000	(1,000,000)	39,950,000
Automobiles and trucks	4,400,000	500,000	500,000		4,400,000
	42,400,000	4,550,000	1,500,000	(1,100,000)	44,350,000
Total	$76,400,000(2)	$7,950,000(1)	$1,500,000	$(1,900,000)(4)	$80,950,000

(1) Additions principally relate to building and equipping a new plant in Burgtown, Texas and replacements for existing equipment.

(2) January 1, 19IX3 account balances have been restated to reflect XYZ, Inc. acquired in a pooling of interests transaction.

(3) The annual provisions for depreciation have been computed principally in accordance with the following ranges of rates:

Buildings and building equipment   3% to 10%
Machinery and equipment   7% to 20%
Automobiles and trucks   20% to 33%

(4) Deduction is due to the effect of exchange rate changes on translating property, plant and equipment of foreign subsidiaries in accordance with FASB Statement No. 52, "Foreign Currency Translation."

SCHEDULE VI—ACCUMULATED DEPRECIAITON, DEPLETION AND AMORTIZATION

OF PROPERTY, PLANT AND EQUIPMENT

ABC, INC. AND SUBSIDIARIES

YEAR ENDED DECEMBER 31, 19X5

COL. A DESCRIPTION	COL. B Balance at Beginning of Period	COL. C Additions Charged to Costs and Expenses	COL. D Retirements	COL. E Other Changes-Add (Deduct)-Describe	COL. F Balance at End of Period
Buildings	$ 6,725,000	$2,400,000	$ 200,000	$ 400,000	$ 9,325,000
Building equipment	1,700,000	500,000	500,000		1,700,000
	8,425,000	2,900,000	700,000	400,000	11,025,000
Machinery and equipment	18,125,000	3,100,000	2,500,000	600,000	20,325,000
Automobiles and trucks	3,000,000	2,000,000	800,000		4,200,000
	22,125,000	5,100,000	3,300,000	600,000	24,525,000
Total	$30,550,000	$8,000,000	$4,000,000	$1,000,000[1]	$35,550,000

(1) Addition is due to the effect of exchange rate changes on translating accumulated depreciation of foreign subsidiaries in accordance with FASB Statement No. 52, "Foreign Currency Translation."

SCHEDULE VI—ACCUMULATED DEPRECIATION, DEPLETION AND AMORTIZATION OF PROPERTY, PLANT AND EQUIPMENT

ABC, INC. AND SUBSIDIARIES

YEAR ENDED DECEMBER 31, 19X4

COL. A	COL. B	COL. C	COL. D	COL. E	COL. F
DESCRIPTION	Balance at Beginning of Period	Additions Charged to Costs and Expenses	Retirements	Other Changes-Add (Deduct)-Describe	Balance at End of Period
Buildings	$ 5,100,000	$2,000,000		$(375,000)	$ 6,725,000
Building supplies	1,300,00	400,00			1,300,000
Machinery and equipment	16,950,000	3,600,000	$ 900,000	(515,000)	19,125,000
Automobiles and trucks	2,400,000	1,500,000	900,000	(525,000)	3,000,000
	19,350,000	5,100,000	1,800,000		22,125,000
Total	$25,750,000	$7,500,000	$1,800,000	$(900,000)(1)	$30,550,000

(1) Deduction is due to the effect of exchange rate changes on translating accumulated depreciation foreign subsidiaries in accordance with FASB Statement No. 52, "Foreign Currency Translation."

SCHEDULE VI—ACCUMULATED DEPRECIATION, DEPLETION AND AMORTIZATION OF PROPERTY, PLANT AND EQUIPMENT

ABC, INC. AND SUBSIDIARIES

YEAR ENDED DECEMBER 31, 19X3

COL. A	COL. B	COL. C	COL. D	COL. E	COL. F
DESCRIPTION	Balance at Beginning of Period	Additions Charged to Costs and Expenses	Retirements	Other Changes-Add (Deduct)-Describe	Balance at End of Period
Buildings	$ 3,500,000	$2,000,000		$(400,000)	$ 5,100,000
Building equipment	1,000,000	300,000			1,300,000
	4,500,000	2,300,000		(400,000)	6,400,000
Machinery and equipment	14,900,000	3,600,000	$1,000,000	(550,000)	16,950,000
Automobiles and trucks	1,100,000	1,400,000	100,000		2,400,000
	16,000,000	5,000,000	1,100,000	(550,000)	19,350,000
Total	$20,500,000[1]	$7,300,000	$1,100,000	$(950,000)[2]	$25,750,000

(1) January 1, 19X3 account balances have been restated to reflect XYZ, Inc. acquired in a pooling of interests transaction.

(2) Deduction is due to the effect of exchange rate changes on translating accumulated depreciation of foreign subsidiaries in accordance with FASB Statement No. 52, "Foreign Currency Translation."

SCHEDULE VIII—VALUATION AND QUALIFYING ACCOUNTS

ABC INC. AND SUBSIDIARIES

COL. A	COL. B	COL. C		COL. D	COL. E
		ADDITIONS			
		(1)	(2)		
DESCRIPTION	Balance at Beginning of Period	Charged to Costs and Expenses	Charged to Other Accounts-Describe	Deductions-Describe	Balance at End of Period
YEAR ENDED DECEMBER 31, 19X5:					
Reserves and allowances deducted from asset accounts:					
Allowance for uncollectible accounts	$300,000	$35,000		$35,000[1]	$300,000
YEAR ENDED DECEMBER 31, 19X4:					
Reserves and allowances deducted from asset accounts:					
Allowance for uncollectible accounts	285,000	35,000		20,000[1]	300,000

YEAR ENDED DECEMBER 31, 19X3:

Reserves and allowances deducted from asset accounts:

Allowance for uncollectible accounts	285,000[2]	25,000	25,000[1]	285,000

(1) Uncollectible accounts written off, not of recoveries.

(2) January 1, 19X3 account balance has been restated to reflect XYZ, Inc., acquired in a pooling of interests transaction.

SCHEDULE IX—SHORT-TERM BORROWINGS

ABC, INC. AND SUBSIDIARIES

COL. A	COL. B	COL. C	COL. D	COL. E[1]	COL. F[1]
CATEGORY OF AGGREGATE SHORT-TERM BORROWINGS	Balance at End of Period	Weighed Average Interest Rate	Maximum Amount Outstanding During the Period	Average Amount Outstanding Duirng the Period	Weighed Average Interest rate During the Period
YEAR ENDED DECEMBER 31, 19X5:					
Note payable to bank[1]	$3,000,000	12.25%	$5,400,000	$2,000,000	11.58%
Commercial paper[2]	3,000,000	12.10	3,600,000	1,400,000	11.27
YEAR ENDED DECEMBER 31, 19X4:					
Notes payable to bank[1]	$7,000,000	9.62%	$7,000,000	$6,975,000	8.14%
Commercial paper[2]	2,000,000	9.32	2,500,000	2,000,000	8.05
YEAR ENDED DECEMBER 31, 19X3:					
Notes payable to bank[1]	$9,500,000	7.53%	$9,500,000	$3,000,000	7.43%
Commerial paper[2]	2,000,000	7.25	4,200,000	2,750,000	7.25

(1) Notes payable to bank represent borrowings under lines of credit borrowing arrangements which have no termination date but are reviewed annually for renewal.

(2) Commercial paper matures generally six months from date of issue with no provisions for the extension of its maturity.

(3) The average amount outstanding during the period was computed by dividing the total of month-end outstanding principal balances by 12.

(4) The weighted average interest rate during the period was computed by dividing the actual interest expense by average short-term debt outstanding.

Note: If the information required by this schedule is included in Management's Discusison and Analysis, the schedule may incorporate the information by reference.

SCHEDULE X—SUPPLEMENTARY INCOME STATEMENT INFORMATION

ABC, INC. AND SUBSIDIARIES

COL. A	COL. B		
ITEM	Charged to Cost and Expenses		
	Year ended December 31		
	19X5	19X4	19X3
Maintenance and repairs	$1,700,000	$1,600,000	$1,500,000
Depreciation and amortization of intangible assets	None	None	None
Taxes, other than payroll and income taxes:			
Real estate	1,000,000	900,000	800,000
Personal property	1,900,000	1,800,000	1,700,000
Royalties	None	None	None
Advertising costs	2,250,000	6,000,000	1,500,000

Note: Amounts called for by Column B need not be given if they are less than 1% of total sales and revenues. Depreciation and amortizan of intangible assets and royalties could be delected from the above table and the following disclosure made: "Amounts for depriciation and amortization of intangible assets and royalties are not presented as such amounts are less than 1% of total sales and revenues."

EXHIBIT 11—STATEMENT
RE: COMPUTATION OF PER SHARE EARNINGS

	Year Ended December 31		
	19X5	19X4	19X3
	(Amounts in thousands, except per share data)		
Primary			
Average shares outstanding	2,950	2,900	2,900
Net effect of dilutive stock options— based on the treasury stock method using average market price	70	55	40
Total	3,020	2,955	2,940
Net income	$8,000	$5,000	$6,500
Per share amount	$2.65	$1.69	$2.21
Fully Diluted			
Average shares outstanding	2,950	2,900	2,900
Net effect of dilutive stock options— based on the treasury stock method using the year-end market price, if higher than average market price	70	55	45
Assumed conversion of 7% convertible sinking fund debentures	350	375	400
Total	3,370	3,330	3,345
Net income	$8,000	$5,000	$6,500
Add 7% convertible sinking fund debenture interest, net of federal income tax effect	529	567	605
Total	$8,529	$5,567	$7,105
Per share amount	$2.53	$1.67	$2.12

Note: This computation is required by Regulation S-K Item 601 and is filed as an exhibit under Item 14a(3) of Form 10-K. It is not necessary that this exhibit support the earnings per share from continuing operations shown in the table of selected financial data for five years.

SEC Release No. 33-5133 provides in part as follows: "... when per share earnings are disclosed, ... the information with respect to the computation of per share earnings on both primary and fully diluted bases, presented by exhibit or otherwise, must be furnished even though the amounts of per share earnings on the fully diluted basis are not required to be stated under the provisions of Accounting Principles Board Opinion No. 15."

US GAAP Pronouncements[1]

Accounting Research Bulletins

Statements of the Accounting Principles Board

---

[1] Pronouncements in effect and not superceded through March 31, 1992. Since parts of these pronouncements may be superceded even though the entire prouncement has not been superceded, and since GAAP can change based on FASB pronouncements, caution should be exercised when using this listing.

Opinions of the Accounting Principles Board

Accounting Principles Board Interpretations

Statements of Financial Accounting Standards

FASB Statements of Financial Accounting Concepts

FASB Interpretations

FASB Special Reports

FASB Emerging Issues Task Force Abstracts

AICPA Statements of Position

AICPA Practice Bulletins

AICPA Audit Guides

Bibliography

Accounting and Financial Analysis

American Institute of Certified Public Accountants. *Accounting Trends and Techniques: Annual Survey of Accounting Practices Followed in 600 Stockholders' Reports.* This book summarizes and comments on reporting practices, using relevant examples from actual financial reports.

Bernstein, Leopole A. *Financial Statement Analysis: Theory, Application and Interpretation.* 4th ed. (1989). This comprehensive text is recommended by the Association for Investment Management and Research to candidates for the chartered financial analyst designation. It is weak in some areas and outdated in others, but addresses most issues well from an analyst's point of view.

Brown, Stephen J. and Mark Kritzman, eds. *Quantitative Methods for Financial Analysis.* Institute of Chartered Financial Analysts. Homewood, Ill.: Dow, Jones, Irwin (1990).

Financial Accounting Standards Board. *Current Text/Accounting Standards.* Volume 1 ("General Standards") and Volume 2 ("Industry Standards") define GAAP, cite sources for existing standards, and cross-reference other relevant publications and statements, including audit and accounting guides. Each topic includes examples and a brief glossary.

Gleim, Irvin N. and Patrick R. Delaney. *CPA Examination Review*. New York: John Wiley & Sons. This sound, basic two-volume review text uses examples from prior CPA examinations.

Annual Statement Studies. Robert Morris Associates. This is a very useful annual reference for common-size financial statement. The studies present financial data on a percentages basis to facilitate comparison of similar companies. Data is also presented by industry and company size.

Miller Comprehensive GAAP. Harcourt, Brace Jovanovich. This annual publication is a straightforward restatement of accounting standards with references to authoritative sources. The examples are easy to follow.

Miller Comprehensive GAAS Guide. Harcourt, Brace Jovanovich. This annual publication is a comprehensive restatement of generally accepted auditing standards.

SEC Guidelines, Rules and Regulations. Englewood Cliffs, N.J.: Prentice-Hall. This is an annual compilation of Securities and Exchange Commission filing requirements used most frequently by accountants, with comments.

Trial Testimony

Hamlin, Sonya. *What Makes Juries Listen*. Harcourt, Brace Jovanovich, 1985. This book is written primarily for lawyers, but several chapters are good sources for expert witnesses.

Lloyd, Terry. "Juries and Numbers: Why They Just Don't Get It." *Trial Diplomacy Journal* (March/April 1992).

Lustberg, Arch. *Testifying with Impact*. Washington, D.C.: U.S. Chamber of Commerce (1982). This brief booklet contains generally good advice.

Taylor, Barbara G. and Lane K. Anderson. "Misleading Graphs: Guidelines for the Accountant." *Journal of Accountancy* 126 (October 1986).

Tufte, Edward R. *The Visual Display of Quantitative Information*. Cheshire, Conn.: Graphics Press. This book contains excellent examples of turning data into appealing and educational visuals.

Jury Comprehension in Complex Cases. Chicago: American Bar Association Section of Litigation (1990). This is the report of the A.B.A.

Section of Litigation's special committee on jury comprehension, issued at its March 22, 1990 seminar of the same name.

"The Numbers Racket: How Polls and Statistics Lie." *U.S. News and World Report,* July 11, 1988, 44–47.

Financial References

Ibbotson, Roger G. and Rex A. Sinquefield. *Stocks, Bonds, Bills and Inflation: Historical Returns (1926–1987).* Charlottesville, Va: Financial Analysts Research Foundation (1989).

Sheppard, Howard R. *Litigation Services Resource Directory.* Colorado Springs: Wiley Law Publications (1992). This is an annual compilation of publications, articles, and information sources organized by subject headings crucial to litigation support.

Troy, Leo. *Almanac of Business and Industrial Financial Ratios.* Englewood Cliffs, N.J.: Prentice-Hall (1988).

Annual Statement Studies. Robert Morris Associates. Published annually.

Business Conditions Digest. U.S. Bureau of Economic Analysis. Published monthly.

Conference Board Business Record. National Industrial Conference Board.

Consumer Price Index. Bureau of Labor Statistics, U.S. Department of Labor. Published monthly.

Economic Indicators. White House Council of Economic Advisors. Published monthly.

Encyclopedia of Associations. 27th ed. Detroit: Gale Research, (1993). This publication facilitates finding associations which can provide information on industries and products, no matter how obscure or mundane. It is also available through DIALOG Information Services as File 114.

Federal Reserve Bulletin. Board of Governors of the Federal Reserve System. Published monthly.

Key Business Failure Record. New York: Dun & Bradstreet, Inc. Published biennially.

Key Business Ratios. New York: Dun & Bradstreet, Inc. Published annually.

Life Tables: Vital Statistics of the United States. U.S. Department of Health and Human Services (1980).

Selected Interest Rates. Board of Governors of the Federal Reserve System. This statistical release is published monthly.

Standard and Poor's Industry Surveys. New York: Standard and Poor Corporation. Published in quarterly and annual editions.

Statistical Abstract of the United States. Bureau of the Census, U.S. Department of Commerce. Published annually.

U.S. Industrial Outlook. Industry and Trade Administration, U.S. Department of Commerce. Published annually.

Damages

Cerillo, William A. *Proving Business Damages.* 2d ed. Colorado Springs: Wiley Law Publications (1991). This clear, concise book contains easily understood examples, and will be of interest both to lawyers and to nonlawyer damages experts.

DeGroot, Morris H., Stephen E. Fienberg, Joseph B. Kadane, ed. *Statistics and the Law.* New York: John Wiley & Sons. (1986). This book contains citations and excellent examples of how to use statistics to prove liability and damages.

Dobbs, Dan B. *Remedies—Damages, Equity and Restitution.* St. Paul: West Publishing Co. (1973). This book is recommended both for financial experts on damages and for lawyers proving or defending against damage theories.

Finklestein, Michael O., and Bruce Levin; *Statistics for Lawyers*; Springer-Verlag, New York (1990). A detailed text of this type of statistical analysis used by lawyers with good graphic illustrations.

Love, Vincent J. and Steven Alan Reiss. "Guidelines for Calculating Damages." Vol. LX/No. 10 *CPA Journal* (October 1990). This "how to do it" article is written for CPAs, but will also be of interest to attorneys working with financial experts.

INDEX

A

Acceleration, matching, financial reporting fundamentals, 13

Accountant, auditor contrasted, 73. *See also* Certified Public Accountant (CPA)

Accounting basis, financial statement notes, 46. *See also* Accrual versus cash accounting methods

Accounting policies:
consolidated financial statement, sample of financial statement notes, 221-222
financial statement notes, 46-47, 48-49

Accounting Principles Board (APB, AICPA):
generally accepted accounting principles (GAAP), 4
interpretations, GAAP pronouncements, 314-315
opinions, GAAP pronouncements, 314
opinions, generally accepted accounting principles (GAAP), 5, 6
statements, GAAP pronouncements, 313
statements, generally accepted accounting principles (GAAP), 6

Accounting Research Bulletins (ARBs), 4, 5, 313

Accounting Standards Executive Committee (AcSEC), 6

Accounting terminology, financial language in legal documents and, 157-159. *See also* Financial language in legal documents

Accounts receivable:
assets, current assets, 27
balance sheet
financial language in legal documents, 162
reading financial statements, 93

Accrual versus cash accounting methods:
cash flow analysis, 121-122
financial reporting fundamentals, 11-12
financial statement notes, 46

Accrued income and expenses:
liabilities, financial statements, 30

Accured income and expenses:
financial reporting fundamentals, 17-18

Acid test or quick ratio, ratio analysis, 103, 119

Acquisitions:
financial language in legal documents, 158, 161
reading financial statements, balance sheet, 95

Activity ratios, 105-108, 119
days payable outstanding, 105, 119
days receivable outstanding, 106, 119
inventory turnover ratio, 106-107, 119
sales to assets ratio, 107-108, 119
sales to employees ratio, 107, 119

Acts of God, financial statement notes, 61, 62